The Evolution of Mass Culture
in America —
1877 to the Present

The Evolution of Mass Culture in America — 1877 to the Present

Gerald R. Baydo, Editor

FORUM PRESS

Published simultaneously in Canada

Printed in the United States of America

Library of Congress Catalog Card Number: 81-69861

ISBN: 0-88273-260-9

Cover Design by Phil Wiseman

Contents

General Introduction
Section I — The Rise of Urban-Industrial America 1
    The Birth of Urban America — from Town to City 3
        Tom Kinnersley
    The Origins of the Corporate State 17
        Howard A. DeWitt
    The Black Politician — The Years of Frustration 35
        Henry A. Bryant, Jr.
    A Religion for Every Taste 49
        Mike Zalampas

Section II — World War I to World War II 62
    The Dream Factory — The Story of the American Film Industry   63
        Sheldon Nagel
    The Emergence of the Modern Woman 81
        Barbara Peterson
    Sports in the Twenties 101
        Douglas A. Noverr – Lawrence E. Ziewacz
    Business and the Mass Mind 119
        Ted C. Hinckley

Section III — World War II to the Present 134
    The Moon of Red Cherries 135
        R. J. Lenarcic
    Television — Reflection of Modern America 159
        James C. Williams
    The Space Age 179
        Tom Heiting
    Battling the Environment: Conservation Turns to Ecology 197
        Warren B. Johnson

General Introduction

The Civil War was a bloody struggle of Americans against Americans; when the smoke had finally cleared, America was on the verge of a new era. America the land of the farmer was fast becoming industrial, urban America. Big business, national labor unions, growing cities with slums and minority problems, a national railroad system, women's colleges, urban churches, mass literature, baseball and football games all characterized life in America in this post-Civil War era. To be sure, this sounds much like life in America today, for the culture of early America with its rural value system was giving way to the evolution of the mass society of modern America.

At the center of this cultural change was the philosophy of self-achievement and a national industrial boom. A growing population, abundant resources, and key captains of industry led the way to the rise of big business. America now became one of the world's leading industrial nations. The rapidly growing businesses demanded more workers who saw themselves at the mercy of the industrial giants and who decided that they must form national combinations as the only way to challenge big business. National unions such as the National Labor Union and the Knights of Labor rose and fell during this era. By the arrival of the twentieth century big business still stood supreme.

When the Civil War took place only 20 percent of the population was urban; by 1920 the majority of Americans lived in cities. Urbanization had become central to the growth of modern American culture. The cities of the late 1800s witnessed the creation of ghettoes filled with immigrants from Southern and Eastern Europe, overcrowding, and crime. These urban dwellers began to demand a religion which met their daily needs and helped to solve their social problems. There was also a need for a popular culture for this growing population. Spectator sports, the theater, and popular music served to entertain these urban masses.

Other social changes were also evident in this urban-industrial era. Technological advances drastically altered the role of the American woman. Women found teaching an acceptable profession; women's colleges were meeting their needs for higher education. Many women became involved in oganizations which worked to bring about social reform. Education was also catering to a mass society. Secondary education now became public, teaching methods were changing, and higher education offered further and varied educational possibilities. Science was on the rise with the birth of the medical school; trends in literature featured regionalism, realism and popular literature with themes such as cowboy-versus-Indian. Daily newspapers ran sensational headlines and competed with mass circulation magazines for readers.

With the arrival of the twentieth century the existence of a mass culture for a mass society was obvious in virtually every phase of American life. Modern American culture involves corporations, the metropolis, pollution, the women's movement, a variety of religions, technology and science, mass education, serious and popular literature, and mass amusements. Those tendencies which appeared in the post-Civil War period and led to an urban-industrial America now burst full blown in the twentieth century.

The corporations with trained executives and advertising campaigns dominate American business. These economic giants greatly influence the types of television shows people watch and even the kinds of food they eat. Convenience stores, chain department stores, and fast food restaurants have become part of normal living in America. The American businessman is concerned with inflation, interest rates, and a possible recession, yet also with expansion. Many American industrial giants have now formed into multi-national corporations.

Urbanization is also a dominant trend in American culture today. The vast majority of Americans now live in cities. With the introduction of the automobile the pattern of urban settlement changed and the flight to the suburbs began in earnest. Today more Americans actually live in suburbs than in cities. Urban living is typical but hardly ideal. Cities are beset with major problems such as crime, bankruptcy, and deterioration of their central core. Pollution, of course, has been one of the major problems identified with urban living. While the federal government has attempted to develop a cohesive energy program that will deal with pollution, this program has not yet solved the problem.

Mass culture has seen a drastic change in the role of American women. The suffrage movement of the early 1900s achieved a victory with the passage of the nineteenth amendment. This was merely the beginning of a women's liberation movement which burst on the scene in the 1960s. Women's groups were formed, the stereotype of the ideal woman came under attack, and a unified push was undertaken for an Equal Rights Amendment.

Modern religion offers something for everyone. Americans can search for

God in their traditional churches, on television, and even outside in sports stadiums. The variety of American religion is characterized by a continuing struggle between those fundamentalists who wish to follow the literal truth of the Bible and those modernists who are attempting to reconcile the writings of Charles Darwin which emphasize evolution and modern science with the Bible and traditional religion. This variety also includes the evangelist with his universal church, the Jesus movement, and an interest in Hindu teachings and beliefs. Mass culture is clearly evident in a mass religion.

Twentieth century technology has greatly contributed to the existence of a mass society. Man on the moon, organ transplants, and computers are all part and parcel of this age of science. Technology has also helped to entertain Americans. Motion pictures, radio, and television have greatly satisfied the American desire for mass entertainment. Spectator sports such as football and baseball have lured thousands of fans to stadiums. The changes which technology has brought to modern America are reflected in American literature and its complex themes. The creation of national book clubs and a paperback revolution have accelerated an interest in a mass literature.

American culture has come a long way from the days of pre-Civil War America. Corporations now struggle to control the consumer dollar; cities are struggling with environmental and fiscal problems. Women look for complete equality, while many Americans seek solace in their religion and escape in their literature. Television has literally brought mass amusements into the home. America now truly features a mass culture for a mass society.

Section I
The Rise
of Urban-Industrial America

While the Civil War temporarily interrupted American industrial growth, the conclusion of the war saw an industrial boom which stimulated a new industrial revolution. This economic revolution coupled with the rapid growth of urban centers led to major cultural changes in American society. The four essays in this section describe in detail these changes. Tom Kinnersley focuses upon the rapid growth of cities and the changes that took place in these cities. He describes the important link between businesses and cities and then focuses upon labor developments, the New Immigration, transportation systems, popular amusements and related facets of these burgeoning cities. Howard DeWitt finds the origins of the corporate state in big business in the late 1800s. His essay describes the importance of new technology and the captains of industry in the business boom. The abuses of big business in that laissez-faire era led to critics such as George Norris. Finally, DeWitt shows the relationship between the businessmen and national politics. Henry Bryant in his essay focuses upon the brief rise and eventual fall of the black politicians. This essay focuses upon the careers of certain black politicians such as Robert Brown Elliott, Blanche Kelso Bruce and Pinckney Benton Stewart Pinchback. Bryant describes how the black politician and blacks in general were removed from the political process. Mike Zalampas concludes this section with his essay which focuses upon the diversity of religion during this period. His essay shows the relationship between the social changes and organized religion. Religious diversity is obvious in his descriptions of the holiness movement, comparative religions, and urban churches.

New York's great "shopping" district and elevated railway, Sixth Avenue from 18th Street, 1899. (Collection of the International Museum of Photography)

The Birth of Urban America — From Town to City

Tom Kinnersley

> The grimy lattice-work of the drawbridge swung to slowly, the steam-tug
> blackened the dull air and roiled the turbid water as it dragged its schooner on
> towards the lumber-yards of the South Branch, and a long line of waiting
> vehicles took up their interrupted course through the smoke and the stench as
> they filed across the stream into the thick of business beyond: . . .

Thus Henry B. Fuller depicted the Chicago of the 1890s in his urban
orientated novel *With the Procession* (1895).

By 1900 American cities were a hodgepodge. They were centers of business and finance; most industrial and political developments took place
there, railroads providing the most important connecting links. Most labor
activity was urban based; and cities were entrepôts of culture. Unfortunately, however, poverty was most obvious in large metropolitan regions.
Having insufficient funds to move on, many immigrants congregated
in urban slums, shocking contrasts to the more affluent neighborhoods.
Other urbanites traveled from city to city searching for greater opportunity, making late nineteenth century American society one of the most
mobile in history.

The relationship between business-industrial growth and urbanization
was intimate. As urbanization accelerated in the 1880s and 1890s, so did
business. By the end of the Civil War there were business negotiations
involving millions of dollars; however, by the end of the nineteenth century

hundreds of millions of dollars were sometimes involved. And in 1901 America's first billion dollar company was organized, the United States Steel Corporation.

The 1880s and 1890s are a transition point for the American economy, as industry overtakes agriculture as the predominant element in economic growth. Statistics make this change intelligible. In 1880, for instance, the United States produced 43 million tons of bituminous coal; in 1900 212 million tons were produced. Likewise, anthracite coal production rose from 30 million tons to 57 million tons during the same period. Pig iron and steel further illustrate this trend. In 1880 four million tons of pig iron were produced; twenty years later production increased to 14 million tons. Soaring from one million tons in 1880 to ten million tons in 1900, steel—perhaps more than anything else—ushered the United States into the twentieth century. Between 1880 and 1900, America's industrial production doubled. Overtaking England in the 1890s, the United States assumed the industrial leadership of the world.

To previous generations, the size and power of America's newly created business-industrial conglomerates would have been unbelievable. Perhaps frightening might be the word that some would have applied to the change. By means both fair and foul, Philip D. Armour (meat packing), Andrew Carnegie (steel), James B. Duke (tobacco), Charles R. Pillsbury (milling), John D. Rockefeller (oil), and other so-called robber barons, became multi-millionaires. While the end result of their production undoubtedly contributed to a rising standard of living, this handful of men created business combines that seemed above and beyond the law. It was said they controlled the best politicians money could buy. Monopoly was theoretically outlawed by the Sherman Anti-Trust Act (1890). It was not, however, effectively enforced within the time period covered by this essay.

All of this rapid growth was accompanied by urbanization; one could not have occurred without the other. Among other things, cities provided business with a labor force and a market. Eventually certain cities were identified with specific types of business-industrial development. For example, Chicago became related with meat packing, Milwaukee with brewing, Minneapolis with milling, New York City with banking and finance, Pittsburgh with iron and steel, and Toledo with natural gas.

During the last twenty years of the nineteenth century American cities were changing. Previously most were commercially orientated; trade was their *raison d'être*. However, by the 1880s industry was beginning to dominate many cities, particularly the largest. As industry meant jobs and jobs meant prosperity, city governments—and often chambers of commerce—made valiant efforts (land grants, tax exemptions, etc.) to provide the incentives thought necessary for industrial growth. Again, by presenting statistics, a significant increase in urban factory workers can be illustrated. There were thirty cities in the United States claiming more than 10,000 factory employees in 1880; there were 54 in 1900. Moreover, within the same time frame, those cities with 5,000 to 10,000 factory workers rose from forty-five to eighty-one.

To take advantage of a growing urban market as well as declining postal rates, American business launched nationwide advertising campaigns, mostly through newspapers. From 1865 to 1900 advertising expenditures increased ten times, the 1880s and 1890s accounting for the greatest expansion. Name brands were born. Urbanites were told they could wash the dirt and grime of the factory from their bodies—and by implication from their souls—by using Ivory soap. Coca Cola, Dr. Lyon's (tooth powder), Kellogg's (dry cereal), Kodak (film and cameras), Lydia Pinkham's Vegetable Compound (a nostrum, 21 percent alcohol), and others became equally as well known and as widely used.

Technology's role in the business-industrial development of the American city was vital. Some technology related directly to industrial production. For example, improvements were devised for manufacturing steel (open-hearth process and furnace linings) and aluminum (electrolytic process); paper (wood pulp) and cement (rotary kiln) were made more efficiently. And by 1900 the electric engine was just beginning to replace the steam engine (5 percent of all engines).

Other technology was more directly related to physical changes in urban environments. New uses of steel and concrete, for instance, led to the development of the skyscraper (Home Insurance Building, Chicago, 1885) and in general to the more economic use of center city land. Such inventions as the telephone (1876), the incandescent electric light (1879), and the electric elevator (1889) combined to make the skyscraper, soaring ten stories or more in height, into a veritable nerve center for business-industrial enterprise. Additionally, the cash register (1879) and the pneumatic tube (1893) helped businessmen market their products, while thousands of typewriters (1867) and adding machines (1885) revolutionized the American office, by the end of the nineteenth century.

American business protected its property with relentless persistence. For precisely this reason, specific municipal services were improved. While professional police departments predated the Civil War, additional advances were made later: for example, police became more specialized (detective divisions, bicycle patrols, etc.) and communications grew more efficient (telephone call boxes). The Bertillon system of classification was introduced (criminal classification by precise physical measurements) and mug books expanded. With the support and encouragement of business, professional fire departments provided better training and added new equipment, much of it steam-powered. Telegraph alarms replaced manual bell alarms, thus improving fire warning systems. Also, water—perhaps the single most essential ingredient for urban survival—was supplied by both private and municipal companies in increasing quantities. Piping in water some forty miles, New York City's Croton system was one of the more impressive urban projects of this nature.

Labor developments are also part of this story. Before the Civil War employer-employee relationships were frequently close. Although industrialization speeded up in the 1850s, most factories remained small, and much manufacturing was in shops where business was conducted informally. Often, everyone was on a first-name basis. But the war spurred factory development. As a result of the growth of and subsequent impersonalization of the factory, owners hired managers and superintendents, and the gap between employer and employee widened. Following the war, this trend continued. Then, as city growth became more and more evident, urban workers emerged with problems different from those of their predecessors.

The American worker sought what he considered his fair share of the national bounty. Advertising informed him of innumerable consumer goods, and naturally there were some he wanted. He simply desired a better life than his parents had; he hoped his children would enjoy better ones still. This is the American dream. After the Civil War, pay and working conditions improved. However, by 1900 the salary for many workers was still but one to two dollars per day; the average annual wage for industrial work was $435. Work weeks averaged fifty-seven hours and were six days long. Moreover, 150,000 children, according to the 1890 census, were employed in factories. Also, many jobs were extremely dangerous. Because of employers' disregard for safety, there were workers being forced to take unnecessary risks. For example, in 1893 one railroad employee in ten was injured, one in 115 killed. Mining was another of the more hazardous occupations. For each year in the 1890s one miner in 150 was injured, one in 400 killed.

Urban workers most effectively dealt with the growing size and power of their employers through unionization. In some respects unions functioned as clubs, lodges, and other fraternal associations. As workers left the countryside, something had to replace their accustomed harvest festivals and fishing, hunting, and swimming outings. But, of course, the pursuit of higher wages and better working conditions was of paramount importance.

First of the post-war national unions, was the National Labor Union (1866). However, its life was short. Not long after transforming itself into a political party in the early 1870s, it died. Next the Knights of Labor (1869) was organized. At first, growth was slow and membership even declined during the Depression of 1873, but with the return of prosperity in the early 1880s, the Union won some victories and gained considerable power. Unfortunately, the Knights were associated with, and even blamed for, the Haymarket Square bombing in 1886. Membership subsequently tumbled and the influence of the organization rapidly declined. The largest and most successful of all nineteenth century unions, however, was the American Federation of Labor (1886). Avoiding the "socialistic" cooperatives of the two previous nationals, the AFL concentrated on improving the economic position of its membership, which was monopolized by the most highly skilled workers. Under the leadership of Samuel Gompers, the AFL rose to 500,000 members by 1900. But at the same time there were only a million and a half union members out of 17 million non-agricultural workers in the United States. Still in its infancy, unionization had a long way to go.

Along with boycotts, strikes were a major union weapon. As most union members were city dwellers, most strikes were urban based. According to a report of an industrial commission in 1900, there were more than 20,000 strikes in the United States in the 1880s and 1890s alone. In late nineteenth century America, however, four big strikes stand out. The Baltimore and Ohio Strike (1877) resulted from a wage cut. Troops were dispatched to Pittsburgh to quell mob violence, and additional forces were sent to Philadelphia where twenty-six persons were killed as soldiers attempted to clear the streets. Sympathetic strikes eventually broke out as far away as San Francisco. The previously mentioned Haymarket Square bombing grew out of a nationwide strike for the eight-hour day. Centering in Chicago, where 80,000 workers struck, a bomb exploded at a protest meeting, killing a policeman and wounding many others.

Receiving extensive press coverage were two extremely prominent strikes in the 1890s. Like so many others the Homestead Strike (1892) was precipitated by wage reductions. Before it was settled the manager of the Carnegie Steel Company, Henry Clay Frick, hired 300 Pinkerton detectives, resulting in a "battle" with workers; there were deaths on both sides. The later Pullman Strike (1894) resulted from several grievances; wages were cut while rents and other services in Pullman's "model" town remained stationary. Sympathic to the strikers, Eugene Debs ordered his American Railway Union to boycott Pullman property. Subsequently, 150,000 workers left their jobs. Unfortunately, as was the case in so many instances of labor protest at this time, the army was called in to break the strike. Under the guise that such was necessary for property protection, this was standard procedure.

Patterns of immigration are also vital to the subject of this essay. From 1845 to 1860 the first great wave of immigrants arrived in the United States. During this fifteen-year period, approximately three million immigrants came from Northern and Western Europe. For primarily economic reasons, they migrated from the British Isles, Germany, Ireland, and Scandinavia. After the Civil War, this same pattern continued for twenty years. In the mid-1880s, however, a switch took place. Immigrants now began arriving from Southern and Eastern Europe: they came from Greece, Italy, Poland, Russia, and Syria; Jews came from various nations. The yearly arrival of these new immigrants, as they were called, began to outnumber the old immigrants in the 1890s, and this trend continued into the twentieth century. Although coming to America for economic reasons as well—supposedly the streets were paved with gold—the new immigrants were also motivated by other factors; fear of military conscription and religious persecution headed the list. Again, statistics show change. From the Austro-Hungarian Empire, for instance, 17,000 immigrants arrived in the United States in 1880; 114,000 came in 1900. In 1880 12,000 Italians migrated to America; in 1900 the figure rose to 52,000. From 1865 to 1900 13 million immigrants came to this country, the bulk in the 1880s and 1890s.

Most of the immigrants were city dwellers. Among the old immigrants, the Irish and Germans were largely city based. However, an even higher percentage of the new immigrants lived in cities. More than 80 percent of Russians, for example, lived there; 75 percent of Italians and 65 percent of Greeks were urbanites; almost 100 percent of Jews lived in cities. Cities were chosen for reasons of comfort and convenience, or because farming skills were lacking, or sometimes because immigrants simply did not have the money necessary to move away from their port of entry.

At the end of the nineteenth century, American cities had a higher percentage of foreign born than at any previous time in their history. Census records reveal that one third of Boston was foreign born; so was one fourth of Philadelphia. Undoubtedly the most cosmopolitan city in the United States, New York City possessed a population that was 80 percent foreign born or second generation. Within the city limits, there were one half the Italians of Naples, one half the Germans of Hamburg, and one half the Jews of Warsaw; there were twice the Irish of Dublin. By the turn of the twentieth century, most large eastern cities had a "little" Italy or a "little" Poland. On the West Coast there were numerous Chinatowns.

Most immigrants were welcomed, at least at first. They offered cheap labor, something much in demand in a land undergoing extensive business-industrial growth. Furthermore, railroads saw immigrants as potential clients for their western lands, and of course, both railroads and steamship lines welcomed immigrant fares. However, nativism inevitably developed. Prior to the Civil War, it evolved as a reaction to the old immigrants, and from the mid-1880s onward, it rose again as a reaction to the new immigrants. Led by the American Protective Association (1887), restrictionists claimed the new arrivals were dirty and unkempt. There were allegations that they could not be assimilated, supposedly because most were atheists who were importing the isms: socialism, communism, and anarchism. Although the goals of the APA were not fulfilled until the 1920s, when restrictive quotas were established, Chinese exclusion was provided in 1882 and contract labor forbidden in 1885. Moreover, during the latter nineteenth century, specific legislation prohibited the immigration of prostitutes, alcoholics, polygamists, and other so-called undesirables. To demonstrate their allegiance to the cause, some states even outlawed the teaching of foreign languages by 1900.

The deprived life-style of many of these newcomers encouraged prejudice. For principally economic reasons, many lived in congested urban slums. By the 1880s rows of three- and four-story tenements had gone up in all of America's larger eastern cities. Not all were occupied by the newest arrivals, but they predominated. Manhattan—as one of the most obvious examples—had 30,000 tenements by 1890. They served as home for approximately one million residents, and two or three families to a single unit was "normal." Often there was only one water faucet to a floor, and if there was an inside toilet it was usually on the ground floor or in the basement. Such facilities were normally outside. Only three to six feet separated one tenement from the next. Periodically, tenement-house laws were passed. However, interest groups made most ineffective, and this problem remained unsolved as the United States entered the twentieth century.

Upon their arrival in America, immigrants desperately sought acceptance, security, and support. For this reason, among others, they herded together in ghettos. For a time, customs from the old country were retained through dress, food, and religious observance; "foreign" language newspapers were published to inform them of news back home. But adjustment to the new country was imperative and this was where the ubiquitous political boss most often came in. Although normally not an officeholder himself, his money and influence controlled many who were. Boss rule was frequently sunk in a foundation of gambling, liquor, and prostitution. Many times streetcar leases were boss controlled, as were many gas, electric light, and telephone franchises. Boss William Marcy Tweed of New York City was probably the most famous or infamous, but there were others. For example, there was "King" James McManes of Philadelphia, "Czar" Martin Lomasney of Boston, and Christopher Magee of Pittsburgh.

Not long after passing quarantine inspections, most immigrants were greeted by a representative of the local machine, the ward heeler who did the footwork for these political armies. Often a place to live was provided, and most new arrivals were given some groceries. Perhaps a job interview was arranged. Moreover, the favors would continue in the days ahead. There would be a turkey at Thanksgiving, and dance tickets and baseball passes were frequently gifts from the machine. For the very poor, wedding and funeral expenses were paid. The machine bailed drunks out of jail; when illness struck or when hospitalization was required, the machine was there to help. Somehow the machine found husbands for even the most unattractive daughters. In return for all this the machine asked for unquestioning political support. For obvious reasons that support was generally given.

Interconnecting America's growing urban centers, was a varied transportation network. For barges there were miles of canals. Hard surface roads were serviced by stagecoaches, carrying both passengers and freight. Teamsters specialized in heavier cargos. On water, steampower was antiquating sailpower, and all "modern" ships were now being built with steel hulls. But by the 1880s and 1890s the railroad had become the predominant mode of transportation. During the 1880s—"the railroad decade"—some 70,000 miles of track were laid as the number of transcontinentals rose from one to four. Time zones were established for the convenience of intercity scheduling. Although much of this work was poorly done, necessitating later reconstruction, by 1900 the United States had almost 200,000 miles of track, 40 percent of the world total.

As in industry, many of the railroad conglomerates acquired enormous power. Jay Gould and William Vanderbilt, just to name two of the owners, were known for both their wealth and ruthlessness. While some of the roads went bankrupt during the Depression of 1893, most were reorganized by big city bankers, like J. P. Morgan, and they again rose to dominance. Like industry, government attempted regulation. State laws established maximum rates until struck down by the Supreme Court in the Wabash case (1886). Congress then passed the Interstate Commerce Act (1887), but the powers of this new commission were insufficient. More effective regulation awaited the twentieth century.

Intracity transportation is also important during this period. Despite their slowness, horse-car lines provided intracity services before the Civil War. They were satisfactory because even the largest pre-war cities seldom had a radius exceeding three or four miles. But, as cities grew after the Civil War, intracity transportation improvements became imperative. Steam-powered cable cars (San Francisco) and elevated railroads (New York City) were introduced in the 1870s, both of which were later electrified. The first electric streetcar line was opened in Richmond, Virginia (1887), and was so successful that twenty-five more lines were in operation within a year. By 1890 electric streetcar systems had laid 15,000 miles of track in the United States; by way of comparison, there were but 4,000 miles of horse-car track. Moreover, completion of the Brooklyn Bridge (1883) and others, eased urban access into the hinterland. Two new forms of urban transportation emerged as the twentieth century approached: the horseless carriage (1893) and the subway (Boston, 1897).

As American cities industrialized, their appearance changed. In addition to the technological changes already described, certain urban sectors became more specialized. Some zones became exclusively factory-oriented. Other districts were associated with banking and finance, and still others with department stores and various retail establishments or with theaters, restaurants, and hotels. Furthermore, transportation improvements stimulated the geographic expansion of cities. For example, the radius of Boston grew from three miles in 1860 to ten miles in 1900. Also, suburbs boomed and "satellite cities" were born along intraurban or interurban railroad lines. Gary, Indiana, is but one example. The site of considerable labor turmoil in the 1890s, Pullman, Illinois, is another. With new rail systems feeding into the countryside, some companies began moving away from the city core. Fleeing central city congestion, Procter & Gamble of Cincinnati, for instance, is just one case of a company taking this action.

To understand the phenomenon of urbanization, geographic mobility must at least be introduced. For many years, it was one of the most misunderstood forces affecting the growth of American cities. Historians used to believe that cities grew like a pile of wood: throw forty to fifty sticks on the pile and it grew that much larger. Or, in other words, if 50,000 persons entered a city, the population increased by 50,000. But this assumed that migration was a one-step process; it assumed that cities were very stable, even stagnant. It assumed there was no outward migration.

Urban migratory patterns are of various sorts. First, there are immigrants entering the United States from abroad. There is also intercity migration, and the importance of the movement from the farm to the urban factory has long been recognized. It is difficult to keep young people in the country once they have seen the bright lights of New York City, Boston, Philadelphia, Chicago, or even of Indianapolis for that matter. Although more difficult to measure, there is intracity migration as well; people have always moved from neighborhood to neighborhood. From all historical studies, late nineteenth century American cities were extraordinarily mobile. Anything but stable, they were like busy way-stations with passengers coming and going en masse.

Several studies indicate the mobility of large eastern cities. For example, one reveals that only 64 percent of Boston's 1880 male population was still in town in 1890. Work dealing with a somewhat earlier period in two New York cities, Poughkeepsie and Rochester, shows higher mobility still. The information suggests that many of the poor refused to stagnate in big city slums. It is likely, on the contrary, that many urbanites traveled from city to city searching for greater opportunity.

Even the Midwest, long thought to be the personification of stability, was highly mobile. For instance, from 1880 to 1895 only 22 percent of the households in five Wisconsin townships stayed put. Mining cities were probably the most mobile of all. A recent study indicates that only 19 percent of the 1870 residents of Virginia City, Nevada, were still there in 1880. Furthermore, it is estimated that more than 120,000 persons entered the town during the 1870s, although the population gain was but 4,000. People were constantly coming in and going out; the city appears like a revolving door in a busy department store.

Aside from industry and labor, aside from immigration, transportation, and mobility, by 1900 American cities were creating a new life-style. Its influence, however, extended beyond urban centers; it was piped into the countryside via the mail-order catalogue as well as through magazines, journals, and newspapers. Imitation of city ways was the order of the day.

While America's food was grown by the farmer (and often preserved by him in the mason jar, 1858), technology eventually made a balanced diet possible for urbanites. Before canning became common most city dwellers ate few fruits or green vegetables from autumn to spring. Instead large quantities of starches were consumed: for example, pies, doughnuts, potatoes, and bread. Before the Civil War, Gail Borden began canning evaporated milk; later Gilbert Van Camp grew rich canning food for Union troops (pork and beans in tomato sauce among others). But after the invention of the pressure kettle (1875) for reliable sterilizing, sales in canned foods zoomed. Tomatoes, tomato ketchup, salt herring, sweet corn, etc., were soon being canned on an assembly line basis.

Further diet changes occurred in the 1880s with the improvement of the refrigerator railroad car and the development of dry cereals (Granola, Shredded Wheat, Grape Nuts, etc.) and other packaged foods. By the close of the nineteenth century the urban diet approached the balance of today. Furthermore, as farming grew more specialized, farmers began to buy some canned and packaged urban food products. In some respects the tables were being reversed—farmers were buying the finished product from the city and not vice versa.

But perhaps the most imitated element of the new urban life-style was fashion. Although only World War I would bring revolutionary change, by 1900 there were omens of the future. As women increasingly participated in athletics and rode the new "safety" bicycles, some clothes became less confining. In 1900, for example, Sears Roebuck and Co. sold sport outfits with skirts slightly shorter than standard. Also, stays and corsets were modified. Unfortunately, however, more formal dress was less functional, running to "smallness." Tight-laced corsets, tight kid gloves, and shoes usually a size or more too small were typical. Moreover, style dictated a wide-brimmed hat, a high choking collar, and a flaring skirt that swept the ground on all sides. Hair was always long, although frequently piled on top of the head or tortured into ringlets; wearing the hair "up" was most popular with older women.

For men, dress was more sensible, but often uncomfortable as well. When "dressed up," the 1900 man wore a dark woolen suit and a derby hat. The coat would have padded shoulders; the collar and cuffs would be stiffly laundered and the shirt held together at the bosom with studs. Dress shoes or boots and heavy socks completed the outfit, although the more affluent frequently complemented their dress with a gold-headed cane or an umbrella. Most everyone owned a pocket watch; sometimes it was an heirloom. Being the male status symbol of the era, beards were still worn, but they were beginning to go out as the twentieth century dawned.

Late nineteenth century American urban architecture was a combination of earlier styles. Both the heavy Romanesque and the somewhat lighter Gothic appeared, and in the 1890s there was a revival of Renaissance Classical. Of course, the functional skyscraper was truly an American contribution. The architecture of the typical home, called Victorian, was stark and box-like. Homes were composites of cupolas, dormers, balconies, and gimcrackery. A covered porch dominated the front approach; often, iron deer decorated the yard, which was in turn encircled by a grate fence.

Wood was the most common building material, although brick was used and the affluent were identified with brownstone. Inside, style was over-balanced on the side of tawdry ornateness. Wealthy Americans crammed their rooms with a variety of settees, divans, and armchairs; horsehair and plush were popular fabrics. And an eye-boggling collection of knickknacks and stuffed pillows abounded. The more cluttered the appearance, the better. On the floor, padded carpets softened the step; floral designs were the style. Of the numerous paintings that were hung on the walls, land-scapes and idyllic children were the subjects most often chosen.

Other than public buildings and monuments, the finer hotels were perhaps the most noticeable aspect of urban architecture. Among the best were the Plaza, the Savoy, and the Waldorf-Astoria in New York City. Philadelphia bragged of the Lafayette; the Palmer House was Chicago's finest. The Vendome was where the well-heeled stayed in Boston. These luxurious hostels advertised private baths, electric elevators, electric call service, and other "modern" conveniences. All offered a banquet hall or ballroom, club rooms, beauty parlors, barber shops, and exquisite boutiques, but activity centered on the lobby, that bustling interior court where news counters and porter's stands flanked a registration desk. Then at a short distance, there was an array of expensive chairs and sofas for guests making last-minute plans or involved in important business discussions. However, this was also home base for idlers, those guests content to watch the world go by.

Then as now, a night on the town was one of the more popular urban amusements. The more cosmopolitan cities offered a wide choice of restau-rants: American, French, Italian, and sometimes Chinese. Catering to the well-to-do, Delmonico's in New York City was a splendid place for dinner. It had earned a worldwide reputation for expertly prepared meals and for a refined atmosphere. If fast food at low cost was desired, by 1900 cafeterias were just coming on the scene (Chicago, 1895).

After dining, the possible diversions were almost limitless. Most towns had skating rinks, both ice and roller. Often there were circuses, wild west shows, and minstrel shows. Although mostly shown in peep-show machines, there were some motion pictures as well. For the musically oriented, bands played in public parks. Some cities were associated with particular types of music: for example, New Orleans with jazz, Memphis with the blues, and St. Louis with ragtime. Of course, all towns contained a red light district, where amusement was found in low class saloons, gambling dens, and brothels. For a more cultured evening, there were live theatrical perfor-mances. Improvements in transportation enabled traveling players to entertain in most towns, although New York City was tops. Sometimes visitors came to the city just to see their favorite thespian. Among the most popular were Ethel Barrymore ("The Country Mouse"), Sarah Bernhardt ("Trelawney of The Wells"), Richard Mansfield ("Cyrano de Bergerac"), and William Gillette ("Sherlock Holmes"). Additional entertainment for the more sophisticated, at least in larger cities, included ballets, operas, and symphony orchestras.

However, to the "average" city dweller, urban culture increasingly meant spectator sports, which were just beginning their rise in popularity. Golf, polo, rowing, tennis, and yachting were all popular, but as they were dominated by the rich, their following was limited. Horse racing and trotting gained in appeal—and all large cities had one or more track—but, again, they were sports of the rich. Basketball (1891) had just been invented, and its popularity awaited the future. Bicycling reached "craze" proportions, and many towns built ovals for competitive racing. However, this was as much a participatory sport as one for the fans.

The big three spectator sports were baseball, boxing, and football. After the first professional baseball team (the Cincinnati Red Stockings) was organized in 1869, the National League was formed in 1876. Composed of eight teams, the league coordinated schedules and standardized rules. Born in 1882, the competitive American Association participated in a post-season tournament with its rival until the Association folded in 1891. But soon after the American League emerged (1901), the "world" series began again. Included among the "stars" were such as Albert Spaulding (1874, 52 wins and 18 losses), Cy Young (511 lifetime wins), and Wee Willie Keeler ("I hit 'em where they ain't."). Although brutal and often illegal, boxing was also enormously popular. And all sports fans argued the merits of heavyweight champions John L. Sullivan ("the Boston Strong Boy"), James J. Corbett ("Gentleman Jim"), and Bob Fitzsimmons ("a fighting machine on stilts"). Football evolved from English rugby and field hockey, at first little resembling the "modern" game. But changes came after Walter Camp wrote the first rule book (1891); the twentieth century brought further change still. At the time the Ivy League produced the superior teams (Harvard, Yale, and Princeton, "The Big Three") and by almost unanimous choice, Walter W. (Pudge) Heffelfinger (Yale, 1888-1891) was the outstanding player of the era.

At this point a summary is in order. Change is the key word in describing late nineteenth-century American urbanization. America was once a nation dominated by farmers and small shopkeepers. However, by 1900 their influence was fast diminishing. The failure of the Populists in the 1890s illustrates at least this much. Once agrarian in politics and provincial in spirit, the country had become a land of cities. Although still only 39.7 percent urban in 1900, the United States was well on its way toward an urban majority.

America's rapid urbanization created enormous problems. Most cities had grown too fast, and most urbanites seemed to have had little over-all understanding of the speed and force of the urbanizing process. Capitalizing on the insecurity of newly arrived immigrants, political bosses used their votes to install corrupt politicians in public office. From city governments, some bosses extracted 999-year streetcar leases or inflated contracts for construction of municipal buildings. While improvements had been made by the turn of the twentieth century, it was still often difficult for cities to provide adequate police, water, and fire services. Inadequate sanitation resulted in the spread of disease, frequently at epidemic rates. Yet another problem was urban congestion. Before cities placed utility lines underground, a jungle of telephone and electric wires marred the landscape. Zoning ordinances were tightened, but that did not prevent the growth of slums. As central city areas deteriorated, the more affluent fled to the suburbs, leaving the city core to the very poorest.

By the close of the nineteenth century, fortunately, movements had begun (National Municipal League, 1892, and League of American Municipalities, 1897) to clean up city governments and beautify urban environments. Furthermore, the Chicago World's Fair (1893) and the work of such reform mayors as Tom Johnson (Cleveland) and "Golden Rule" Samuel Jones (Toledo) were supportive of these efforts. In the near future, Progressivism would further reform and democratize American cities. For example, new types of city government (commission and city-manager forms) were introduced and soon the initiative, referendum, and recall was applied to municipal politics.

It should never be forgotten that cities have always been at the center of action in this country. While they have had problems—and still do—they are the heart of the nation; they are where the most vital decisions are made. The best newspapers and schools, and virtually all the art galleries, bookstores, libraries, museums, etc., are urban. Urbanization has long been the wave of the future; from all indications, it is not going to go away. As in 1900, the United States must deal with this phenomenon, sink or swim.

Suggested Readings

Although a relatively new specialization, there are numerous American Urban History selections that can be recommended. For students interested in urban history within the context of a general social history of the United States, there are several good books to chose from. Gerald R. Baydo's *A Topical History of The United States*, as the title suggests, presents American History topically. For instance, there are chapters on industrialization, labor, Indians, etc., as well as one on the city. Nelson Manfred Blake's *A History of American Life and Thought* and J. C. Furnas' *The Americans; A Social History of The United States 1587-1914*, although dealing with various social history subjects, also include much urban material.

For students of late nineteenth century American Urban History, there are at least a half dozen reading musts. On urban immigration there is Humbert S. Nelli's *The Italians in Chicago*; on transportation developments there is Sam B. Warner's *Streetcar Suburbs*; and on labor there is Stanley Buder's *Pullman*. Easily the best works in their respective fields are Stephan Thernstrom's *Poverty and Progress*, a brilliant study of nineteenth century urban geographic mobility, and James F. Richardson's *The New York Police Colonial Times to 1901*. For information regarding the growth and development of boss rule, Alexander B. Callow's *The Tweed Ring* is about the best.

However, for those urban history students whose needs can best be fulfilled via a textbook approach, there are four standouts. Constance McLaughlin Green's *American Cities*, Blake McKelvey's *The Urbanization of America* (which has about everything in it), Zane L. Miller's *The Urbanization of Modern America*, and Arthur M. Schlesinger's *The Rise of The City, 1878-1898* (although more than 35 years old, still excellent). Both the Green and Miller books are in paperback.

The Origins
of the Corporate State

Howard A. DeWitt

The triumph of industrial America and the rise of the corporate state is associated with the post-Civil War change in intellectual attitudes. The belief that anyone could rise from rags to riches glorified the role of the businessman and deified the values of the banking community. By the 1870s the growth of the transcontinental railroad, the emergence of a modern factory system, the rapid burst of technological innovation, the availability of accumulated capital, and the extensive supply of various classes of skilled and unskilled laborers made the success of big business inevitable in the American experience. There were many reasons for the triumph of corporate ideas during the last three decades of the nineteenth century. The military needs of the Civil War, for example, stimulated demands for increased industrial production as well as the scientific distribution and marketing of consumer goods. The triumph of the corporate state led to surplus production which created new foreign markets in Asia, Europe, and Latin America for American goods. The dominance of business in domestic and foreign affairs created a strong demand for reform in American politics. Thus, virtually every social-intellectual, economic, or political change in the United States could be traced to the corporate state, and the result was to create a nationwide debate over the role of economic change in American life.

There was an element of conflict between free enterprise capitalists and the common man in the late nineteenth century. There was a widespread belief among intellectuals that American institutions should meet social

The first transcontinental United States railroad was completed on May 10, 1869, in Promontory, Utah. Central Pacific and Union Pacific railroad officials drove in the last spike. (The Bancroft Library, University of California, Berkeley)

needs and provide material wealth for all levels of society. A number of reform-minded ministers like Washington Gladden and Walter Rauschenbusch wrote and preached that improved working conditions, slum clearance, temperance, and decent employee-industrial relations would lead to greater prosperity and defuse the revolutionary impulse in American society. This intellectual hostility to the rising corporate state was known as the social gospel movement. As religious activism declined in the city, zealous Catholics, Protestants and Jews organized to generate new life into urban religious institutions. The social gospel movement was a reaction against uncontrolled individualism and unrestrained capitalism. The popularity of public charities, schools for destitute children, and aid for senior citizens marked an important change in American values. Washington Gladden, who became known as the Father of Social Christianity, urged church leaders to develop responsible attitudes toward labor and urban problems. Gladden believed that a revitalized, reform-minded urban religion could improve the welfare of the working classes.

In response to these developing reform attitudes the defenders of individualism and unrestrained competition argued that business concentration did not influence the mobility of business-minded entrepreneurs. Drawing freely upon the Horatio Alger myth that anyone could make a million dollars, defenders of the corporate state argued persuasively that the only responsibility of big business was to continue to provide an expanding economy. This argument was supported by the growth of the factory system. In 1860 slightly more than 100,000 factories operated in America, but by 1900 over 200,000 manufacturing plants were creating the impression that individual corporate initiative was open to anyone. Yet these statistics were misleading. By 1900, when only ten percent of all manufacturing plants had annual production of a million dollars, one percent of the nation's factories produced over two-thirds of all U.S. goods. To fully appreciate the triumph of business concentration, it is necessary to examine the rise of the transcontinental railroad and the monopolistic tendencies that it stimulated in the American economy.

In 1860 railroads were the most significant economic enterprise in the United States. As new track was laid, freight and passenger trains created a quiet revolution in settlement and the distribution of consumer goods. Of all the railroad projects that occupied the public imagination none was more exciting than the transcontinental line. In 1862 Congress granted the Central Pacific railroad the right to build east from Sacramento, and the Union Pacific was chartered to build westward from Omaha, Nebraska. After a great deal of controversy over excess federal aid to the railroad industry and a strong anti-Chinese movement due to the use of Asian labor the transcontinental railroad was completed. On May 10, 1869, the two railroads linked their tracks before a wildly drunken crowd in Promontory, Utah. As a large crowd gathered boisterously cheering, a young lady with a radiant smile provided a spike of gold, silver, and iron to begin the elaborate ceremony which completed the railroad system. There was a feeling that the transcontinental railroad was the beginning of an unlimited era of techno-logical triumph. A telegraph wire was placed around each spike, and every barroom in America exploded with cheers as they heard the "tap-tap-tap" driving the last spike into the ground. This cataclysmic event marked a new era of economic growth in American civilization.

In the 1870s Pullman sleeping cars, steel rails, uniform gauges, improved tracks, and terminal facilities made the railroad an impressive national transportation network. The invention of cold-storage railroad cars pro-vided a link for Chicago meat packers to all parts of the United States. The cold storage warehouses in the Middle West created a revolution in the distribution of agricultural goods and led to increasingly sophisticated marketing techniques.

The corruption and monopolistic tendencies of the Union Pacific and Central Pacific lines did not escape the scrutiny of public opinion. Despite the economic advantages of the transcontinental railroad, its critics argued that the railroads each owned the construction company which built their lines. The result of this convenient economic arrangement was to siphon millions of dollars from state and federal government. The Crédit Mobilier, the company which built the Union Pacific, billed the railroad for $73 million for construction work that cost less than $50 million to complete. The Central Pacific and Union Pacific received twenty million acres of land and $60 million in government loans to complete their project. The state and county governments provided $528 million and graciously donated fifty million acres of land to the two railroads. In most cases these subsidies encouraged railroads to overbuild in order to enlarge construction profits.

The need for improved transportation stifled much of the criticism of the railroad industry. By 1883 the Northern Pacific completed its line to Port-land, Oregon, and the Atchison, Topeka and Santa Fe railroad connected Kansas and Nebraska. In 1893 James J. Hill's Great Northern Railroad coupled Seattle with the Middle West, and the presence of five major railway systems throughout the United States created new demands for consumer goods and intensified business activity. Yet, large numbers of railroads experienced financial problems or quietly went bankrupt and were bought up by investment bankers. As one critic suggested, free-enterprise capitalism failed long before monopolistic bankers gained control of key transportation systems. It was the greed of easy short-term profits which condemned the railroad barons to long-term economic failure.

In the 1890s it was apparent that the railroad industry was overbuilt and in shallow financial water. The panic and depression of 1893 caused 318 companies to experience bankruptcy, and this allowed two New York in-vestment banking firms to gain control of most major railroads. Typical of the investment banker was J. P. Morgan who financed the consolidation of a number of railroads to prevent irresponsible financial and investment schemes. However, Morgan insisted that bank representatives be placed on the management of leading railroads, and this increased monopolistic tendencies in the transportation industry. By 1900 a few major railroad systems, controlled by Wall Street banking houses, controlled over half the mileage in the nation.

The railroad industry is an excellent example of how finance capitalism led to the rise of uncontrolled oligarchical monopolies. As wealth accumulated it was reinvested in corporate endeavors which led to aggregations of capital which hampered competition in the marketplace. Wall Street bankers argued that pooling of business resources guaranteed greater prosperity, but the average citizen believed that economic controls in the hands of a few individuals would destroy the fabric of American democracy. As a result, fears of "Robber Barons" or "Captains of Industry," as they were commonly known, reached epidemic proportions. The big businessman created a new level of economic monopoly from 1870 to 1900.

John D. Rockefeller's rise to power aptly demonstrates this dominant development in late nineteenth century America, the rise of monopolistic business practices. In response to Rockefeller's legendary early speculative exploits in the oil industry, Americans coined the term "robber baron" to describe his business character. During the Civil War, he financed his first oil refinery. By 1867 he was the most prosperous oil magnate in the Cleveland area. In 1870 Rockefeller formed the Standard Oil Company of Ohio in which he introduced modern technical and managerial skills to squeeze out the competition. Since the oil industry was highly competitive, transportation costs cut heavily into profits. To increase Standard Oil's earnings, Rockefeller guaranteed large scale shipments to railroads in return for rebates which reduced his company's transportation costs.

By 1880 Standard Oil controlled more than 90 percent of all refined oil in the United States. Rockefeller's ingenious business tactics had virtually ended all competition. In 1882 Rockefeller and his partners formed the country's first trust, which was a company that controlled an industry through consolidation, spies, industrial sabotage, rebates, and other unscrupulous business tactics. By consolidating twenty-seven different companies into a single corporation, Rockefeller created America's first corporate giant. The Ohio courts responded by declaring Standard Oil a company which illegally restrained trade. This forced Rockefeller to re-create his oil trust under New Jersey's liberal corporate laws.

As he rose to power, Rockefeller created numerous enemies in private business and federal government agencies. As a result of his tactics, the United States Supreme Court forced the Standard Oil Company to reorganize its business interests to avoid trust prosecution. In 1911 Rockefeller grudgingly formed thirty separate firms to satisfy federal laws. The irony of Rockefeller's Standard Oil story is that the company contributed to the growth of the American economy while fostering federal regulation of big business.

As much as Rockefeller dominated the oil field, Andrew Carnegie, a poor Scottish immigrant, revolutionized the steel industry. Prior to investing in the steel business, Carnegie became a wealthy man from investments in railroad construction, bridge building, and oil refining. On a business trip to England, he witnessed the Bessemer process for producing steel. This inexpensive production technique made it highly profitable to invest in the steel industry, and soon the Pennsylvania countryside was dotted with steel mills. When the Panic of 1873 caused financial difficulty, Carnegie bought out many of his competitors.

The significance of Carnegie's business success came in the area of scientific management. He introduced cost conscious production techniques. Business expenses were reduced by mechanization and revolutionary accounting procedures. In a few years the price of steel declined so rapidly that it replaced iron, wood, and stone in construction. In 1900 Carnegie sold his steel holdings to the investment broker, J. P. Morgan, for half a billion dollars, thus paving the way for the creation of the powerful United States Steel Corporation.

Many myths were perpetuated about Carnegie's life. His defenders suggested that he was typical of the poor immigrant who made millions, then devoted the rest of his life to philanthropic causes. In 1889 Carnegie wrote "The Gospel of Wealth," a popular pamphlet, which argued that the rich had a moral obligation to spend their money for the welfare of the general public. Many industrial barons were civic-minded individuals who supported the arts and helped to establish a tradition which linked wealth to cultural advancement. Prior to his death, Carnegie used his massive fortune to create libraries, charitable institutions, research foundations, and endowments for peace and international cooperation. Since such philanthropy was not tax deductible, Carnegie was supporting his belief that corporate wealth would create a better world.

John Pierpont Morgan was a late nineteenth-century businessman who made his fortune providing investment capital for fledgling corporations. The post-Civil War banking system made it unlawful for large banks to accept land as security for a loan. Many banks lacked the funds to lend money to legitimate business enterprises. As a result, the J. P. Morgan Company became one of the investment corporations which provided loans for business expansion. The general pattern was for a new or expanding company to sell stock or bonds, and the J. P. Morgan Company would then act as a broker for these economic devices.

Thomas A. Edison, a young inventor, prospered from the financial support of the J. P. Morgan Company. As a young inventor in the telegraph and telephone fields, Edison was well known for his scientific genius. Without J. P. Morgan's financial support, however, Edison's technology would not have spread to every part of the United States. In 1877, at age thirty, Edison worked on an incandescent light and the phonograph. These diverse inventions indicate the scope and breadth of Edison's mind.

In October 1878, Edison perfected the theory of the incandescent light and founded the Edison Electric Company. He theorized that the light produced by electricity could be broken into small units and distributed to homes and businesses. On September 4, 1882, the first commercial electrical station opened at Pearl Street near New York City's financial district. J. P. Morgan's financial support helped the Edison Company to open its business with 85 customers and 400 lamps. To help publicize electricity, Morgan installed his own electrical plant in his Manhattan home. In a few years electrical lighting stations were constructed in Boston, Chicago, and Philadelphia with Morgan's financial support.

The key to Morgan's financial success is that he provided the financial resources for new corporate enterprises. Until Morgan entered the investment market, the sale of stocks in a corporation was considered a risky venture. By the 1880s the reputation of the J. P.Morgan Company guaranteed the confidence of eager investors. As a result of his financial reputation, Morgan was able to bring about the merger of many corporations and to control these business interests by placing his men on the boards of directors. Investors would eagerly purchase stock in Morgan-controlled companies, because they believed that his management skills assured high profits.

The relationship between Rockefeller, Carnegie, and Morgan is an important element in understanding the rise of the corporate state. Carnegie was the cost-conscious steel master who built a major American industry, and Rockefeller carried these ideas one step further by seeking out the best methods to expand the oil industry. Morgan was the banker who financed financial undertakings by entrepreneurs like Carnegie and Rockefeller. Between 1898 and 1901 Carnegie and Morgan struggled for control of the steel industry. In 1901 Morgan and his partners bought out Carnegie's steel interests for an inflated price of $447 million and formed the first billion dollar trust—United States Steel. The billion dollar trust which Morgan organized was the capstone to the monopolistic triumphs of the robber barons.

The high noon of monopoly occurred just after the turn of the century as more than 300 trusts emerged in the aftermath of the formation of United States Steel. Yet, it would have been impossible to consolidate this level of wealth had it not been for the inventors and technological change. The economic revolution was a result of more than 440,000 new inventions from 1870 to 1900. A review of the most important inventions indicates the degree of technological innovation which aided the rise of business values. In 1866 Cyrus W. Field was successful in laying a transatlantic cable to Europe. Alexander Graham Bell's telephone was operating by the 1890s, and the American Telephone and Telegraph Company made American business a worldwide phenomenon. To speed the pace of business success, Christopher L. Sholes invented the typewriter, James Ritty the cash register, and William S. Burroughs the adding machine. These inventions were an important catalyst to the general technological revolution during the late nineteenth century.

Much of the economic productivity of America was due to the rise of the city. One of the key elements in cities was the large number of immigrants who arrived from Europe. In the 1880s more than five million foreigners entered the United States to seek their fortunes. Many immigrants found it difficult to adjust to American life, and this helped to give rise to city bosses. In New York City the Tammany Hall political machine secured jobs and housing and provided social contacts for the new immigrants. In return the boss requested and received political support from the alien once he was naturalized. By the late 1880s immigrant votes furnished the base for the power of the successful city machines. The city boss acted as a mediator between the poor immigrant and the law. Tammany Hall leader George Washington Plunkitt suggested that this was a social service organization designed to aid the poor. In many respects city bosses were power brokers insuring the adequate function of urban government and society. While there was prosperity and full-employment the city boss found little competition from high-minded reformers. The prospect of a lengthy depression, however, threatened to challenge the urban machine.

In each decade from 1870 to 1900 there were three- to four-year periods of economic disaster which created unemployment, bankruptcy, and business failures. Although progress, prosperity, and economic growth were generally the hallmarks of the rise of the corporate state there were reformers who argued that the lack of business competition threatened the fiber of American democracy. The "Goo-Goos," as the reformers were known, pointed out that the Panic of 1893 caused 500 banks and 16,000 business to fail. In June 1894, the Federal Government announced that one-fourth of railroad capital was in receivership, and federal officials painted a gloomy picture for the future of the American economy. The question of who was to blame for the roller-coaster-like economy occupied the minds of most people in the 1890s.

Many Americans blamed the business practices of the robber barons for the catalysmic changes in employment and business. The press and reform-minded politicians charged that unscrupulous business practices by J. P. Morgan's United States Steel trust and John D. Rockefeller's Standard Oil Company made it impossible for the common man to compete in the business world. The defenders of the industrial barons quoted Charles Darwin's *Origins of the Species* (1859) to argue that the strongest and most capable individual made millions of dollars while the weak fell by the wayside. Herbert Spencer, a popular English philosopher and writer, delighted American advocates of the corporate system with his Social Darwinism. This theory argued that commerce and trade must flow without interference from government. In Spencer's view the rich deserved their wealth, and the poor were simply the product of laziness, vice, and general lack of ability. Social Darwinism was a convenient rationale to explain the extremes of wealth and poverty present in America's new industrial society.

The critics of the American economy were an important force in creating a public demand for reform. The most popular protest themes during the late nineteenth century centered around railroad and land monopolies.

Henry George, a transplanted New Yorker, rose to prominence in California during the 1870s as a critic of the Central Pacific and Southern Pacific railroads. The California Democratic Party hired George to edit the *Oakland Transcript*. He used his position to call for an end to the unbridled economic power of the railroads and to plead for the election of reform-minded Democratic politicians. In his writings, George linked the railroads' use of inexpensive Chinese labor with huge profits and monopolistic business practices. Thus George also advocated the enactment of legislation to curb Chinese immigration. The railroad barons and the land speculators, George argued, did not profit from the benefits of their own labor. Although George viciously attacked the practices of big business, he did not gain an immediate audience for his ideas.

Then one day as he was riding his horse in the Oakland hills, Henry George developed an economic theory which reflected the hostility of middle-class Americans toward the new corporate wealth. George speculated that land prices were rising for reasons he believed to be economically catastrophic. In a moment of spontaneous reflection, George suggested that as progress and wealth increase in society, a twin emerges in the form of poverty. If wealth is created without hard work, it inevitably results in unemployment and blue-collar dissatisfaction. The rise of land values made it virtually impossible for the average person to purchase a home, or to succesfully operate a small farm. George believed that the traditional mobility of the landowner was vanishing as land barons and corporate interests dominated the economy.

In a series of pamphlets, George suggested that the large land grants to railroads were unfair because they accentuated the drift toward monopoly. It was George's premise that a portion of public lands should be returned to the people. In the depression-ridden 1870s this was an unusually popular idea. It could be accomplished by a single massive tax on land speculation. In a finely argued piece of logic, George demonstrated that wages no longer had the purchasing power that they had in the past. In a time of spiraling inflation and declining wages, George's theories attracted a substantial public following.

The most important weapon in Henry George's intellectual arsenal was a device called the single tax. It was a plan to tax the "unearned increments" on the rise of land values. In other words, if a person held a piece of land for speculative purposes, there would be a still tax upon the property. In this way, George argued, excessive unearned profits would disappear and free economic competition would remain a standard practice. One of the key arguments in George's philosophy was the idea that the railroads' power was due to monopolistic practices aided by federal money and land grants. This was the perfect argument to connect hostility toward both the railroads and th federal government.

In 1879 George's best-selling book, *Progress and Poverty,* popularized the single tax and sold a record-breaking five million copies. There was little sophistication in George's work. He asked a simple question: "Why should an individual be rewarded for simply selling land in an inflationary market?" This question exploited the growing middle-class fears that the unemployed and business interests would engage in a revolutionary conflict. In many respects *Progress and Poverty* recognized the triumph of the corporate state, and it called for a public campaign to restore individual initiative to the American dream. George believed that the sturdy pioneer and the yeoman farmer were no longer the backbone of the nation. He was right, for the industrial order had transformed America from a rural, agricultural state into an urban, industrial complex.

As America lost its pioneer charm and became cynical over the triumph of business values, a new form of literature began to emerge. Suddenly bitter, acid-penned critics began to examine the new corporate civilization. Among the most satiric writers was a nasty, sharp-tongued San Francisco news-paperman, Ambrose Bierce. As a reporter for the *San Francisco News Letter*, Bierce wrote a titillating gossip column, "The Town Crier," in which he satirized local culture and reported sexual scandals. In 1911, Bierce's *The Devil's Dictionary* became an immediate best-seller although it contained little more than a collection of ironic definitions and nonsense statements. Bierce's work was a perfect reflection of the cultural anarchy of industrial America. In an age of business dominance, Bierce's writings provided a comic-opera tone to relieve the misery of vanishing economic opportunity.

The decline of farm prices and the increasing difficulty of the American farm also became a popular theme. Frank Norris, the product of a wealthy Chicago family, moved to California and became an eyewitness to the emergence of the railroad's control of the American West. After a year of studying creative writing at Harvard, Norris wrote a series of books on the battle between the farmer and the railroad monopoly. His epic novel, *The Octopus*, published in 1901, was a dissection of California agricultural problems during the golden age of corporate growth.

In *The Octopus* Norris fictionalized the Battle of Mussel Slough. In 1880 near Hanford, California, local farmers and the railroad argued over home-steader claims. The Southern Pacific railroad published a series of promotional pamphlets encouraging settlement on less than desirable railroad land. Southern Pacific managers then constructed a rail line through the San Joaquin Valley and confidently predicted that the influx of marginal land settlers would turn a large profit for Southern Pacific. This land scheme was also to the railroad's tax advantage, because Southern Pacific did not take possession of the land. This delayed state land taxes to the railroad's advantage. In a complicated legal maneuver the railroad reached a gentleman's agreement with local homesteaders by which the farmers leased the land. It was, however, an extralegal agreement which allowed the Southern Pacific to evict the tenant farmers.

Although local citizens referred to Mussel Slough as "Starvation Valley," the land prospered. This prompted the railroad to bill the tenant farmers twenty-five to forty-two dollars an acre for the land. Local settlers pointed to elaborate irrigation systems, extensive land improvements, and railroad promises to sell the land as reasons for not paying the assessed prices. When the local sheriff came to evict the settlers there was a bloody shooting, and seven people were killed in the so-called Battle of Mussel Slough. Frank Norris's novel, *The Octopus,* while fictionalizing the incident, also helped to keep alive bitter memories of agricultural strife. The hostility to corporate interests was reflected in the rapid sale of the book and its long survival as a best-seller. There were numerous novels which were critical of big business interests in the late nineteenth century, and this is a strong indication of a revolutionary intellectual mentality in the midst of the triumph of the corporate state.

In order to place the origins of the corporate state in a proper perspective, it is necessary to examine a number of changes in the city and the subtle influences of immigrants and religion. This resulted in a great degree of political change and a shift in traditional American voting patterns. The major political parties found that this intellectual change brought third-party challenges, new attitudes upon foreign affairs, and an increased pressure from fledgling labor unions to control the economy. The effects and challenges of the corporate state led to the birth of reform sentiment and the twentieth century conflict between government and business. These changes were subtle but they began to appear in the major American cities in the 1890s.

The city dominated American politics in the late nineteenth century. The rapid growth of major urban centers made it difficult for traditional politicians to exercise power. As a result, bosses who directed urban political machines arose as power brokers in the Gilded Age. American voters were passionate in their participation in the political arena in an era when the Republican Party usually predominated. In many respects there was a theatrical air to the political spectrum as witty, nattily-dressed Republican and Democratic bosses provided jobs for European immigrants. By 1890 one of four Philadelphians and one of three Bostonians were foreign born. In New York City, four of five residents were foreigners or born of foreign parents. The immigrants supplied a ready source of cheap labor for expanding American industry—soon sweat shops grew up in every major city—as well as a source of new votes for the period's political brokers.

During the Gilded Age, with its influx of large numbers of immigrants, ethnic and religious influences were an important factor in American society. The Democratic Party depended heavily upon German and Irish Catholics to control some northern cities. Yet, the Democratic Party was also strongly supported by Episcopalians, Jews, and Lutherans. Since all ethnic and religious groups were interested in personal freedom, Democratic Party bosses were able to trade votes for promises of freedom to worship, work, and practice any cultural trait common to an ethnic group. The Republican Party was not as fully represented by cultural, ethnic, or religious factors. In general, Republican voters were fundamentalist Christians with strong business interests. They were native born Baptists, Methodists, and Presbyterians who believed that politics was a means of controlling public morals.

It was inevitable that the clash between Republican and Democratic politicians would lead to anti-foreign sentiment. In the 1880s an anti-Catholic pressure group, the American Protective Association, was formed to fight the Roman Catholic Church and advance the Protestant faith. The A.P.A. staged the first serious modern attempt by right-wing politicians to infiltrate the mainstream of the American political system, and in the 1890s it lent its support to hundreds of anti-alien demonstrations. In local politics it was easy for white, Anglo-Saxon, Protestant politicians to control public opinion, because the federal government was not involved in education, consumer protection, or other social issues which touched the daily lives of Americans. Only during presidential elections did the national Republican and Democratic party machines organize local communities. This helps explain why there was such a narrow view of American life in non-presidential years.

Although Republican presidents generally captured the White House from 1877 to 1900, there was still a vibrant two-party political system. Between 1874 and 1892 the Democratic Party controlled the House of Representatives by sizable majorities, and only in 1880 and 1888 did the Republicans eke out a slim majority in the lower house of Congress. Yet, there were few political issues of consequence raised by the major parties, both of which were frequently dissension ridden. The general division in American politics allowed big business to exert undue influence. Corporate lobbyists often manipulated politicians into supporting business-minded legislation.

There were few politicians who were reform-oriented. The most significant changes in American politics were aimed at curbing the role of party patronage. For years it had been customary to reward the party faithful with appointive political office. In return, officeholders kicked back part of their salaries to the party to finance elections. The increase in the size of the federal bureaucracy prompted President Ulysses S. Grant to introduce competitive examinations for civil service positions. The use of patronage to build party loyalty often led to state political machines dominating the presidency. In the late 1870s President Rutherford B. Hayes challenged the New York Republican machine by demanding that customhouse officials be fired for incompetence and public drunkenness. In 1883 the Pendleton Civil Service Act culminated the drive for government efficiency by creating a three-member commission to supervise competitive examinations for federal employment. The Pendleton Act prevented the collection of mandatory campaign funds from federal officeholders, and by 1900 almost 50 percent of all federal jobs were controlled by the Civil Service Commission.

In the 1880s American public opinion became increasingly sensitive over the importation of foreign goods. The Republican Party argued that a high tariff on goods imported into the United States would foster the growth of

American industry. The Democrats responded that low tariffs and less federal regulation would maintain low prices and readily available consumer goods. The importance of the tariff issue to Americans was demonstrated in 1888 when President Grover Cleveland, a Democrat, lost his bid for a second term. Cleveland did not believe that he should wage an active campaign, and the Democratic Party underestimated public demand for a strong stand on the tariff question. Benjamin Harrison, the Republican candidate, campaigned strenuously for a high tariff and suggested that industrialists and factory workers could not expect decent profits and wages without protection from foreign competition. The pro-tariff states provided Harrison with a narrow victory and an indication of strong American feeling about foreign goods.

Since the Republican Party was the most business-minded of the two major parties, the G.O.P. reflected the belief that a high tariff encouraged the increased production and consumption of American goods. In control of the presidency and both houses of Congress, the Republican leadership passed the McKinley Tariff of 1890 which extended tariff coverage to goods that had previously entered the United States without duties. In order to foster the growth of agricultural products, the McKinley Tariff provided protective duties for key crops. The Democratic party used the tariff issue in the congressional elections of 1890 to argue that high consumer prices and reduced buying power resulted from Republican unwillingness to recognize that a protective tariff hurt the economy more than it helped it. The voters agreed and elected a Democratic Congress. This was a prelude to the return of Democratic political power.

In 1892 Grover Cleveland was elected to a second presidential term due to serious public concern over the economy. The decline in prices for agricultural and manufactured goods created pressure for an adjustment in the national supply of money. The Sherman Purchase Act of 1890 had increased the supply of silver that the federal government would purchase each month, but the Depression of 1893 was blamed upon silver speculation and the Sherman Act was repealed. The controversy over silver was one of the reasons the People's Party of America, or the Populists, as they were known, emerged as a potent third party force. The Populists were disgruntled farmers, supported by a few urban workers, who believed that increased silver coinage and sweeping political change would reform the economy. In the spring of 1893 the stock market hit a new low, and the following year Jacob Coxey led an army of unemployed blue-collar workers in a march upon Washington, D.C., as discontent over economic dislocation became increasingly widespread throughout the country.

In local elections in 1893 the Populists won numerous state government seats, and in 1894 a small number were elected to Congress. The major parties were braced for a strong challenge from the Populist Party in the election of 1896. The controversy over silver coinage led to the emergence of a young, powerful Nebraskan, William Jennings Bryan, who argued with the intensity of a Baptist preacher that free silver was a cure for the nation's economic ills. Although he was only thirty-six years old, young Bryan captured both the Democratic and Populist party nominations for the presidency. A large number of tradition-minded Democrats deserted the party because they believed that Bryan's views were too radical on the money question. This forced Bryan to campaign as the candidate of the common person and to promise to rebuild the Democratic party.

The 1896 presidential election was an exciting affair as Bryan's supporters organized "silver clubs" in every state. Bryan himself delivered almost six hundred speeches to more than three million Americans. A short, stocky man with a rumpled appearance, Bryan used his great oratory skills to further his cause. As the campaign intensified, Bryan's watchword became, "You shall not crucify mankind upon a cross of gold!" The fervent moral tone of Bryan's politics appealed to a large number of Americans who believed that political and business corruption must be controlled by the federal government.

Small-town bankers, businessmen, immigrants, and almost all those living in the urban-industrial Northeast were frightened by Bryan's campaign. The Republican party exploited these fears of Democratic-Populist radicalism by suggesting that free silver would destroy the nation's economy. Church leaders called Bryan a dangerous radical as the election of 1896 degenerated into a name-calling contest, and the Republican party proved extremely skillful in blaming the current economic depression upon President Cleveland's Democratic politics.

The Republican candidate, William McKinley, was an appealing candidate, because he was able to exude sincerity and honesty. A tall, imposing man, McKinley soothingly lectured the nation on the problems of the economy. He seemed much like a kindly grandfather ready to lead the United States back toward prosperity. The smooth direction of the 1896 Republican campaign was the work of Mark Hanna, a wealthy Ohio crony of McKinley's. The key to Republican Party success was the organization of thousands of small McKinley clubs throughout the nation. A large number of Democrats in the Middle West defected to the Republican Party, and McKinley's overwhelming election brought a surprising number of Midwestern farmers into the G.O.P. Perhaps the best example of Hanna's campaign skills was the Republican Party flag day held two weeks before the presidential election. The significance of the flag day is that it conjured up images of the Republican Party as the savior of the Union. Although the Civil War had been over for more than thirty years, Hanna used the G.O.P.'s reputation for saving the Union to help elect McKinley president.

In 1897 prosperity returned to American life, and the farmers and urban laborers ignored the protests of third-party candidates. Many historians believe that there has never been a history of radical change supported by working-class Americans, and the election of 1896 surely seemed to reaffirm the appeal of staid, business-minded conservatism to most blue-collar workers. Yet, the Socialist Party grew almost continually in the decade after

1900, and almost a million Americans voted for the party's presidential candidate in 1912. As the corporate state stood on the verge of triumph, radical politics presented at least a temporary challenge.

One of the most important changes in American life during the period of the origins of the corporate state was the rise of organized labor. In the late nineteenth century America's longest surviving unions were formed along craft lines. The employer resisted union demands, and there was a great deal of violence in the 1870s between the worker and business. As a result, workers grew increasingly militant by the mid-1880s. The most powerful early industrial union was the Knights of Labor, formed in Philadelphia as a secret society. In 1881 Terrence V. Powderly, a Scranton, Pennsylvania, machinist became the leader of this organization, His influence was to promote worker cooperative efforts, boycotts, and nationwide demonstrations as tools to achieve economic justice for American toilers. Thousands of the more than 600,000 members of the Knights of Labor participated in strikes in the 1880s. This served to concentrate public attention upon the fledgling labor movement. Yet, the Knights of Labor did not fully establish itself as the mainstream American labor organization because the union's leadership failed to organize workers to engage primarily in collective bargaining along craft lines. Since the Knights failed to adjust their structure to the emerging corporate economy, a weakness developed which contributed to the loss of membership and eventual decline in power.

In May 1886, during a picketing demonstration at the McCormick Harvester Company in Chicago, local police killed four strikers. To protest this violence, a mass meeting was held at Haymarket Square. After a series of moderate speeches the police attempted to break up the meeting and a riot ensued. A small bomb was thrown from an unknown source, killing a policeman and six other bystanders. The business community and the press blamed the Haymarket riot upon labor, and this incident contributed to the rapid disintegration of the Knights of Labor.

The American Federation of Labor, organized in 1886 by Samuel Gompers, was the most realistic and successful trade union of its time. The AFL promoted a union program which worked for the best interests of skilled workers. Rejecting the utopian idealism of the Knights of Labor, the AFL believed that labor had to form a tight-knit coalition to achieve better wages and improved working conditions through collective bargaining. Much of Gompers' rhetoric was aimed at making the skilled laborer a well paid and respected worker. By 1897 more than 400,000 workers were members of the AFL. The growth of the American Federation of Labor highlighted the general dissatisfaction of the American worker in the late nineteenth century.

In the 1890s a series of dramatic and violent strikes caused public opinion to react negatively to organized labor. The high level of unemployment in the 1890s due to a prolonged depression from 1893 to 1898 created middle-class fears of labor violence. In 1892 Andrew Carnegie's Homestead steel plant in Pennsylvania was struck by workers reacting against wage cuts and poor working conditions. More than three hundred Pinkerton detectives were called in to escort strikebreakers—or scabs, as they were known—into Carnegie's plant. There was some public sympathy for the strikers, but it vanished when Russian Anarchist, Alexander Berkman, attempted to assassinate the plant manager. The strike failed, and union activity in the steel industry ended for several years.

An equally disasterous setback for labor followed in the Pullman strike of 1894. When the Depression of 1893 hit, there were increased wage cuts, layoffs and strikes. In 1894 more workers were unemployed due to strikes than at any time before in American history. The most significant strike occurred in George M. Pullman's company town, Pullman, Illinois. This model company city located south of Chicago was struck by Eugene V. Debs' New American Railway Union. When Debs demanded that Pullman accept arbitration and the company refused, a lengthy strike ensued. The Pullman Company persuaded President Cleveland to use federal troops to break the strike. The ruse used to invoke federal intervention was that the United States mails were being illegally disrupted by the Pullman strike. On July 4, 1894, President Cleveland dispatched 2000 federal troops to Chicago to end the Pullman strike by demanding that the trains run to deliver the mail. The union lost control of the strike and public attitudes were strongly anti-union by 1900. Despite this failure, Gomper's American Federation of Labor was the first major union federation to survive a large scale economic depression. It would retain its position as the dominant American trade union organization in the next century.

By 1900 the corporate state was fully developed and in control of the political-economic structure of American life. Labor, agrarian protesters, and the small business interests were no longer able to challenge big business. The stage was set for the final conflict between corporate capitalism and the federal government. This would lead to the modern political and economic system that the United States embraces in the present day.

Suggested Readings

For an excellent study of businessmen's attitudes on the economy and government, see Edward C. Kirkland, *Dream and Thought in the Business Community* (1956). The influence of Andrew Carnegie is brilliantly documented in Harold C. Livesay, *Andrew Carnegie and the Rise of Big Business* (1975). A pioneer study using quantification to examine the attitudes of wealthy mining barons is Richard H. Peterson, *The Bonanza Kings: The Social Origins and Business Behavior of Western Mining Entrepreneurs, 1870-1900* (1977). For pioneering studies of the business community, see Thomas C. Cochran and William Miller, *The Age of Enterprise: A Social History of Industrial America* (1942) and E. C. Kirkland, *Industry Comes of Age: Business, Labor and Public Policy, 1860-1897* (1961).

The varied phases of political activity in the late nineteenth century are examined in ten essays dealing with a wide variety of topics, H. Wayne Morgan, editor, *The Gilded Age: A Reappraisal* (1970). Richard J. Jensen, *The Winning of The Midwest: Social and Political Conflict, 1886-1896* (1971) is an important study emphasizing the importance of social and religious values upon politics. For reform in the Gilded Age see John G. Sproat, *The Best Men: Liberal Reformers in the Gilded Age* (1968). For the nativist reaction to Catholics, Jews, and eastern European immigrants see John Higham, *Strangers in the Land: Patterns of American Nativism, 1860-1925* (1955) and Harvey Schwartz, *Era of Intolerance: The Tradition of Anti-Radical Nativism, 1875-1920* (1966).

A useful study of rising labor and declining agricultural influences is Grant McConnell, *The Decline of Agrarian America* (1969). For a brief look at farmer hostility see, Howard A. DeWitt, "Manufacturers in Iowa—A Note on Iowa Agriculture in 1873," *Annals of Iowa,* XXXVII (Spring, 1965). For conflict between the Knights of Labor and the AFL see Gerald N. Grob, *Workers and Utopia: A Study of Ideological Conflict in the American Labor Movement, 1865-1900* (1961).

"The First Colored Senator and Representatives" by Currier & Ives, lithograph 1872. From left to right (front) U.S. Senator H. R. Revels of Mississippi, Benjamin S. Turner, M.C. of Alabama, Josiah T. Walls, M.C. of Florida, Joseph H. Rainy, M.C. of South Carolina, R. Brown Elliott, M.C. of South Carolina; (back) Robert C. De Large, M.C. of South Carolina, Jefferson H. Long, M.C. of Georgia. (The New York Public Library)

The Black Politician

The Years of Frustration

Henry A. Bryant, Jr.

The Thirteenth Amendment to the Constitution, passed in 1865, abolished slavery in the United States. With the demise of slavery, blacks felt that they were free to enjoy all the privileges and rights of other freemen. This newly gained position should have been proof enough to their former masters that slavery was a serious error in humanity. This, however, was not the situation.

With the end of slavery Congress found it necessary to propose and pass more laws for the protection of the former slave. In the summer of 1866 the Fourteenth Amendment was passed making blacks citizens with certain specified safeguards for their protection. Could it be assumed that this was enough protection? This did not prove to be the case. The passage of the Thirteenth and Fourteenth Amendments alone did not give blacks complete political rights.

In February 1869, the Fifteenth Amendment was passed which gave blacks the right to vote. With the passage of this amendment, blacks were now allowed to participate in state and national politics. Certain blacks had, of course, participated to some degree in political action before the Civil War. The deeds of Frederick Douglass, John Mercer Langston, and Sojourner Truth are well known. They, however, worked outside the established political system in their efforts to abolish slavery. No black was a citizen prior to the passage of the Fifteenth Amendment, even in the North where slavery had been abolished. It would be safe to say that black Americans were outside the American political system until the 1870s.

The South was obviously reluctant to pass the Thirteenth, Fourteenth and Fifteenth Amendments, so Congress, dominated by the Republican Party, passed the Reconstruction Acts of 1867. These laws led to the military occupation of the South, protection of the blacks, and the formation of new state governments. Under the protection of the military, blacks in the South now began to exercise their right to vote. These votes brought in black sheriffs, mayors, judges, and national legislators. The black politician was now becoming a reality.

The whole nation had watched Mississippi since the year 1865. It was here that blacks were showing so much political potential. By 1867, registration figures in Mississippi showed sixty thousand whites and forty thousand blacks registered to vote. Black voters were a majority in thirty-three of sixty-one counties in the state. This meant that blacks had a better opportunity in this state than any other Southern state. Mississippi, in fact, had the only black senators during the Reconstruction period in the persons of Hiram Revels and Blanche Kelso Bruce.

Because of the Reconstruction Acts of 1867, Mississippi had to call a state constitutional convention to make sure they kept within the framework of these laws. Sixteen blacks were selected along with eighty-four whites to attend the convention set for September 1868. It was here that they wrote a constitution which would allow blacks to participate in the political process of the state, selecting forty of them for their first state legislature. In January 1870, these forty blacks and seventy whites met in the first legislative session in Mississippi's history where blacks were involved.

Hiram Revels, a minister, opened the convention with a brief prayer, again a first for blacks in Mississippi politics. Revels came to be nominated as United States senator through a compromise. He was not well known but appeared intelligent and able, and a great deal of respect was accorded him because he was an African Methodist Episcopal minister of some reputation in Natchez, Mississippi. Due to the slave restrictions, he had no prior political experience. White politicians felt, however, that he would be the most likely candidate to fill the seat vacated by Jefferson Davis. Davis, a senator from Mississippi and later president of the Southern states during the war, was now confined to prison. Whenever a senator is not able to fulfill his six-year term, the state legislature must appoint a replacement. There were now two vacant seats. Black legislators insisted that one of the seats be given to a black. The Mississippi whites were willing to compromise and give Revels the short term still left from Jefferson Davis's term, if it was agreed that a white man would be given the long term. It was further agreed that Revels' seat would return to a white man when his term was finished. Blacks supported Revels' nomination.

Almost every state, with the exception of Georgia and Texas, produced outstanding black politicians. However, to highlight the careers of all would be beyond the scope of this essay. Some of these do deserve special merit, such as Robert Brown Elliott from South Carolina, Blanche Kelso

Bruce from Mississippi, and P. B. S. Pinchback from Louisiana. Robert Brown Elliott from South Carolina was probably the outstanding politician of the era. He was from the state of South Carolina which produced the most black members to serve in the United States Congress. In South Carolina by the year 1867, blacks were in the majority of those registered to vote with eighty thousand registrants to forty thousand whites. In the state constitutional convention of 1868, seventy-six blacks and eighty-four whites were selected to attend. Eighty-four blacks were selected to serve in the state assembly. Blacks in South Carolina, therefore, had an excellent opportunity to be elected to a national office. With this advantage Robert Brown Elliott would rise to heights never dreamed possible for a black man.

Elliott was born in Boston on August 11, 1842, of parents with unmixed African blood. Well preserved photographs of him reveal his ancestry. Like many other well educated blacks of that time, Elliott attended school abroad, enrolling in High Hollow Academy in England and graduating from Eton College. He studied law and was admitted to the South Carolina bar and then entered politics. He was an excellent scholar, having one of the largest private libraries in the state.

Still in his twenties, he was elected to the state legislature, rising to the rank of speaker. At twenty-eight he was elected to Congress, and represented South Carolina in the forty-second and forty-third congresses.

Political experts and critics alike agreed to the brilliance and skill of Elliott. He was an exceptional speaker who could hold his audience entranced for hours. His speeches covered a variety of subjects, frequently in defense of his people. During his first session of congress, he argued for a grant of $12,000 for the poor and needy blacks of the District of Columbia, and finally received the grant after fighting long and hard for it. In the next session, as a member of the education and labor committee, he spoke for money for poor blacks in South Carolina and blamed all of the trouble in his state on the Democratic Party, who had ruled the state before the war. He was concerned most of all with the poor financial position of the state of South Carolina.

Certain of Elliott's speeches reveal a deep concern for all people, black or white, and a dislike for the prejudice and racial discrimination which separated blacks and whites. Although he strongly denounced government policies, he often stated that he had not given up on America and felt that it could fulfill its promise to humanity.

Elliott even stood against the majority of his fellow black politicians on some occasions when he openly attacked the Northern Republicans for their "cloak and dagger" support of Southern policies. He felt that it wasn't just the Southern whites, who violated the rights of blacks, but that white Northerners were their willing allies on many occasions.

During his second session, he was frequently absent because of his busy schedule. This absence caused some writers to accuse him unjustly of laxity. It was during this period in his political career that he was most interested in being reelected in 1872. Many politicians felt that he had a good chance at reelection for he had been elected by twenty thousand votes over his opponent in the last congressional election. Everything seemed to point to success for him. In this election he was contested by two whites, a situation which seemed to heighten his chances, because it appeared that the whites would split their votes and cancel each other. However, when the final tally came in, it showed that Elliott had run second to a white named Patterson. Many blacks as well as whites voiced their outrage at the vote. *The Charleston Courier*, the leading white newspaper in South Carolina, preferred Elliott to the mediocre Patterson. This defeat was a very frustrating one for Elliott. It tended to destroy his motivation to continue his present position in Congress. In January 1873 he resigned from Congress.

In October 1874 he was elected chairman of the Republican State Committee, and later was reelected to the South Carolina House of Representatives. During this period the state governor gave him a free hand in the reform of the state, which he did so well that he was awarded a sum of $1,000 by the state legislature. In 1876 he was nominated for attorney general, but his nomination was rejected by white Republicans. Another chance to become United States Senator presented itself, but he could not muster enough votes to win. On May 1, 1877, Robert Brown Elliott was forced to surrender his last elected office. Everything appeared to be going downhill, not only for Elliott, but black politicians in other states as well had begun to see the "handwriting on the wall." The period of political frustration and defeat had set in. Republicans were being thrown out and the Democrats were again regaining power in the South. In 1880 he resigned from public life. Through some political friends he was appointed special agent for the United States Treasury Department, with headquarters in Charleston, but his political enemies seemed out to ruin him. He was accused of stealing $4,000 and became a branded man. To forestall further trouble, the Treasury Department transferred him to New Orleans, where his troubles continued. Finally President Chester A. Arthur removed him from his position.

Elliott now turned to legal practice but was continually frustrated by the power of the white bar. He was then forced to seek a living in the city courts as an attorney. On August 9, 1884 Robert Brown Elliott, sick and in poverty, died, an inglorious end to a glorious beginning. This was to be the lot of many black politicians, who were forced by racism to a similar fate.

Blanche Kelso Bruce was born a slave in Prince Edward County, Virginia, on March 1, 1841. Bruce's father was a white planter and his mother a mixed-blood black woman. Being a "house slave," Bruce experienced none of the terror of his less fortunate darker-skinned brothers. He received a good education from a tutor, something almost impossible for the vast majority of slaves. He was taken to Missouri a few years before the Civil War began, where he studied the printers' trade. In 1861 Bruce's young master, who was also his brother, entered the Confederate Army. A short time later Bruce escaped to Hannibal, Missouri. It was here that he organized an all-black school, which was the first of its kind in that state. After the conclusion of the Civil War, he entered Oberlin College where he studied for two years and then decided to migrate to the state of Mississippi. It was an opportune time for a capable and intelligent black man, since Mississippi and the South in general, was ready for the black politician. Once in Mississippi, he quickly entered politics. Bruce was an impressive physical specimen, standing over six feet and weighing over two hundred pounds. He had a very handsome and commanding appearance.

Beginning his political career in 1869, he became sergeant-at-arms of the state senate, county tax assessor, tax collector, sheriff, superintendent of schools and a member of the levee board. He also bought property, began planting crops, and became a rich man. In 1873 he was nominated for lieutenant governor, but he refused this position because he wanted a much higher political office, that of United States senator. On March 5, 1875 Blanche Kelso Bruce became the first black senator ever to be elected to a full term. He would become a model for all aspiring black politicians.

Bruce's entrance into the Senate gave forewarning that his stay there would be a very difficult one. The senior senator from Mississippi Alcorn was so upset at Bruce's election that he broke with tradition and refused to escort the newly-elected senator from his state to take the oath of office. Roscoe Conklin escorted Bruce in his place.

Bruce's record in the Senate, however, was one to be admired as he fought hard and consistently to secure complete representation for blacks all over the country. In 1878 he introduced a bill to provide for payment of bounty to black soldiers, sailors, their wives and children. The bill went to the Senate committee on military affairs, where it was defeated. In March 1876 he presented a resolution to the Sons of Temperance of the District of Columbia asking for the passage of a law to stop the importation of liquor. This action was taken because many blacks were drinking heavily which led to their involvement in fights and other disorders. Many of them were destitute and experiencing great hardships. Bruce felt that the bottle hindered rather than helped. The measure showed marked foresight and concern, although it was not acted upon.

He was also concerned with the number of black orphans left destitute by the war. In January 1877 Bruce referred a petition from one Mary Ann Lynch, orphan daughter of a black soldier, John Lynch, to the appropriations committee for payment, which was granted.

Bruce served during a time when sentiment against blacks was beginning to run high. However, he was still quick to defend their honor against anyone, anywhere. In one particular instance, Senator Key from Tennessee spoke about the murders of a woman called Eliza Pinkston and her husband, stating that the crime was so brutal that it could not have been the work of white men. Bruce asked him to explain himself, as he logically assumed that Mr. Key was saying that it was done by blacks. When Bruce confronted Key about the implications of his remarks, Key apologized. Bruce served on the special sessions committee on manufactures, the pension committee, the education and labor committee, and the improvement of Mississippi River and tributaries committee. An avowed enemy of theft in high places, Bruce sought to protect the depositors of the badly managed Freedman's Savings and Trust Company, by serving as chairman of the investigating committee. He and his committee were successful in eliminating graft from the bank commissioner's salaries. However, he was unable to reimburse the depositors. He also opposed the exclusion of Chinese from America, and fought for the rights of Indians as full-fledged citizens.

Bruce, although respected, "never had it made"; he was a senator during the period when white racism was on the rise. He served in Congress under President Rutherford B. Hayes who ended the military occupation of the South in 1877. After leaving the senate in 1881, he found that the era of the black politician was nearly over. He later was appointed Register of the Treasury by President James Garfield. President Benjamin Harrison appointed him Recorder of Deeds and President William McKinley re-appointed him as Register of the Treasury in 1897. His health, however, was failing, and he died in March 1898.

Pinckney Benton Stewart Pinchback was born a slave in the state of Mississippi in 1841, the son of a white planter and a black woman. He was given an early education by a tutor but was sent north to Cincinnati to finish high school. During the Civil War, he recruited and organized two black regiments but left this service in 1863 because of extreme racism shown toward black soldiers. Moving to the state of Louisiana after the war, he was appointed Inspector of Customs for the Port of New Orleans and became a delegate to the State Convention to write a new constitution. He was also a delegate to the Republican National Convention in 1868. He was then elected state senator and Lieutenant Governor of Louisiana. When the white governor of that state was removed for alleged theft, Pinchback briefly served as governor. He was then elected to the United States Senate, but his own state refused to let him take his seat. White racism was now on the rise. While his elected career now ended, his public career continued. President Chester Arthur appointed him to the position of Surveyor of Customs for the Port of New Orleans. In 1921 he peacefully died there.

The black politicians have been blamed for many of the abuses committed during the period of military occupation of the South, commonly called Reconstruction. These politicians have been pictured as being gullible, ignorant, and superstitious. The problems in the South after the war, however, can hardly be explained in terms of black politicians. Take, for example, the state of Louisiana. While a white governor was in control of that state, it is estimated that over four million dollars disappeared from the state treasury. This situation also occurred in other states where fiscal control lay not in the hands of blacks but in the hands of white politicians. Actually, many black politicians sought to bring some fiscal responsibility to government, to grant civil rights provisions, and to institute a public school system. In fact black politicians such as Robert Brown Elliott, William T. Greener, F. L. Cardozo, and Edward R. Bassett were outstanding politicians and were also highly educated men. The myth of the black politician and his leadership role in graft and corruption in the postwar South is exactly that—a myth.

By the year 1875, black politics was on its way out. By that time only South Carolina, Florida, Louisiana and Mississippi were still voting Republican, and the Democrats were taking over. The southern white establishment was again taking control. Black politicians suddenly became devils; homes of blacks were searched and weapons were taken in the name of the law. In the state of Mississippi, whites illegally came across the line from Louisiana to help vote out blacks, as blacks were intimidated and kept from the polls through violence. The political base which had kept the black politician in office was being destroyed. It was just a matter of time until the black politician would disappear.

Blacks attempted to counterattack in different ways. Black women refused to marry wavering blacks who deserted the Republican Party, but white Democrats were getting more control of politics, property, and the economic system. If a black man wanted to survive he had to make some changes, and most of the changes would involve getting out of politics.

Blacks were increasingly becoming the victims of outright violence. The whip, the knife, and the gun added to black misery. Whites wanted black political activity completely crushed. The Ku Klux Klan, the Knights of the White Camelia, and other notorious groups burned, murdered, and pillaged, as blacks were at the mercy of Southern whites.

The result of the national election of 1876 was a turning point in the exit of the black politician. The outcome of this election hinged upon disputed results in Louisiana, South Carolina, and Florida. Rutherford B. Hayes, the Republican candidate, who was running against Samuel Tilden, the Democratic candidate, claimed the victory in these states. Senators who had supported and helped black politicians began to turn their backs on them. Political leaders such as George A. Julian, Charles Sumner, and Thaddeus Stevens were being replaced by men who took a dimmer view of black politics such as James Garfield and Oliver P. Morton.

Instead of endorsing voting rights and other civil rights originally advocated by Republican Radicals, these new politicians now merely gave lip service to black needs, for both the North and the South were disinterested in civil rights. The issue of civil rights was getting in the way of the Northern businessmen making large profits in the South. They couldn't make money if they had to be concerned with human rights at the same time.

After the election of 1876, Southern Democrats refused to allow the presidential ballots to be counted. The South wanted a political deal; they would permit the votes to be counted if the North would permit the South the privilege of ruling themselves the way they desired to. The Democratic candidate Samuel Tilden was willing to go along with the compromise if his party would receive certain economic and political concessions. The North needed stability for its markets, and cheap labor for its factories. Businessmen could get this down South, but they would have to let the South control its blacks and its politics. This meant that the Reconstruction Acts would have to be nullified and the troops pulled out of the South, thus leaving the blacks at the mercy of the South. Although an electoral commission awarded the election to Republican Hayes, he followed the dictates of the compromise. Military occupation of the South ended, the Southern Democrats now took control.

One thing was now very clear; the sun which had shown so brightly in 1867 had now passed beyond the horizon. Election to congress became increasingly difficult for black politicians; a few, however, managed to survive despite the bitter frustration that was constantly present. Richard Cain of South Carolina served from 1873-79. Charles Nash of Louisiana served from 1875 through 1877, and George A. White, who served from 1897-1901, was the very last of this breed. In all, twenty-two elected blacks served on the national level between 1869 to 1901.

Those black politicians who had attracted considerable national publicity found their political careers frustrated but were chosen to serve in other capacities. We have mentioned the appointments of Pinchback and Bruce; there also were others. Hiram Revels was appointed at the expiration of his term to fill the office of president of the newly founded Alcorn A & M College in Mississippi. He worked hard to make Alcorn an outstanding institution until his death in 1901.

Frederick Douglass, who never served in elected politics, became an outstanding appointed politician. Douglass served as presidential advisor to Abraham Lincoln during the war, and afterwards was appointed Marshall of the District of Columbia in 1877 by President Ulysses Grant. He was later appointed Minister of Haiti by President Benjamin Harrison. Many of the black appointed politicians did not assert themselves because of the strong feelings against blacks during that period; Douglass, however, was a true soldier and a constant threat to the establishment, with his strong devotion to the welfare of his people. All foreign political appointments made to blacks outside of the United States were usually made to black Haiti. Ebenezer Bassett, John Mercer Langston, George W. Williams, William F. Powell, and others served with distinction in this position. The most noteworthy foreign appointment was made to Mifflin W. Gibbs, the first black municipal judge, who later became ambassador to Madagascar, an island nation in South East Africa.

Black political activity, though severely limited after 1877, did not disappear. The black politicians were men with strong character who did not give up easily. Organizations continued to be founded to represent black political interests. In August 1875 the first convention of Negro newsmen was held becoming the forerunner of the Negro Press Association. P. B. S.

Pinchback was the keynote speaker at this function. In 1885 Frederick Douglass, Bruce, and Pinchback signed a petition calling for a conference for the organization of industrial schools for black people, which was to meet the following year. In 1890 the Convention of Colored Americans met in Washington, D.C., and voted to send a representative to the United States Senate for the citizens of the Equal Rights Association.

In the year 1880 Blanche K. Bruce was present at the Republican National Convention, was nominated for vice-president of the United States, and received eight votes. Bruce actually received more votes than James Alcorn, who had refused to escort him to the Senate. In the Republican convention of 1888 he was again nominated for Vice-President and received eleven votes, placing fourth. Bruce thus became the first black to be nominated for Vice-President.

In the same 1888 convention, James Roy Lynch, secretary of state for Mississippi, was appointed as temporary chairman of the convention after he was nominated by Henry Cabot Lodge. Powell Clayton of Arkansas was also nominated. Lynch received 424 votes to 384 for Clayton.

The 1888 convention marked a return of blacks to the Republican Party. In 1883, blacks had met in the National Colored Convention in Louisville, Kentucky, and voiced their sentiments against the Republican Party who had all but deserted blacks. In 1884 at the Republican National Convention, blacks were not enthusiastic at all. Only the old timers remained committed to the Republicans.

In the election of 1884, blacks voted for Democratic candidate Grover Cleveland, and the Republican Party went down to defeat. This served as a lesson to the Republicans, by showing them that blacks would no longer tolerate their indifference. Cleveland's policies were not favorable to blacks, as he represented the Southern Democrats. The Democratic Party blew its chance for a lasting political relationship, and blacks now returned to the Republicans in 1888. The Republican gestures toward Bruce and Lynch were no more than political moves to bring blacks back to the party.

However, by the end of the 1880s the Republican national political structure tended to do away with blacks altogether. Here was another frustrating experience. Although blacks had worked hard to become loyal Republicans, they were again betrayed as their political utility lessened. The black political experience rose and fell, depending on the party in power and the sentiments of white majority. The strain of this relationship would soon take its toll.

Now, out of sheer frustration, blacks turned to organized farm alliances with disgruntled Southern white farmers; blacks even formed with white farmers a National Alliance in 1888. Blacks now formed black cooperative unions which spread into the Indian territories and covered at least nine states. However, racism tended to cut the coalition short. Blacks supported the Henry Cabot Lodge federal elections bill, but whites were strongly against the bill, which would give black voters protection in federal elections.

In the year 1890 blacks were very much concerned about their votes, which were being sought by three political parties: the Democrats, Republicans and a rising new political party, the Populist Party. The Populists said that they wanted blacks admitted to their party councils on an equal basis. This party incorporated into its platform a provision for the dropping of the convict-lease system and other violations of human rights. However, the Populists went down to defeat in 1892 and were never able to regroup again.

Despite the covert opposition of the Southern Democrats, blacks also had to cope with strong anti-black organizations. The most notorious of these groups was the Ku Klux Klan, a brutal organization started in Pulaski, Tennessee, on December 24, 1865. Its very name stood for whippings, maulings, and constant threats. This group more than others, kept blacks out of politics and away from the polls.

These overt brutal policies, however, tended to bring about an outcry against such tactics by people who were concerned with the constant bloodletting which was taking place in the South. It was felt that savage lynchings and other forms of mayhem were simply not enough to crush black politics. Much more sophisticated devices with longer range effects had to be found that would meet these objectives. The state of Mississippi, which led the way in black political accomplishment, would also lead the way in black political destruction. It has the distinction of having lynched more blacks than any other state of the union, murdering them almost at will. Blacks had continued to vote during the 1870s and 1880s despite the intimidation and murders. It was this persistence which made Mississippi decide to call a Constitutional Convention for the purpose of completely destroying black political participation. It was to be held in the summer of 1890 and would spell doom for all the black electorate in that state and the sister Southern states.

The first tactic adopted by the Mississippians was the two dollar poll tax, which was payable before one could vote, a virtual impossibility for many poor black sharecroppers. These people might not see two dollars in a whole year's time. The literacy test was the next device, which required a registrant to read a section of the Constitution, and give reasonable interpretations of that section. This "reasonable interpretation" was to be determined by the person giving the examination, and many blacks were simply not certified as qualified to vote by the examiner, no matter what they said. Of course, most blacks could not read at all; this measure alone would eliminate thousands of black voters.

Under Section 244 of the new constitution, registrants were required to live at least a whole year in a precinct. This particular section was aimed at the disposition of young blacks to change their homes each year due to the insistent harassment of the Klan and other organizations. Whites observed this and sought to take maximum advantage of it at the convention. As a result of crimes such as theft or arson and obtaining goods by fraud the vote was taken away from many blacks. Crimes such as murder, rape, or assault were not included, because of the great number of whites they would have excluded from the polls.

In 1902 the state of Mississippi instituted the white primary which held that party nominations for state and local officers should be made by primary elections. The state executive committee was authorized to exclude anyone from its primary, consequently they kept out blacks. The state of Texas would make this device famous right down to the 1940s, when the Supreme Court threw it out in the case of *Smith* v. *Alwright*.

How effective were these devices in destroying blacks politically? One illustrative example is that of Mississippi in 1867 when 98,726 blacks were of voting age. There were 60,167 registered to vote in contrast to 46,636 whites. In 1899 out of a possible 198,747 blacks eligible to vote, only 18,170 managed to do so. Blacks who had constituted fifty-five percent of the electorate in 1867, were now only a little more than nine percent of the electorate in 1899. This was a drastic reduction.

The state of South Carolina's ballot box election of 1882 deserves some mention. It required a special ballot box in every voting place for every office. The boxes were properly labeled and the election officer would read the election slate aloud. The trick was that no one was allowed to speak to the voter or insert his ballot for him. If the ballot was inserted in the wrong box, it didn't count. Most blacks couldn't read, and therefore most of their ballots were vetoed. This reduced black voters to almost nothing.

In Louisiana in the 1896 election, there were 130,344 blacks registered to vote; blacks were in the majority in twenty-six parishes. In the 1900 election, only four years later, there were only 5,320 blacks registered to vote. Black registrants declined from over 130,000 to just over 5,000 in only four years. Many blame it on the famous *Plessy* v. *Ferguson* decision which originated in Louisiana in 1896. This was the decision which made "Jim Crowism" legal throughout the United States, by stating that it was perfectly all right to segregate blacks and whites as long as they were given "equal" facilities. Equal facilities were never given to blacks; they drank from water fountains labelled "colored," went to inferior "colored" schools, and were forced to sit in the back of the bus. This was done by the Supreme Court, the highest court in the land. With all of the violence and political gimmicks used against blacks, the apparent concurrence of the Supreme Court was the final crushing blow.

By 1900 only one black politician was left in Washington, George H. White, who would be thrown out in 1901. After this date it would be thirty years before a black would attempt election again. It appeared that white bigotry had triumphed over black politics. With the Klan, the white primary, lynchings, poll taxes and the like, blacks didn't have a chance. To make matters worse, the Supreme Court was upholding these restrictions. Blacks couldn't appeal to the sheriffs, the legislators, or policemen because many of them were klansmen and anti-black. Fear would become the way of life for blacks, and politics would become "white folks business." The ramifications of this period still haunt blacks.

Conclusion and Summary

Through the Thirteenth, Fourteenth, and Fifteenth Amendments, blacks were freed, became citizens, and were allowed to vote. The Radical Republicans in Congress passed the Reconstruction Acts which led to the military occupation of the South, the rewriting of state constitutions, and the implementation of the "black" amendments.

This period saw the rise of black sheriffs, state legislators, judges, county officials, and national legislators. Two black senators Hiram Revels and Blanche K. Bruce, both from Mississippi, went to Washington and served admirably. Robert Brown Elliott, congressman from South Carolina, and Pinckney Benton Stewart Pinchback, congressman from Louisiana were excellent examples of black political involvement on a national level.

However, by 1875, white Democrats were regaining power, and were determined virtually to re-enslave blacks. Through organizations such as the Ku Klux Klan and others, blacks became the victims of concentrated violence, which was designed to drive them from political office for good. In 1876, with the election of Rutherford B. Hayes, Union soldiers were pulled out of the South, leaving blacks without protection.

Although it became increasingly difficult to be elected, notable blacks such as Pinchback, Douglass, and Bruce stayed in politics through the appointment route. They attended conventions, organized their own conventions, and stayed active. White Southerners continued to use violence and added the poll tax, the literacy test, and other sophisticated devices to their arsenal. The 1896 Plessy decision of "separate but equal" by the United States Supreme Court, gave a resounding victory to legalized segregation. Against overwhelming odds, black politics was doomed to failure. In fact, after 1901, not one black politician was left. The years of frustration would continue well into the twentieth century.

Suggested Readings

For years the role of the black politician in the period of Reconstruction was overlooked completely in works on this era. The following books describe the positive contribution of black politicians. Robert Cruden in *The Negro in Reconstruction* (1969) gives a brief but overall view of the role of blacks in the process of reconstructing the South. *Reconstruction, 1865-1877* (1965) Richard N. Current, editor, is a book of primary documents dealing with the period after the Civil War in the South. These documents reveal the white racism toward blacks in general and black politicians in particular. John Hope Franklin in *Reconstruction After the Civil War* (1961) presents a revisionist interpretation of reconstruction. He shows how blacks took great pains to educate themselves in the process of assuming political liberty and power.

Kenneth M. Stampp in *The Era of Reconstruction* (1965) presents a brief political history of reconstruction. He doesn't give as much space in this book to the role of black reconstructionists. W. E. B. Dubois in *Black Reconstruction in America* (1968) shows the positive efforts of the black politicians. *Black Power U.S.A.* (1969) by Lerone Bennett is one of the best contemporary works on reconstruction. It provides extensive research into the role of blacks in reconstruction. In *The Radical Republicans and Reconstruction, 1861-1870* (1967) author Harold M. Hyman presents an intense study of the role of the Republicans in Congress and their involvement in passing legislation which led to the rise of black politicians.

The Great Revival—Mr. Moody preaching at the Hippodrome. (The Library of Congress)

A Religion for Every Taste

Mike Zalampas

When Lee surrendered to Grant at Appomattox Court House, most Americans worshipped the same God, read the same Bible, hoped for the same heaven and feared the same hell. They differed only on theological details and the organizational structures of their churches. Most Americans were Protestants affiliated with denominations that had initially developed in Europe—Baptist, Methodist, Episcopalian, or Congregational. The catholic Christian tradition was represented by a relatively small Roman Catholic Church.

By 1914 a series of seismic shocks had fragmented the American religious landscape and an astounding number of radically divergent churches, faiths, and movements were active in the United States. There had appeared "a God for every man, a religion for every taste." This uniquely American pluralism was occasioned and accompanied by equally tremendous changes in the intellectual, economic, social, and demographical make-up of the United States.

Although Darwin had published his *Origins of Species* in 1859, it was not until the end of the Civil War that Americans turned their attention to it. A furious religious debate immediately erupted in full force. Most Americans, in spite of their denominational differences, had agreed on the acceptance of the Bible as the divinely-inspired, inerrant Word of God. Interpreting the Bible literally, they affirmed the divine creation of the earth and its inhabitants in six days. Geologists had already called into question the age of the earth by demonstrating that it was millions of years old. Some clergy had replied that to God "a day was as a thousand years and a thousand years a day."

Darwin's concept of evolution, however, dealt not only with the question of the when but the how of creation. Darwin drew on geology to show that the fossils in earlier rock formations were biologically simpler than the later, more complex fossil forms. There had thus been a slow development and a biological continuity among all living species. The most fit specimens for survival in every generation were those that could most successfully adapt to their environment. The adaptations were passed to successive generations as species became increasingly complex and adapted to their surroundings. Man, argued Darwin, was the end product of one of these lines of biological development.

Battle was immediately joined. Darwinism was taken by many clergymen to be a direct attack on the Bible and was rejected outright—a rejection that is still a fundamental article of faith for Protestant conservatives. Charles Hodge of Princeton Seminary declared biological evolution to be "absolutely incredible" while Mark Hopkins, president of Williams College, declared it to be "atheistic." Their sentiments were shared by most ministers of the day. There were those, such as Ralph Ingersoll, who became doctrinaire Darwinists and abandoned the Christian faith. While this latter position was widespread in Europe, a mediating position developed in the United States. Lyman Abbott, the influential Brooklyn pastor, accepted the principle of evolution, declaring evolution to be a divine process, not a product. In his *Ascent of Man,* Henry Drummond reinterpreted divine creation to mean the presence of God in history, giving it direction and meaning as mankind struggled upward to a deeper, more spiritual understanding. Their direction was followed by many in the east and midwest. In the south, however, the struggle against evolution was to continue until it culminated in the Scopes Trial in the 1920s. Since that time, evolutionists and theological conservatives occasionally pass one another, though they seldom speak.

This debate was further heightened when the general principle of evolution was applied to the Bible and the great creeds of the Christian faith. Biblical scholars in western Europe, particularly those of Germany, were increasingly interpreting the Bible as the final product of a thousand year long evolutionary process. Julius Wellhausen, for example, demonstrated that Genesis could not be the work of one author but, rather, was the union of several literary sources over a period of time. The Bible was thus the written expression of the religious beliefs of just one group of ancient peoples. The creeds of Christendom were similarly examined and presented as solutions to historical disputes within the church rather than as statements of eternal truths.

Catholics were less troubled than Protestants over this apparent weakening of what had been regarded as the infallible Word of God. As early as the Council of Trent (1545-1563) the faith of the Catholic Church was defined as resting as much on Catholic tradition as on the Bible. Further, the new biblical criticism was forbidden to Catholic scholars by papal edict.

Protestants, on the other hand, were uniquely wedded to an infallible Bible as the source of their theology. Any questioning of the Bible was, therefore, especially threatening to their entire theological system. Several distinct responses were made by American theologians.

The most radical attitude was that adopted by the "scientific modernists." It is not too great an exaggeration to say that this group replaced the former belief in an infallible Bible with an infallible faith in science and scientific progress. The Divinity School at the University of Chicago was a leading center of "modernism." Under the leadership of outstanding scholars such as William R. Harper, Shailer Mathews, and G. B. Foster there developed a distinctive "Chicago Theology." The religious experience was interpreted empirically in psychological and sociological terms while creeds and church organizations and practices were viewed as the result of historical forces and social environments. Any religious statement had to be made solely within the context of scientific insights. Some completely abandoned a Christo-centric theology for one essentially non-theistic. In Mathew's words, "The God of the scientifically minded will assume the patterns of science."

Although relatively few in number, they exercised a significant influence on theological education as many other seminaries sent their faculties to Chicago for their graduate training. Furthermore, they remained quite active in church affairs. Mathews, for example, was president of the Council of Churches for four years and president of the Northern Baptist Convention in 1915.

Evangelical liberals assumed a more mediatory position toward the new scientific and historical insights. Committed to a firm Christocentric theology, they sought to replace the external authority of the Bible with an emphasis on the primacy of the inner experience of Christ. This approach allowed them to accept the results of biblical criticism, the concept of evolution and other scientific insights, without abandoning what they saw as the ultimate Christ-centered truths of Christianity.

They drew partially upon the German theologian Albrecht Ritschl but more directly upon the American Horace Bushnell. Bushnell viewed the Bible as the record of a religious experience which every believer could enter and reproduce in his own life. The ultimate validation of the Christian faith was neither the Bible nor science, but in the "spiritual consciousness of man." Christ they conceived to be the divine redemptor of a world scarred by human waywardness and sin. Redeemed individuals constituted the kingdom of God which was being progressively realized in history. In their own eyes, they did not so much profess a new theology as a "progressive orthodoxy" which sought to present an eternal Christ to the world.

A large and quite diffuse group, evangelical liberalism included in its ranks professors, pastors, and laymen. The seminaries at Bangor, Andover, and Yale educated an entire generation of young pastors in this theological approach. Methodists, Presbyterians and Congregationalists, especially those in the north, were all deeply affected by the movement. Under the editorship of Charles C. Morrison, the *Christian Century* journal was effective in interpreting the new theological emphasis to laymen. Evangelical liberalism was thus optimistic in its outlook and was able to retain a deep Christian faith while coming to intellectual terms with science.

Protestant conservatism developed in part as a defense of the older Christian consensus and in part as a reaction against those liberals and modernists who accepted biological evolution and biblical criticism. Charles Hodge, in his *What Is Darwinism?*, attacked the principle of evolution by defending the trustworthiness of a divinely-inspired Bible in a scholarly fashion. Most conservatives, however, were simply content to dogmatically affirm the inerrancy of the Bible.

Large interdenominational Bible conferences were held at which a literal view of Scripture was stressed. The Niagara Bible Conference became an annual summer retreat which attracted thousands. In an effort to counteract the influence of the more liberal seminaries, Bible schools were founded to teach "the Bible, the whole Bible, and only the Bible." As they were willing to accept students with a minimum of education, they were able to attract large numbers of young men who aspired to the ministry. Their graduates returned home to preach a message based on an inerrant Bible.

While there were occasionally heated debates between conservatives and liberals at their denominational conventions, Congregationalists and Episcopalians generally proved to be flexible enough to weather the theological tensions. Lutherans were generally successful in avoiding a rupture as they demanded and received a rigid theological conformity. Methodists, Baptists, and Presbyterians experienced greater difficulties. As conservatives had generally remained closer to the laypeople in their churches, they were able to insist on a number of heresy trials and seminary faculty dismissals.

In 1893 the Presbyterian General Assembly demanded the dismissal of Charles H. Briggs from the faculty of Union Seminary in New York. In his inaugural address to the faculty and students of the seminary, Briggs had taken a liberal attitude toward biblical authority. Rather than dismiss Briggs, the seminary responded by severing its ties to the Assembly—Briggs chose to be re-ordained as an Episcopalian minister. Henry Preserved Smith, who had defended Briggs, was forced from Lane Seminary and went to the faculty at Union. The Methodist Alexander Winchell was dismissed by Vanderbilt University in 1878 while James Woodrow was ousted from the Presbyterian Seminary of South Carolina in 1886. Crawford H. Toy in 1879 and William H. Whitsett in 1898 were dismissed by the Southern Baptist Seminary in Louisville.

Conservatives took these actions in an effort to contain and punish liberal theologians. The end result of these ousters, however, was to publicize the newer theological views and to gain widespread sympathy for those who had been attacked. Most laypeople thought of themselves as moderates and were dismayed by the controversies. By the turn of the century, although there were to be sporadic dismissals, most denominations had placed heresy trials behind them.

In the midst of these controversies which were fragmenting the general Protestant tradition, there appeared several new movements that further broadened the religious spectrum in the United States. Each of these new groups claimed to possess the only true Christian faith, were intensely evangelistic, and were generally antagnostic toward their parent groups.

The conservative commitment to an inerrant Bible had been reinforced by the preaching of the Englishman J. N. Darby. Darby, a self-taught Bible student, toured widely in the United States, preaching an interpretation of biblical prophecy which divided history into specific periods of "dispensations." Each dispensation represented a distinct step in God's unfolding plan for the salvation of humanity. The present period of "grace through faith" is the Age of the Church. It constitutes the final dispensation prior to the return of Jesus Christ to the earth to establish the kingdom of God. This theology was orthodox in most other respects. Based as it was on an interpretation of "infallible prophecies," dispensationalism buttressed the conservative view of the Bible and was warmly received and taught at Prophecy Conferences and at the new Bible schools. The annotated Bible of C. I. Schofield, which was quite rigid in imposing the dispensationalist views on Scripture, was influential in disseminating this theology among conservatives. Popular preachers such as R. A. Torry, J. W. Chapman, and A. T. Pierson, all of whom were associated with the Moody Bible Institute, were vehement in their attack on all "liberalism"—which all too often meant all others who refused to accept their dispensational theology.

Between 1910-1915 the dispensationalists published a number of volumes entitled *The Fundamentals*. Interspersed with articles on dispensationalism were ones defending the inerrancy of the Bible. More importantly, the fundamentals of the Christian faith were defined as the acceptance of a literal interpretation of the Bible, the virgin birth, a substitutionary view of the atonement of Christ, and the physical resurrection and earthly return of Christ. While not all conservatives accepted the dispensationalist theology, most did adopt these articles as a test of orthodoxy. Those who refused assent to a literal interpretation of these dogmas were declared to be heretical. In 1910 the Presbyterian General Assembly formally adopted similar articles as a test of faith. In large areas of the south, the "fundamentals" were continued informally as a test of orthodoxy well into the twentieth century.

Another group arose out of the union of elements of dispensationalist and Adventist theology. In 1884 Charles T. Russell organized the International Bible Students Association, more commonly known today as Jehovah's Witnesses. Russell interpreted biblical prophecy to mean that 1914 would mark the end of the world as Christ returned to earth. When this event failed to take place, Russell insisted Christ had returned "invisibly" and that World

War I represented the beginning of the final struggle between God and Satan. As the victory of God would occur within a generation, "millions now living will never die."

Under the leadership of Russell and his successor Joseph F. Rutherford, the Witnesses directed a bitter campaign against all other religious groups. Extremely zealous in all their efforts, the Witnesses grew quickly, especially among lower-income disaffected Protestants. Rejecting all earthly governments as satanic, members of the movement have proved willing to endure persecution rather than recognize the sovereignty of those governments.

In the decades following the Civil War, American churches shared in the general prosperity and increase in wealth. The traditional Protestant denominations were rapidly converted into upper middle-class churches and, in the process, lost some of the biting edge of their earlier commitment to a distinctive Christian life. There were those who felt the mainline churches had become too "worldly."

One result was the Holiness Movement which had its roots in the teaching of John Wesley. Wesley had insisted that the initial blessing of God, salvation, was to be followed by the "second blessing" of sanctification. Sanctification was the divine gift of perfect love and freedom from sin which made it possible for the believer to live a holy life. As early as 1860 the demand for an emphasis on sanctification and holy living led to the foundation of a Free Methodist Church in New York. Charles G. Finney at Oberlin College had long insisted on a theology which stressed sanctification and in 1867 a National Association for the Promotion of Holiness was established.

Initially centered among Methodists, the Holiness Movement soon began to cut across denominational lines and attracted lower income, rural following. In time separatist tendencies began to develop as the parent denominations began to criticize the extremism of holiness leaders and as those leaders sought to dissociate themselves from the "worldly" and apostate traditional churches. In 1881 Daniel S. Warner founded the "Church of God Reformation Movement." Warner was devoted to both a holiness theology and a desire for Christian unity. This desire for unity was gradually displaced by a growing tendency to denominational separatism. Ultimately Warner's work produced the Church of God (Anderson, Indiana).

Similarly, Albert B. Simpson combined a desire for sanctification with faith in divine healing and a stress on missionary activity. In 1887 he established the Christian and Missionary Alliance. Although intended as an interdenominational group for Protestants, it too developed with time into a separate organization. If the Church of God enjoyed its greatest success among the rural poor, the Alliance found its support among the urban poor. The fastest growing holiness group was founded by Phineas Brese in 1908 as the Church of the Nazarene. Stressing an emotional, revivalistic theology based upon sanctification and an emphasis on holy living, the Nazarenes were soon prominent in the west and the south. As was true of the earlier holiness groups, the Nazarenes enlisted most of their followers from among the disaffected of the regular churches rather than the previously un-churched.

The Holiness Movement was, in turn, splintered by the erruption of Pentecostalism. While Pentecostalism shared the Holiness emphases upon a literal interpretation of the Bible, the second blessing and a strict moral life, it added a belief in a "third blessing." This third blessing, the baptism of the Holy Spirit, was the gift of *glossolalia* or speaking in unknown tongues. Originally known as the Latter Rain Movement because of an emphasis on *glossolalia* as interpreted from Joel 2:23, it began in 1901 at C. F. Parham's Bible School in Kansas. It was not until the Azusa Street revival in Los Angeles in 1906 that the movement attracted public notice. The Azusa revival was a biracial phenomenon under the leadership of W. J. Seymour, a black former student of Parham, but it split into separate, segregated de-nominations as it spread through the south and west. Today the movement has further fragmented into a number of groups, the largest of which are the Church of God (Cleveland, Tennessee), the Church of God in Christ and the Church of God of Prophecy. Although the Pentecostal churches suffered a relative decline following World War II, they began a resurgence in the decade of the sixties and an interest in *glossolalia* has arisen among both Protestants and Catholics.

In addition to these generally Christian responses to the theological ten-sions and needs of the period following the Civil War, there appeared a number of new groups quite radical in their separation from the Christian tradition. None was numerically important in its origins, but they were quite visible and did point to religious directions that enjoy some success at the present time.

Following the Civil War Americans developed a tremendous interest in the study of comparative religions. Capitalizing on this interest, Helena P. Blavatsky established the Theosophical Society in 1875. Blavatsky, a recent Russian immigrant, insisted she had been taught the eternal Wisdom of the Ages by "Adepts" who lived in Tibetan monasteries. These Adepts, in turn, had been taught by Moses, Confucius, Buddah, and Christ. Elements of Buddhism and Spiritualism were woven into a theological mixture which identified re-incarnation as an extension of the principle of evolution. Blavatsky attempted to combine this theology with an acceptance of science and technology. Her purpose was to promote universal brotherhood with-out regard for race, sex, caste or creeds. When Blavatsky went to England to establish a Theosophical Society the movement was taken over by Annie Besant who introduced Hindu concepts into its theology.

Insignificant numerically, theosophy is important as it represents the first effort to convert Americans to an oriental type of religious faith. When the World Parliament of Religions met at the Columbian Exposition of 1892, some 150,000 persons attended one or more of its programs. Other oriental and Near Eastern faiths were quickly established. In 1894 Swami Vivek-ananda founded the Hindu Vedanta Society to promote the Hindu religion in the United States. Yoga was soon being taught by the Yogoda Sat-Sanga Fellowship. The Muslim religious tradition was represented by Baha'ism which stressed the ultimate unity of all religions and the brotherhood of men.

Each of these religions, it will be noticed, was a synthesis of oriental religious concepts, stressed the brotherhood of man and attempted an accommodation with scientific insights. Groups such as Hare Krishna, Suni, and the Church of Unity are their direct descendants. They were also influential in leading many Americans to believe there was a common denominator among all religions and that, somehow, this commonality represented the "truth" to be found in theology.

A totally different religious approach was formulated by the Christian Science movement. Drawing on the hypnotic experiments of Franz Mesmer, Phineas P. Quimby taught that diseases were the result of negative thinking. Healthy mental attitudes, on the other hand, dispelled illness and disease. Mary Baker Eddy, a former patient of Quimby, became convinced that the Mind of God sustains all creation, matter exists only in the unhealthy mind, and disease is only the product of faulty thinking. In 1875 Eddy established the Christian Science Society and published her *Science and Health with Key to the Scripture.* By 1914 over one hundred thousand members had accepted the faith, and there were Christian Science Reading Rooms and churches in every major American city. The *Christian Science Monitor* became one of the most respected newspapers in the United States. Present "power through positive thinking" groups are the indirect descendents of Eddy's teaching.

Added to these theological divisions produced by new intellectual currents were the profound social and economic changes initiated by the industrial revolution and the mass immigration which overtook the United States between 1865 and 1914. These also introduced major changes into American religious life.

American cities experienced an explosive growth in the years following the Civil War. Minneapolis grew fiftyfold, Los Angeles twentyfold. Older urban areas such as New York and Philadelphia, starting from a larger initial base, doubled in size. While much of this growth came from a rural movement to the cities, even more was occasioned by the massive wave of immigrants reaching the United States. Between 1865 and 1900 fourteen million new Americans arrived from Europe. In the decade following 1900, nine million additional immigrants arrived—two-thirds of them settling in cities. The number of new immigrants in Chicago in 1890 equaled its population in 1880. This human flood was added to an American population that numbered only thirty million in 1865.

The period also marks what has charitably been called the "age of big business" but which Mark Twain less charitably designated as "the gilded age." Industrialization, with its concurrent placement of enormous wealth in the hands of a few, combined with urbanization to create slums, massive poverty, and corruption. A unique series of challenges was thrust upon the churches. These new urban masses were largely unchurched and increasingly indifferent to religion. Several responses were made to meet this need.

As urban areas increasingly became the focus of commercial life and the refuge of the poor and underprivileged, many churches were faced with the choice of following the middle classes to the suburbs or dwindling and dying. In one effort to combat this trend, Thomas Beecher in 1872 developed the concept of the institutional church at Elmira, New York. Added to the church's more traditional ministries of worship and evangelism were athletic programs, day nurseries, libraries, medical and legal clinics, educational classes, and musical and dramatic associations. This pattern was adopted by many inner city churches irrespective of denomination.

Initially these institutional churches enjoyed an amazing success. St. George's Episcopal Church in New York, which had shrunk to a membership of six families, grew to a membership of five thousand in only a few years. By 1900 the Baptist Temple of Philadelphia was the largest single congregation in the United States. The institutional churches, however, were enormously expensive and could not all depend, as did St. George's, on the support of a J. P. Morgan. In time, they became a tremendous drain upon their denominations as budget deficits had to be made up by contributions from the hinterland. Furthermore, these institutional churches tended to become non-denominational in theology and more humanitarian than evangelistic in their goals. They did little to Christianize the urban masses.

Another approach was attempted by the Salvation Army. Founded in England in 1878 by William Booth, the Army immigrated to the United States two years later. Initially designed as an evangelistic arm for the regular churches, it soon became a separate denomination. Preceded by its brass bands and spearheaded by dynamic preaching, it penetrated urban slum areas to provide the poor with food, shelter, and work. Joined to its holiness and revivalistic theology were a wide range of social services, including legal aid, day nurseries, and employment bureaus. The Army soon acquired a reputation for a willingness to go into urban areas where no other group would work and so gained the respect of all classes of society.

In 1896 Booth's son Ballington, who had led the Army in the United States for ten years, refused his father's orders to return to England. He resigned to found the rival Volunteers of America, which stressed a Christian ministry to the poor, ex-convicts, and unwed mothers. The Volunteers stressed democratic participation rather than the rigid discipline of the army and placed relatively less emphasis on preaching and the conversion of the individual.

The same industrial, social, and urban problems which produced the institutional churches and groups such as the Salvation Army, gave birth to the Social Gospel movement. Traditionally, Protestantism had stressed the salvation of the individual, believing the injustices of this world would be redressed in the next world. Convinced that society needed a basic readjustment here and now, the advocates of the Social Gospel sought political and economic reforms to remedy the worst ills of nineteenth-century capitalism.

Washington Gladden, "the father of the Social Gospel," championed the right of labor to organize, laws against child labor, and the reform of unsafe industrial conditions. The leading spokesman for the movement, however, was Walter Rauschenbush. Initially a Baptist pastor in Hell's Kitchen, New York City, Rauschenbush joined the faculty of the Rochester Theological Seminary. Drawing on his personal experiences, he produced a series of publications which delineated the injustices of society and demanded a Christian effort to ameliorate those abuses. His unique contribution was to bridge theologically the gap between liberals and conservatives. The social consciousness of evangelical Protestantism was raised while liberals were provided with a theology which allowed them to remain within the Christian witness. In time many of the ideas of the Social Gospel movement were widely accepted as seminaries added courses in social ethics and reforming social service organizations were formed along denominational lines.

Revivalism had long been a staple feature of American rural life. The camp meeting was an annual event that attracted thousands. However, evangelism was largely unknown in large cities prior to the Civil War. Increasingly, the cities were becoming unchurched and non-Christian in tone. It was not until Dwight L. Moody, with the singer Ira D. Sankey, returned from a triumphal revival campaign in England in 1872 that serious efforts were made to evangelize urban areas. Moody, a Congregational layman, had been drawn to full-time Christian work through his association with the YMCA in Chicago. He preached a simple, undenominational theology which stressed "Ruin by Sin, Redemption by Christ, and Regeneration by the Holy Spirit." Possessed of a gentle, ecumenical spirit, Moody was not a great theologian. His primary talents lay in a simple message superbly presented and a systematic and efficient organization. Moody was able to unite diverse denominations in his cooperative evangelistic crusades and, in turn, channeled his converts into local churches.

Moody's mass rallies drew huge crowds where tens of thousands professed conversion to the Christian faith. In retrospect it now appears that most of those reached by his crusades had previously attended rural churches before moving to a large city. Therefore, they represented a return to the church rather than fresh converts. The newer non-protestant immigrants from Europe were largely untouched by what was essentially, after all, a Protestant movement.

Moody's crusades were largely confined to northern urban areas. In the south, evangelists like Sam Jones utilized the same approach with great success. It was Billy Sunday, a former baseball player, however, who succeeded to the fame and position of Moody. In 1917 a two-month crusade by Sunday produced one hundred thousand converts. It was these revivalistic efforts which were to issue in the mass evangelistic crusades of the present day.

The enormous tide of immigrants produced the single most dramatic development in American Christianity—the phenomenal growth of the Roman Catholic Church. In 1870 there were four million Catholics in the

United States, by 1880 six million, by 1890 nine million, while by 1900 there were twelve million Catholics. By 1914 every third American church and every sixth person was Catholic. The strain of meeting the religious needs of this great mass was almost overwhelming. Thousands of priests had to be recruited and trained, dozens of dioceses formed and tremendous sums of money raised. Compounding these difficulties were the diverse languages, traditions, and customs of these new Americans.

The influx of European Catholics raised a number of issues for the Church. These issues were not theological in nature but were, rather, questions relating to the goals and methods to be adopted by American Catholicism. Two parties of diffuse make-up emerged within the Church. The "Americanists" argued that the Chruch should adopt a positive attitude toward the assimilation of Catholics into the mainstream of American life, support the concept of religious freedom and become tolerant of religious differences. The "Conservatives" wanted to retain Catholic distinctiveness, traditions, and to refuse accommodation to American culture. These groups were united in their loyalty to the American political system. They disagreed on several specific issues. One was the desire of some Catholics for their own ethnic parishes as opposed to territorial parishes. Allied to this was the demand for greater representation in an essentially Irish hierarchy. The dispute was ultimately referred to Pope Leo XIII who decided against separate parishes and, in time, the hierarchy became more representative.

A second issue revolved around the question of public school versus Catholic parochial education. More liberal Catholics viewed public education as a means of assimilating their children into American life. Archbishop Michael A. Corrigan threw his support behind the parochial system and finally received a papal decision in favor of a Catholic elementary educational system. By 1914 one million pupils were enrolled in parochial schools which generally had a reputation for excellence.

Secret societies, such as the Knights of Labor, also produced tensions within the Church. It was feared by some that the secrecy and semi-religious elements of these organizations might injure the Church. The issue was resolved by papal acceptance of organizations which were directed toward positive social good and did not endanger the unity of the Church.

Ultimately Leo XIII intervened to resolve the tensions between the Americanists and the conservatives. While condemning "Americanism," he defined and treated it in such a way that the loyalty and unity of both parties was preserved. The overwhelming nature of the Catholic task in America was a tremendous force for keeping the Church united. There was, in addition, little time or energy for theological debate when churches had to be provided, schools built, and the religious needs of the laity met. The condemnation in 1907 of "Modernism" by Rome had little effect on American Catholicism which was theologically conservative by nature.

The Eastern Orthodox church also experienced a tremendous growth during this period. As the Orthodox churches in Europe had been organized along national lines, languages and customs, there was little controversy between them. Their common problem was that of providing priests and churches for their laymen. They were largely unmoved by the theological controversies raging among Protestants. In time, Greeks, Bulgars, Russians, and Ukranians developed their own religious communities, which while adding diversity to the American scene, produced little divisiveness.

In 1865 there were perhaps 150,000 Jews in the United States, most of whom were Ashkenazic or German in origin. Generally they leaned to a Reform tradition which relaxed the Talmudic dietary laws, adopted a liberalizing attitude toward scientific thought, and yet, retained the Mosaic ethical code. In 1889 a Central Conference of American Rabbis was organized which unified the Reform congregations.

In reaction there evolved the Conservative congregations which, under the inspiration of Issac Leeser, sought to preserve the Mosaic laws as developed in Talmudic literature. In 1886 the Jewish Theological Seminary of America was established to provide Rabbinical training for Conservative Judaism.

By 1914 Jewish immigrants had increased the number of American Jews some twelve times. The newer group arriving after 1880 were primarily Yiddish speaking, highly orthodox in their devotion, and suspicious of Reform Judaism. By 1900 there were some 1,000 Orthodox congregations which founded the Union of Orthodox Rabbis the same year.

The rise of Zionism near the end of the century produced tension within the Jewish community. Reform synagogues tended to oppose Zionism while the Orthodox retained their hope in the coming of a Messiah. Conservative Judaism was essentially supportive of Zionism but was able to act as a mediating bridge between all Jews. The worldwide rise of anti-Semitism near the end of the century acted to impress upon Jews of all persuasions their common religious heritage and identity. They were able to act cooperatively on a wide number of benevolent and charitable organizations.

Taken together, it may be said that America, in the decades between the Civil War and World War I, experienced a remarkable religious development. At the time the religious diversity was often accompanied by tension and, at times, overt hostility. There can be no doubt in hindsight, however, that this religious diversity acted to enrich American life and to provide a distinctively religious orientation for most Americans. Today there has developed an amazing degree of acceptance and cooperation among Americans of quite divergent religious views.

Suggested Readings

For general treatment of American religious history, see Winthrop S. Hudson, *Religion in America,* second edition (1973); Robert T. Handy, *A History of the Churches in the United States and Canada* (1977); and Sydney E. Ahlstrom, *A Religious History of the American People* (1977). For the development of Protestant liberalism, see Kenneth Cathen, *The Impact of American Religious Liberalism* (1962); for Protestant conservatism, see Ernest Sandeen, *The Roots of Fundamentalism, British and American Millenarianism, 1800-1930* (1970).

For Protestant social Christianity, refer to C. Howard Hopkins, *The Rise of the Social Gospel in American Protestantism, 1865-1915* (1940). For the Holiness Movement, see Vinson Synan, *The Holiness-Pentecostal Movement in the United States* (1971). Robert D. Cross has studied the Americanist crisis in his *The Emergence of Liberal Catholicism in America* (1958). On the Jewish experience in America, see Arthur Gilbert, *A Jew in Christian America* (1966). For sects see, Charles S. Braden, *These Also Believe* (1949); and J. Stillson Judah, *The History and Philosophy of the Metaphysical Movement in America* (1967).

Section II
World War I to World War II

Cultural changes which occurred in the period after the Civil War were accelerated with the arrival of the twentieth century. The federal government began to regulate businesses during the Progressive Era, but regulation did not bring destruction to big business. The American corporation was now on the horizon. The four essays in this section reveal new developments that were taking place in the early 1900s. Sheldon Nagel describes in his essay the business ethic of the film industry and shows the financial power behind the movie stars. His essay initially reveals the importance of changing technology to the movie industry. He then describes the careers of the movie barons such as William Selig, William Fox, and Marcus Loew. His essay gives a new perspective to the rise of the film industry. Barbara Peterson pinpoints the origins of the modern women's liberation movement in the changes in the feminist movement of the early 1900s. The Gibson girl was the liberated woman of the 1890s, but she really wasn't liberated all that much. Barbara Peterson describes the changes that took place with the Gibson girl and the forces of liberation which occurred with the suffrage movement.

Many drastic cultural changes took place during the 1920s and none were so revealing as the rise of mass sports. Douglas A. Noverr and Lawrence Ziewacz describe in their essay the lure of sports in the 1920s, showing why sports were so popular in that era. Most of their essay describes the sports heroes of the 1920s in their respective sports. While Ted Hinckley shows the general relationship between business and the mass mind, much of his essay focuses upon major business changes and the consumer revolution of the 1920s. His essay clearly reveals the birth of the mass business mind.

The Dream Factory

The story of the American Film Industry

Sheldon Nagel

Brilliant men, beautiful jazz babies, champagne baths, midnight revels, petting parties in the purple dawn, all ending in one terrific smashing climax that makes you gasp.

Movie advertisement, 1919

It is the only multimillion dollar business in America that has taught more than three generations how to smoke, make love, and believe in happy endings. Worshiping it as art or cloaking it in a gossamer mantle of nostalgia has become a semi-competitive pastime. But the American film industry was nurtured under the tenets of capitalism and spurred by the profit motive. The fantasies it presented on the screen were no more improbable than the struggles, victories and disappointments that took place behind the screen and remarkably, the beginnings were humble and almost haphazard.

Thomas Alva Edison, the tyrannical tinkerer of Menlo Park, (whose own affectionate image held by the public would later be aided by two film portrayals; one by Mickey Rooney and the other by Spencer Tracy) produced in 1889, the kinetoscope. This device was a cabinet inside of which was machinery capable of showing some fifty feet of film. By dropping a coin into a slot and looking through a tiny hole, the viewer could see either a man

Errol Flynn and Basil Rathbone in *Captain Blood*, 1935. (Warner Bros. Pictures, Inc.)

sneezing, a girl dancing, a boxing match, a horse eating hay, or a number of other simple presentations. Each vignette took less than a minute. The great dream factory began as a penny peep show.

Edison's interest soon drifted to other projects, and he failed to expend the $150 needed to acquire foreign patent protection. This oversight would come back to haunt Edison and his future associates. Not only did foreign manufacturers duplicate the popular kinetoscope, but their subsequent patents became the basis for a growing number of American competitors who used European imports to challenge Edison's later attempts to monopolize the movie industry. The contenders seized upon Greek and Latin sources to name their devices. Anything suggesting life, action, vision, record, or motion was used, and the result was that muto-scopes, bio-scopes, and bio-graphs competed with kinetoscopes for wall space in penny arcades.

The arcade owners quickly realized that these machines were their most profitable attraction, and they quickly absorbed all that could be produced. The cabinets, however, were in short supply as were the cameras used to manufacture the pictures. To fill the demand for films, Edison had constructed the world's first movie studio in West Orange, New Jersey. This small peculiar building was dubbed the "Black Maria" and it rotated on a track in order to follow the sunlight. Edison, in turn, was dependent upon Kodak (a nonsense word made up by George Eastman as his company's trademark) which had only recently superimposed film on celluloid and as a result now dominated the world market.

These limitations on potential profits could be overcome if the projectors could be freed from the cabinets and the images thrown upon a large, single screen. Scores of patrons could then be charged to view the image cast by a single machine and profits would soar. The breakthrough came in 1895 when projection machines were developed almost simultaneously and independently on both sides of the Atlantic.

The premier showings of this technological breakthrough were greeted with wild enthusiasm, and the unexpected reaction of some early viewers was startling. Scenes of waves breaking against the shore caused a few to become seasick. In Paris, the Lumiére brothers projected a train coming toward the camera. As the locomotive grew larger, members of the audience fled in panic. The Edison Company's Vitascope premiered to such accolades as "tremendous," "sensational," and "enormous."

Now the arcade owners became exhibitors. At first, they merely curtained off sections of their arcades, making them suitable for viewing. A few of the more visionary provided chairs for the patrons. The popularity of the "movies" was phenomenal. Vacant shops were engulfed by platoons of would-be entrepreneurs who converted them into storeshows. The fare offered was basically what had been viewed in the old kinetoscopes. (The Lumiére cabinet had been called the cinematograph, giving Europe its label for motion pictures.)

Audiences would pay to see anything that moved and as a result anyone could successfully produce films. Anyone, that is, who could get his hands on a camera. Edison, who believed that only his own patents were legal, regarded all other film producers as thieves or outlaws, and he began the almost endless litigations that still erupt with amusing regularity in the film industry.

By 1900 film was being produced in longer strips. The raw stock extended to 250 unbroken feet or three to four minutes of projection time. Now, simple stories could be told. More would be needed to produce a movie than simply aiming the camera and grinding away. Movie acting, writing, and directing skills in their primitive form were about to receive an introduction to the infant industry.

America's artistic breakthrough in the film industry occurred in 1903 when Edwin S. Porter of the Edison Company shot a complete story on 740 feet of film. Using both indoor sets and the breathtaking landscape of New Jersey, Porter gave to this country all the elements of our classic morality play, the western. This eighteen-minute film, *The Great Train Robbery*, was run continuously by some exhibitors from morning until night and earned them $1,000 a week on five-cent admissions.

By 1905 1000 feet became standard as one reel of film, giving the director, writer, and actors about a quarter of an hour to tell their story. In June 1905 John P. Harris and Harry Davis remodeled a storeshow into a more permanent and pleasant theater. They combined the American word for a five-cent coin (their admission price) with the Greek word for theater. McKeesport, Pennsylvania, had America's first nickelodeon.

The number of movie production companies continued to blossom but with a limited survival rate. The more successful existed either on their own patents which were based upon minor modifications of Edison's original equipment, or they imported foreign equipment protected by the overseas patents resulting from Edison's initial carelessness. One such challenger was the Biograph Company which used a film size slightly larger than that of the Edison Company. Wandering into Biograph's New York studio one day came a young Kentuckian. He hoped to sell some story ideas (writers received a flat fee, seldom more than five dollars, for their inspirations,) and earn enough to maintain basic sustenance until the more legitimate arts recognized his talents. He stayed to do more stories and then reluctantly to appear before the camera and finally to direct some of the one-reelers. As a director, David Wark Griffith brought to Biograph what no other film company or filmmaker had attained. Griffith had a genius for understanding the uniqueness of his medium. He saw that storytelling on film was different from storytelling on the stage. He developed as actors, young men and women who were photogenic. The merciless lens showed youth and beauty only where it existed. Aging ingenues from Broadway, without the filter of distance between the footlights and the audience did not do well in films. Griffith also developed camera angles, the close-up, imaginative editing, and better stories. Griffith brought quality to movie making.

The executives at Biograph were generally pleased with Griffith's work and the favorable reaction it received from the public. But to Edison, Vitagraph, Biograph, Essanay, Kalem, Selig, Lubin, Kleine, Pathé and Melies (these latter two being American branches of French pioneer film companies) quality was a pleasant bonus, neither asked for nor encouraged.

The exhibitors were developing an insatiable demand for films. They purchased them at ten cents per foot regardless of content and changed films daily. This was the poor man's entertainment, simple enough to keep the masses amused and to keep the nickels and dimes coming. Some houses ran a two-hour show, nine reels, each reel different with a complete change in the bill the following day. Quality was not only unnecessary, it actually slowed down production at a time when anything on film sold.

The need for efficient product distribution was met by the development of film exchanges in all the major exhibiting centers of the country. In these cities, companies were created which purchased the prints (by the foot) from the movie manufacturers. These companies, or exchanges, would lease the prints (by the foot) to exhibitors at a profit. From their large stock, culled through purchases from several producers, these exchanges could assure the exhibitors a guaranteed supply for the daily program changes.

Within two decades from its beginnings as a peep show, the film industry had grown and subdivided into its three basic units: production, distribution and exhibition. Now movement began which attempted horizontal and eventually vertical consolidation. The next stage of the movie business had begun.

The decades following the Civil War were among the most imaginative in the history of American business. Combining an almost romantic flair with an instinct for the economic jugular, men such as J. P. Morgan, John D. Rockefeller, and Andrew Carnegie sought to weld together empires impervious to attack and from which impudent competition could be crushed. A key tactic in these struggles had been consolidation. Where one corporation controlled all the essential raw materials of an industry, or dominated all retail outlets or all the methods of distribution, then horizontal consolidation had been achieved. Similarly, if one could control a product from its raw material source, through its manufacture, distribution and sale, then from bottom to top, vertical consolidation had occurred. Rockefeller had achieved both types of control in the oil industry.

These then were both the models and the goals which stood before the aspiring monopolists of the film industry. Consolidation offered production regularity, quality standardization, control of distribution, elimination of competition, and the promise of enormous profits.

Prompted by George Kleine, Edison in 1909 organized the Motion Picture Patents Company. This brought together the ten movie producing companies which all claimed one or more patents on film-making equipment. The Patents Company trust in turn organized the General Film Company to control distribution. Exhibitors quickly signed exclusive contracts with General Film to assure themselves an adequate supply of the one reelers turned out by members of the trust. Fear was the great motivator for the theater owners. Without the license issued by General Film, their source of movies might disappear and they would be forced to close their doors. Producers outside the trust were taken to court for patent infringement and if the courts proved too slow in meting out justice goon squads were sent to smash the equipment of the recalcitrants. It was all very tidy and the trust members divided millions in profits. But they miscalculated. The tried and true formula of consolidation wasn't yet ready to work in the movie business. Uncontrollable variables doomed the organization even while they reaped huge dividends. Not one of the ten trust members survives in the industry today.

The story of the trust's demise is the story of the rise of the great studios and stars which dominated the industry until shortly after World War II. It is also the story of how the tiny provincial community of Los Angeles and nearby environs such as Hollywoodland came to be recognized the world over as simply Hollywood, a term synonymous with motion pictures. Finally, it is the story of how a small group of able, energetic and tenacious men rose from impoverished beginnings to dominate an industry. The tale is both intricate and fascinating, more so in the living than in the telling, and we can touch only upon its highlights.

The members of the trust were businessmen as opposed to showmen. They had built their structure on two principles: the mass audience did not have the intelligence to absorb a story that went beyond one reel and this same audience would not pay more than five or ten cents to see motion pictures. A one-reel movie was needed, therefore, not only to satiate the audience to its maximum but also to derive the maximum profit. Anything such as longer films increased production costs without increasing profits. The masses would still be paying the same prices for films which cost more to make and more to rent. Producers, distributors, and exhibitors would all lose. The nabobs of the trust turned a conservative ear to the pleas of those who argued that better films would draw larger audiences willing to pay higher prices. When D. W. Griffith defied his bosses at Biograph and produced a two reeler, he was promptly fired.

If the trust failed to gauge accurately the public's willingness to pay more in order to get more, there were others who did not. The trust had not frightened away all the competition. Several independent producers continued the struggle on two fronts. They fought the trust in the courts and they fought it in the darkened theaters. They lost the former battle, but by winning the latter they won the whole war. Audiences gravitated to their films so that there were no longer enough paying customers to support one-reel producers. The members of the once powerful trust faded from the business.

The independents were showmen as well as businessmen. They saw that certain actors and certain types of films generated favorable comments from audiences leaving the theaters. The trust producers did not name the actors or directors in their films. They reasoned correctly that name recognition would lead to higher salary demands. The audiences, however, began asking when they could again see the "Biograph girl" or another "Little Mary" picture. Waiting in the wings were the independent producers who sensed a phenomenon in the making. With the allure of name recognition through billing and substantially increased salaries, the premier performers of the trust were snared away by the independents. The star system had begun and the cardinal premise of the movie industry had been established: success lay with those who could accurately judge public taste, failure lay with those who could not.

The life of Carl Laemmle was as unpredictable and episodic as the movie industry, yet his life contained elements common to most of the movie moguls. He was foreign born, emigrating to the United States in search of greater opportunities. He was Jewish. He had no background in show business. He entered the movie industry when most men his age are already ensconced in a career. He had not shown any predilection toward films.

Laemmle was born in 1867 in the South German kingdom of Würtemburg. He was the tenth of thirteen children, and eight of his brothers and sisters died in a single scarlet fever epidemic. At thirteen, the traditional age of Jewish manhood, Carl was apprenticed to a family friend. He mastered the stationery business, becoming the firm's bookkeeper and office manager. One of his surviving brothers had gone to America, and Carl was intrigued by the accounts of the New World that were sent back to the Old. The unexpected death of his mother seemed to lessen any remaining constraints to stay in Europe. Laemmle purchased a $22.50 steerage ticket, and on February 14, 1884, he sailed from Bremerhaven. This five-foot-tall, seventeen-year-old must have appeared as a fly speck in what was then an unending tide of immigrants.

Nothing like it had appeared before in history. Europe spewed out its disaffected, disenchanted, and persecuted. By the tens of millions they left strange and exotic-sounding places such as Laupheim, Kiev, Minsk, Warsaw, Ricse and Krasmashhilz. If the points of origin were diverse, the final destination was shared by all as a single desire: the golden shore. They funneled through Ellis Island and Castle Garden in New York Harbor to swell the cities. America would turn this refuse into protein. Carl Laemmle was one of these.

He went inland. In Chicago he was an office and errand boy. He delivered newspapers and worked as a bookkeeper. There was even a stint on a South Dakota farm. After ten years in America Laemmle was back in a Chicago department store earning $18 a week. His next move was to Oshkosh, Wisconsin, which must have sounded strange and exotic indeed back in Laupheim. He worked as bookkeeper and salesman for the Continental Clothing Company, becoming the store manager and showing an inventive flair for advertising promotions. Volume buyers, for example, could get free turkeys. Laemmle married Recha Stern, the boss's niece. The couple would have two children, a son and a daughter.

Fulfillment seemed near, but Laemmle was stunned when a requested raise in pay was turned down. Disgruntled, he took his family to Chicago and began looking once more for new opportunities. It was 1906, Laemmle was thirty-nine years old, and he announced he was putting his savings into a nickelodeon.

What fascinated him was that customers paid for a product they didn't take away with them. No wrapped packages left the store. The product was, in fact, left behind for reuse with other customers. Best of all, it was cash in advance. The astonishment and apprehension on the part of family and friends over his initial announcement turned to pleasant relief. The venture was so successful that in only two months Laemmle opened a second theater. Noted for their cleanliness and respectability, the theaters prospered. When he felt he was not getting the proper service from the local film exchanges he opened his own. He offered honest, efficient, and courteous service. Within three years the Laemmle Film Service became the largest film distributor in the United States. But he was on a collision course. His film exchange was outside the protective constrictions of Edison's trust. The trust unleashed its vengeance against him. Laemmle fought back and other independent distributors rallied to him. Since films could not be obtained from the trust, he would make his own. He organized the Independent Moving Pictures Company of America, and IMP films began coming out of the company's New York studio.

Laemmle's penchant for promotion was given full play. With great flourish he announced that the Biograph girl had signed with IMP. The world would know her name. The IMP publicity department trumpeted that "the Girl of a Thousand Faces," had been given a life contract at an unheard of $15,000 a year. Laemmle next captured Biograph's other major attraction. Canadian born Gladys Smith and her blond curls were an immense favorite with audiences. IMP offered her $175 a week and billing. Using her stage name, Mary Pickford became the screen's first genuine superstar.

IMP was then merged with Patrick Powers' Universal Film Company. After a chaotic period of infighting, Laemmle and his right hand man, Robert Cochrane, emerged in total control. Carl Laemmle was now ready for his boldest move since his decision to tackle the trust. Universal Pictures was going to center its film production in Los Angeles.

Several film pioneers had already been working in California. The consistent weather with its almost endless sunshine cut down production costs considerably. But northern California, notably the San Francisco Bay area was a greater attraction than Los Angeles. "Baghdad by the Bay" was ideal for exterior shots, it contained a sizeable population available as extras, it had a flourishing theater capable of delivering experienced actors, and it presented a diverting night life for the film workers. Indeed, George K. Spoor and Max Aaronson had built the Essanay studios across the bay in near-by Niles. Using the hills as a backdrop, they created scores of "Broncho Billy" westerns.

To William Selig must go the credit for discovering the singular advantage Los Angeles possessed. Prior to becoming a member of the trust, Selig was seeking a quiet place to produce his films; a place far from the clutches of the Edison lawyers and goon squads. Not only was Los Angeles far from New York, it was also close to Mexico. Lookouts spotting suspicious figures approaching the outdoor sets would yell out warnings. The equipment would be hastily placed in waiting cars and a mad dash for the border and safety would take place. By March 15, 1915, the dangers from the trust had dissipated but the lure of Los Angeles remained. On that date, Carl Laemmle, the president of the Universal Film Manufacturing Company opened Universal City in the San Fernando Valley. Today, Universal City is the largest motion picture manufacturing complex in the world.

Not all the independents who took on the trust were ultimately as successful as Carl Laemmle. But some were meteors, nonetheless.

William Fox was of German-Jewish descent and was brought to this country in 1880 when less than a year old. The family occupied a rear tenement apartment on New York's swarming lower East Side. Twelve more children were born to his parents, only six of whom survived childhood. To help support the family, William sold newspapers, stove polish mixed by his father, candy lozenges with riddles inside, sandwiches, and pretzels. All this before he was eleven. At that age he entered the garment trade, cutting linings for men's suits. He worked from seven to seven for $8 a week. In time, saving penny on top of penny, Fox and a friend named Sol Brill opened a cloth sponging firm which preshrunk material before it was sold to the tailors. The business did well and the hard times seemed past. Just before his twenty-first birthday, Fox married Eva Lee and they soon had two girls.

Suddenly, an opportunity presented itself which would thrust Fox into the ranks of the multimillionaires. Stuart Blackton, one of the founders of the Vitagraph film studio was selling a penny arcade and picture show in Brooklyn. In 1904 Fox depleted his savings of $1,600 and purchased the little enterprise. He was twenty-four years old and in the entertainment business. Fox concentrated on the motion picture aspect of his arcade. He refurbished the viewing room and installed more comfortable chairs. He hired vaudeville acts to attract patrons, and between film showings he had a piano player sing illustrated songs with the audience joining in. He did well enough to buy another theater and another until he owned fifteen in the New York area.

From this plateau Fox could see that the big money was being made by the distributors. He formed the Greater New York Rental Company. William Fox now became a target of the trust. They offered to buy out his film exchange at a price far below its actual value. He refused. The trust countered by revoking his license as an exhibitor. Fox in turn brought a $6 million lawsuit against them declaring that the Patents Company was in violation of the Sherman Anti-Trust Act. The case was settled out of court when Fox agreed to accept $300,000.

Both his theater chain and leasing firm grew. In 1914 he began producing his own films. William Fox became the first man to embrace the three elements of the film industry into a single organization. He was a producer, distributor, and exhibitor. The Fox studio was adept at that most Hollywood of all skills, manufacturing illusions. He took a middle-class Jewish girl from Cincinnati, Theodosia Goodman, and turned her into the screen's first love goddess. Vampire-like she drained the hapless males who fell into her clutches. A screen name befitting this "vamp" was created by Fox. Not only was "Theda Bara" more alluring, the scrambled letters could be rearranged into "Arab Death" and the studio created a fanciful biography to further exploit the mystery. When her immortal line, "Kiss me, my fool," appeared on the screen, male hearts pounded and Fox's profits soared.

William Fox had overcome deprivation, physical infirmity, and educational limitations to become an industrial and commercial colossus. A childhood accident and his family's inability to pay for proper medical attention had caused his left arm to hang uselessly at his side. He became an ardent golfer despite this and learned to play one-handed. Night school barely got him to the sixth grade. He selected stories and edited scripts by having his wife read to him in the evening. Near the end of the silent era the Fox Film Corporation was valued at $200 million. The Fox theater chain of some 800 houses was valued at an additional $50 million. William Fox was now ready for his most rapacious move.

Loew's Incorporated owned a significant chain of theaters and was the parent corporation which controlled the Metro-Goldwyn-Mayer studio. Founder Marcus Loew was dead, and Fox offered the widow and other key stockholders a $50 million package for their shares. The man who had sued the Patents Trust for restraint of trade was now on the threshold of engulfing the film industry. He borrowed from such diverse interests as American Telephone and Telegraph and investment bankers Halsey, Stuart and Company. Suddenly, the whole scheme turned to ashes. On October 29, 1929, Black Tuesday, the stock market collapsed. Fox had planned to use his own earnings to retire the notes that now became due, but stock in the Fox Film Corporation had plummeted from $119 per share to $1. At the same time the government stepped in, declaring that Fox's ownership of Loew's Incorporated violated the anti-monopoly laws of the United States. Continuing lawsuits forced his bankruptcy in 1936 and in 1941 he served six months for bribing a judge. His studios were absorbed by Daryl Zanuck, Spyros Skouras, and Joseph Schenck's Twentieth Century Film Corporation to form Twentieth Century-Fox.

Fox did not die in poverty. Royalties from some of his own early patents provided him with a comfortable existence. But Hollywood's real prize was irretrievably lost. Without influence or power and with no one to pay him deference, he died in May 1952, filmdom's forgotten man.

At the time of America's entry into World War I there were about one hundred companies producing films in the United States. Within a decade less than a dozen film corporations, with headquarters in New York and production facilities in California, dominated not only American but world film output. It is not surprising, then, that the moguls at the top not only knew each other but often had their lives intertwined. Such was the case with Adolph Zukor, Marcus Loew, Jesse Lasky, Samuel Goldfish and Louis B. Mayer.

Adolph Zukor was born in the Hungarian town of Ricse. In 1888, at the age of fifteen, he arrived in America with $40 sewed into his vest. After various odd jobs and a stint in night school he learned the fur business. Establishing a small firm in Chicago, he met and married Lottie Kaufman. Zukor now determined to relocate his business and his growing family in New York. An energetic fur salesman, Marcus Loew, had met Zukor in Chicago and now Loew assisted him in his transition to the East. The Zukors and the Loews became neighbors and intimate friends. Looking for investments beyond the fur business, Zukor became an associate of Loew's in nickelodeons and vaudeville-film theaters. Soon he was operating picture shows on his own.

Zukor's diminutive size and soft-spoken manner hid an iron will and ferocious tenacity from casual observers. His quick mind now seized upon a revolutionary idea. He felt American audiences would be receptive to longer films of better quality, so receptive they would be willing to plunk down more than the usual five- or ten-cent admission price. The higher ticket prices were essential to his concept since a larger gross would be necessary to cover the increased production costs of longer films. The Patents Trust rebuffed his idea, one member commenting that Zukor would "soon be back making buttonholes."

Zukor struck out on his own. In 1912 he organized the Famous Players Company and produced exclusively what became known as "feature pictures." Not only did he produce the longer four-, five- and six-reel features, Zukor correctly assessed the public's desire to see their favorites star in them. He set out to capture the leading players for his production company, including Mary Pickford who had recently left Universal.

"Only in America," the immigrants were fond of muttering, especially whenever they witnessed improbable events resulting in good fortune. What could have been more incredible than the pairing of Jesse Lasky and Samuel Goldfish. Lasky was born in San Jose, California, in 1880. As a young man he played in vaudeville with his sister Blanche. By 1910, he was a leading vaudeville producer. Samuel Goldfish was born in the Jewish ghetto of Warsaw, Poland, in 1882. Fiercely independent, he ran away from home when only eleven. At thirteen, traveling alone in steerage he came to America. He found his way to Gloverville, New York, and eventually became a glove salesman par excellence. Introduced to Blanche Lasky by a mutual friend, Sam soon proposed. In 1910 they were married.

The brothers-in-law were intrigued by the film producing business, especially long features. They organized, in 1913, The Jesse H. Lasky Feature

Play Company with Lasky as president and Goldfish as general manager. Young Cecil B. DeMille, scion of a theatrical family also received a quarter of the new firm and became the director-general. For a remaining share of the company this trio convinced stage star Dustin Farnum to film his Broadway success, *The Squaw Man*. Not one in this quartet had ever produced, directed, or appeared in a film before.

DeMille shifted the shooting locale to Hollywood, renting a barn in the midst of an orange grove at Selma and Vine Streets. Farnum began to lose faith in the operation and demanded $5,000 in cash for his stock. A decade later this proved to be a $2 million mistake. The fledgling producers had put up about $25,000 for the picture and the return doubled their investment. The Lasky Company was on its way, producing twenty-one films during its first year.

Meanwhile, Zukor had not been idle. A group of exhibitors desirous of a steady supply of quality feature films organized under the leadership of William W. Hodkinson. Their objective was to finance film production and guarantee first-run theater showings in return for a percentage of the receipts. Since Zukor's Famous Players was the chief manufacturer of feature films, his company became the cornerstone of the whole operation. Zukor now approached the Lasky, Goldfish, DeMille group and the two merged into Famous Players-Lasky. With Zukor as president, Lasky as vice-president, DeMille as director-general and Goldfish as chairman of the board, this tetrad controlled the industry's leading stars and production facilities. Hodkinson provided exclusive access to the nation's leading theaters. The whole organization was known as the Paramount Pictures Corporation. It dominated the industry and Zukor dominated Paramount.

But all was not well in Lotus Land. The steady tenacity of Zukor conflicted with the bombastic individualism of Goldfish. In 1916 Goldfish, within months of the merger, sold out his interests for $900,000. The following year, Samuel Goldfish joined with the successful Broadway producers, Edgar and Archibald Selwyn, to form a new company. They combined their names and created the Goldwyn Pictures Corporation. Samuel put up his nearly $1 million, and the Selwyns put up their motion picture rights to a mouthwatering collection of hit plays. But Sam did even more. He legally took as his own, his corporation's name. He became Samuel Goldwyn.

Sam had flair, style, and more than just a touch of class. He used the Latin phrase "Ars Gratia Artis" (Art is Beholden to the Artists) as the studio motto. The trademark came from bright, young Howard Dietz. A Columbia University graduate, he took his school's mascot and transferred it to the Goldwyn studio. The lordly lion framed in a loop of film and crowned by the Latin motto would become one of the world's most recognized trademarks. The studio produced quality films but unbridled expenses combined with Sam's inability to share authority caused problems. Taking his new name with him, Sam Goldwyn left the troubled studio and became at last in 1924, an independent producer maintaining absolute control over his product.

Until his death in 1974, he put his imprint on some of Hollywood's most distinguished films, including: *The Dark Angel* (1925); *Stella Dallas* (1925); his first talkie, *Whoopee* (1930) starring Eddie Cantor; *Arrowsmith* (1931) directed by John Ford; *The Kid From Spain* (1932) again with Cantor and choreographed by Busby Berkeley; *Dodsworth* (1936); *These Three* (1936) which was an adaptation of Lillian Hellman's *The Children's Hour; Dead End* (1937), another Hellman play—*The Little Foxes* (1941); *The Best Years of our Lives* (1946) which won twelve Academy Awards; *Guys and Dolls* (1955); and *Porgy and Bess* (1958).

It was a long road from the Warsaw ghetto to Beverly Hills. By traveling it, Samuel Goldwyn attained fame, accumulated wealth, and developed personal elegance. "Hollywood owes me nothing," he once said. "I owe Hollywood everything."

Marcus Loew's story contains all the now familiar ingredients, and his life took the early twists and turns that appear ritualistic for anyone who hoped to become a film tycoon. Although his birth in 1870 was in America, his father had emigrated from Austria only three years earlier. The locale of Marcus' birth is acceptable to the standard scenario. It was at 173 Fourth Street, off Avenue B, in the heart of New York's lower East Side slums.

The family was abysmally poor and six-year-old Marcus was forced to sell newspapers on the street. Over the next six years his life revolved around a variety of jobs, some of which involved a ten-hour day and six-day week for the munificent sum of $2.10. An opportunity at age twelve to earn $4.50 a a week (six 11½-hour days) brought him into the fur trade. By 1894, Loew's first quarter century, he had earned, invested, made and lost money in the fur business. He did establish himself as a successful fur salesman and married Caroline Rosenheim. As Loew enjoyed a moderate prosperity selling furs, he began looking into other investment possibilities. Real estate seemed to offer a profitable stability lacking in the fur business and Marcus began to dabble. By the turn of the century the Zukors had come to New York with Loew's assistance and Marcus' interest was piqued by Adolph's arcade success. When Zukor contemplated expansion, Loew asked to be let in. Within a short time Loew became anxious to get into the arcade business by himself. Culling his own backers, he withdrew his investment in Zukor's arcades and in 1904 started the People's Vaudeville Company. The little furrier was in show business.

Before 1905 had filtered through the calendar Loew had developed a small chain of arcades, not only around New York but as far away as Cincinnati. At his Cincinnati arcade Loew experienced a phenomenon. He leased a five-minute Biograph comedy entitled *Hot Chestnuts*. In an empty upstairs room he and his manager positioned a projector and 110 folding chairs. On opening day nearly 5000 customers came to view the cheap show. The following Sunday they added 200 more chairs and funneled 10,000 patrons through. Loew rushed back to New York and immediately began converting his arcades into screen shows. Less than six years out of the fur business Marcus Loew controlled a chain of theaters specializing in combined vaudeville and film presentations. In 1910 People's Vaudeville gave way to the newly formed Loew's Consolidated, capitalized at $5 million. The subsequent years were profitable beyond Marcus Loew's most fanciful expectations. But he was vulnerable. The personal relationship with Zukor continued to be intimate and friendly. Zukor's daughter was now married to Loew's eldest son. But Paramount could freeze out his independent chain in favor of their own theaters. William Fox avoided this threat through consolidation. Marcus Loew's solution came in part on a cold blast from Canada that deposited in its wake, Louis B. Mayer.

Born in Russia, Mayer came to this continent as a child when his parents immigrated to Canada. By age eight Louis was out collecting scrap iron for his father's business. At thirteen, Louis was running the junk yard. He developed ". . . the shape and texture of a fireplug. He was short, thick and strong." Mayer continued to take over more and more of his father's responsibilities. Business trips brought him into the New England area where he made friends and contacts. In 1904, at the age of nineteen, Mayer married the daughter of a synagogue cantor. He and the former Margaret Schenberg continued their lives in the United States and Louis pursued the scrap metal business.

Three years later, almost on a whim, Mayer purchased a decrepit store show in Haverhill, Massachusetts. He moved his family, which now included two small daughters, to Haverhill and they ran the theater as a family enterprise. Modest profits after a tough start allowed him to purchase another theater and eventually build new ones in the nearby towns of Lowell and Lawrence. He then branched out and opened his own film exchange.

In 1915, a group of independent producers and film exchange owners were attempting to reorganize a floundering motion picture company. Mayer was one of these men, and the name they chose for the new company was The Metro Pictures Corporation. Metro could boast some formidable stars including Lionel and Ethel Barrymore, Francis X. Bushman and Mary Miles Minter. They also had among their extras a Russian émigré and part-time tailor. But Leon Trotsky's fame would come from other than the field of entertainment.

Mayer served faithfully and well as a Metro officer, however, he continued to wheel and deal independently. Despite warnings that the film would be "played out" he invested $25,000 for the New England distribution rights to D. W. Griffith's *Birth of a Nation* after it finished its first run. This epic feature displayed all of Griffith's directoral genius, and the controversy it sparked by stereotyping Negroes and elevating the Ku Klux Klan to the role of heroes caused it to play to packed houses. Mayer's investment returned a quarter of a million dollars.

As with Zukor, Mayer realized that audiences paid to see favorite performers. In 1917 he formed a production company around the lovely Anita Stewart. As soon as her contract with Vitagraph was fulfilled, Mayer took his star, his company, and his family to Hollywood. He became an independent producer and severed his ties with Metro.

Several years after Mayer's departure, the Metro organization fell upon hard times. As they had done once before, the officers began to look for a method of re-organization that would salvage their corporation. It was here that they came into contact with Marcus Loew. Loew was looking for a production company that could assure him an uninterrupted supply of features. Metro offered him a half interest in their firm. Loew wasn't interested in halves. In January 1920 Marcus Loew bought the whole studio.

Metro's first productions achieved all Loew's expectations. In 1921 the studio released *The Four Horsemen of the Apocalypse* featuring the then unknown Rudolph Valentino. The film's reception thrust Metro into the forefront of Hollywood's studios and the picture reaped millions in profits. But then it all hit a snag. Valentino, along with key creative personnel, left for other studios and better deals. By 1923 the quality and profits of Metro's films became so discouraging that Loew's Incorporated began to think seriously of swallowing their losses and closing up the studio.

Metro wasn't the only lot in trouble. The Goldwyn Studios (without Samuel Goldwyn, now an independent producer) was also mismanaging itself toward oblivion. But the Goldwyn Studios had some assets: a big plant in Culver City, a lineup of top directors, and stars such as Marion Davies. Joe Godsol, the Goldwyn head, approached Marcus Loew with the idea of a merger. Loew was receptive but his organization recognized the necessity of new studio management. Loew's legal counsel, Robert Rubin, was also the attorney for Louis B. Mayer. Rubin nominated Mayer. Mayer's reputation as a tough-minded, independent producer was favorable and he would bring with him as head of production the boy genius, Irving Thalberg. On April 17, 1924, Metro-Goldwyn-Mayer, replete with lion, came into existence.

These, then, were Hollywood's "major" studios during the pre-Babel era: Carl Laemmle's Universal Pictures, Adolph Zukor's Paramount, William Fox's Fox Pictures, and Loew's MGM. The studios a notch below in size were United Artists, formed by Mary Pickford and husband Douglas Fairbanks, Sr., along with Charles Chaplin and D. W. Griffith, RKO Pictures controlled by the Radio Corporation of America, and such quality independents as Samuel Goldwyn Productions. They were developing a universal medium of entertainment. Since language was no barrier to the enjoyment of silent films, Chaplin, Keaton, the Keystone Cops, and Garbo could all generate an international appeal. Much of that international appeal was focused right in the United States. The onslaught of immigrants to America produced not only the great tycoons of the film industry, it also provided the audience. Silent films became the only possible medium of mass entertainment for a dispossessed, urban proletariat employing a polyglot of languages. The moguls were able to appeal to the tastes of this audience because they came from their ranks. The techniques of production, distribution, and finance developed after the Civil War became the tools by which the great studios controlled their industry. Their pictures often depicted scenes in which other products aiming for mass consumption were being used with casual familiarity. Motor cars, refrigerators, and elegant clothes became necessities in the minds of audiences desiring to elevate their own shabby existence by emulating the glamor of the stars. Motion pictures had become an integral part of modern America's mass production-consumption economy. Hollywood was not so analytical about itself. It demanded only profits, and most of the profits went to the majors who aimed their output at the broadest possible audience. Economics dictated the mawkish sentimentality that pervaded movie content. In 1928 the majors had to make room for one more. The brothers Warner literally shouted their way into the inner circle.

Krasmashhilz, Poland, saw the last of Benjamin and Pearl Warner in 1882. Settling in Youngstown, Ohio, the couple produced twelve children including brothers Sam, Harry, Albert and Jack. In 1903 the family pooled its meager resources, which included the pawning of Ben's watch, and opened a nickelodeon. The family's business affairs were anything but meteoric. Their various ventures as exhibitors and distributors failed and so they turned to production. The four brothers opened a studio in Burbank, California. Their greatest assets were John Barrymore and Rin Tin Tin. The dog kept them one step ahead of bankruptcy. The financial resources of Warner Brothers were limited and if the studio was to survive some bold innovation would have to be found.

For several years the engineers at Bell Telephone's Western Electric laboratories had been working toward an efficient method of putting sound into movies. The system they developed was named Vitaphone. William Fox had been working toward the same objective and he dubbed his system, Movietone. Sam Warner accepted Bell Telephone's offer for exclusive use of Vitaphone which the other studios had rejected, and he began the exhausting search for financing. Sam found the money but so draining was the ordeal that he would not live to see the fruits of his labors. In 1926 both Movietone and Vitaphone appeared in a few theaters with a series of two-reel vaudeville acts. Theater owners were wary. They were reluctant to commit the thousands of dollars needed to wire for sound if the whole thing was only a passing fad. Warners responded with the feature length *The Jazz Singer* in 1927. It was really a "singie" instead of a "talkie" since there were only two lines of dialog. The rest of the sound was limited to the songs of the star, Al Jolson, who insisted he be paid in advance. The following year, Warners produced *Lights of New York*, the first full length talking picture. The stampede to sound was on and Warner Brothers not only survived, it was a major.

"More stars than there are in heaven," Louis B. Mayer proclaimed at the end of World War II. His reference was to the long list of quality players under contract to MGM. But the dominance of the great studios over the film industry was coming to a close. The rise of television undercut the bread-and-butter market for "B" pictures which were the inexpensive formula films with fixed costs and high profits. The public's "three times a week" movie habit was broken. Even more disastrous was the success of government anti-monopoly lawyers. After decades of litigation, the courts finally ruled that a studio's ownership of theaters represented restraint of trade. The great theater chains built up by the majors would have to be sold off. Hollywood would no longer have an assured distribution market for its product. Without a guaranteed base income the studios could no longer afford to keep a vast stable of stars under contract. One by one the actors were let go to negotiate for themselves on a per picture basis or else go into independent production.

Carl Laemmle's Universal is today owned by the Music Corporation of America, and MCA is in television production as much as theater features. Warner Brothers is part of a conglomerate and often issues films in partnership with other studios. *The Towering Inferno*, for example, was done with Twentieth Century-Fox. This latter studio, once the possessor of Hollywood's largest backlot has sold most of its land holdings. Los Angeles' Century City real estate development is the result. The studio itself was purchased in 1981 by Denver oil tycoon Marvin Davis for $800 million and includes on its board of directors former President Gerald R. Ford. The once mighty Paramount still produces films, including the immensely successful, *The Godfather*, but the studio is a subsidiary of Gulf and Western Industries. Metro-Goldwyn-Mayer now produces fewer pictures in a year than it once did in a week. Without the Loew's theater chain, MGM doesn't even distribute its own pictures, using instead, United Artists. Leo has sniffed profits elsewhere and Metro now builds and operates gambling casinos. In a move reminiscent of William Fox, Kirk Kerkorian the former head of MGM had also controlled a major interest in Columbia Pictures, a studio that rose to prominence in the thirties on the talents of director Frank Capra. Metro is now headed by David Begelman who left a similar position at Columbia Studios over a scandal involving $40,000 in forged checks. The incident resulted in Begelman's receiving a sentence of three years' probation and a $5,000 fine.

A Warner's executive once stated flamboyantly, "It is a fact that civilized man cannot live without motion pictures." Perhaps so, but civilization will have to wait until the accountants determine where and when they shall appear and by whom they shall now be created.

Suggested Readings

For an understanding of the historical forces of which motion pictures are a part, one could do no better than George E. Mowry's, *The Urban Nation-1920-1960*. Russel Nye's, *The Unembarrassed Muse* deals with all aspects of the popular arts in America. Dealing with America's performing arts is the highly entertaining *Show Biz–From Vaude to Video* by Abel Green and Joe Laurie, Jr. This book uses the uniquely descriptive style of Variety, the "show business Bible."

Two books still stand far in front for their treatment of the movies as both an art and a business: Benjamin Hampton's, *History of the American Film Industry-From its Beginnings to 1931* and Lewis Jacobs', *The Rise of the American Film*. For a social history of American film one might look at *Film: The Democratic Art* by Garth Jowett. Not nearly as valuable as any of the above, a thin volume by Juliet P. Schoen, *Silents to Sound—A History of the Movies*, can serve as a quick introduction to the topic. More scholarly is the recent *A History of Film* by Jack C. Ellis who deals with the worldwide artistic development of the medium.

The Moguls by Norman Zierold contains some minor factual errors but contains delightful stories of the studio heads. Deserving serious attention is the narrative history of MGM by critic Bosley Crowther, *The Lion's Share*. For a brief resumé of what became of the majors and their role in television see *Method to the Madness (Hollywood Explained)* by Dick Atkins, et. al.

Autobiographies and general reminiscences of Hollywood's "golden era" are more plentiful than presidential exposés and more fun to read. Among my favorites are Garson Kanin's, *Hollywood*, the autobiography of the legendary director Frank Capra, *The Name Above the Title* and the exceptionally well written *Bring on the Empty Horses* by David Niven. For a diverting collection of amusing and insightful anecdotes, see *The Wit and Wisdom of Hollywood* by Max Wilk.

Th. .Th. .That's all, folks!

The Emergence of the Modern Woman

Barbara Peterson

The "New Woman" of the 1890s, applauded by feminists and ridiculed by anti-feminists,* represents the first stage of what we might call the emergence of modern woman. The New Woman was typified by the popular Gibson girl, the creation of artist Charles Dana Gibson in a series of drawings for *Life* magazine. This New Woman wore a "shirtwaist" blouse with a tailored suit or dark skirt instead of the reams of yardage, petticoats, and ribboned finery worn by former Victorian ladies. She had completely taken off or at least loosened that instrument of physical torture, the corset, which had guaranteed an eighteen-inch waist and almost as certainly had induced fainting spells. From 1890 until the first World War, American women yearned to be like the dazzling New Woman, the Gibson girl, "tall, stately, superbly dressed, artful but never truly wicked," as the authors of *This Fabulous Century* recounted. "Overnight she became the model and idol for a generation. The Gibson girl might work before marriage but ultimately she cherished love, proper courtship and a good husband, the traditional Victorian themes. But she was freer than her Victorian mother had been, certainly in dress, as she was depicted as companion to men—a playful partner in tennis, golf, bicycling, and even driving an automobile." Lois Banner in *Women in Modern America* (1974) appraised, "The Gibson girl was the American virgin-woman, but around her there was a refreshing hint of health, sensuality, and rebellion."

---

*"Feminism is customarily thought of as the theory that women should have political, economic, and social rights equal to those of men," wrote Aileen S. Kraditor in *Up From the Pedestal,* 1970.

From the uplifted nose under the tilting pompadour, to the fall of her chiffon dress, Alice Roosevelt personified the chic but haughty, artful but never truly wicked Gibson girl, the American feminine ideal from 1890 to World War I. (Brown Brothers Photo)

The Gibson girl was the athletic maiden, not vampy, but certainly beguiling as H. L. Mencken, in *This Fabulous Century,* described: "Her skirts have just reached her very trim and pretty ankles; her hair, coiled upon her skull, has just exposed the ravishing whiteness of her neck. A charming creature!" As the New Woman evolved from Gibson girl to the flapper of the twenties, Mencken continued his enthusiasm: "There is something trim and trig and confident about her. She is easy in her manners. There is music in her laugh. She is youth, she is hope, she is romance—she is wisdom!"

Looking back to the Victorian era, we can really see how far the New Woman had come by the 1890s. In the 1870s, the man of the house was a monarch who supervised his domain, and his wife was part of his domain. His wife called him "Mister." His children addressed him as "Sir." The Victorian father was omnipotent, evaluated the editors of *This Fabulous Century, 1870-1900,* "whether he sprawled with his feet and a drink on the table or stood solemn and resplendent in frock coat, a heavy gold watch chain traversing his paunch." The taproots of Victorian ideals concerning women and their proper "place in the home" go all the way back to colonial times. But at the beginning of the Victorian period, (1837-1901), one American male's view stands forth prominently because it represents an ideal expressed so *early* and which was so difficult to change. Thomas R. Dew, a southern gentleman and proslavery pamphleteer, idealized the Victorian concept of "true womanhood" in his "Dissertation on the Characteristic Differences Between the Sexes," which appeared in the *Southern Literary Messenger,* 1835. "The relative positions of the sexes in the social and political world," he proclaimed, "may certainly be looked upon as a result of [Divine] organization. The greater physical strength of man, enables him to occupy the foreground in the picture. He leaves the domestic scenes; he plunges into the turmoil and bustle of an active, selfish world; . . . courage and boldness are his attributes. It is his province, undismayed, to stand against the rude shocks of the world; to meet with a lion's heart, the dangers which threaten him. He is the shield of woman, destined by nature to guard and protect her. . . . Her inferior strength and sedentary habits confine her within the domestic circle; . . . timidity and modesty are her attributes." This Victorian idealism placed the American woman on a pedestal; her proper "place" or sphere was severely circumscribed. But the majority of American women did not complain of this idealism which portrayed the male as lord of creation and the female as clinging vine. Each had been properly *socialized* as to her respective, legitimate role. Woman, through her grace, modesty and charm ennobled herself, her man, and all of society. Her role was to be passive rather than active, especially in sex and politics. The old dime novel which portrayed the mustached villian saying, "You must pay the rent," the fair damsel replying weakly, "But I can't pay the rent," and the hero triumphantly proclaiming, "I'll pay the rent!" is the quintessence of the Victorian social code of chivalrous manhood and feminine dependence.

But not all women believed this romantic mythology. One group of women, later dubbed the suffragettes, had focused their feminist aspirations and activism on securing the vote for women. The event which had heralded the *political* founding of the woman's suffrage (or right to vote) movement was the convention at Seneca Falls, New York, in June 1848. It was called by Elizabeth Cady Stanton, Lucretia Mott, and Martha C. Wright and was dedicated to discussing the rights of women. Their deliberations produced a Declaration of Sentiments which was a list of social grievances for which the organizers believed women should fight. At the heart of the declaration was the crucial statement, "We hold these truths to be self-evident, that all men *and women* are created equal. . . ." The signers of this declaration included sixty-eight women and thirty-two men, and each agreed that women should be granted the right to equal education, to preach, to teach, to practice as physicians and lawyers, and to act as legal guardians for their children upon the death of their husbands. Women were concerned about this last item because by law, a husband might select as guardian for his children someone other than their mother after his death. Women were also concerned with the double standard in divorce laws of the time which allowed a man to divorce his wife for adultery but in most states she could not divorce her husband for the same indiscretion.

The conventioneers also adopted the seminal idea that "it is the sacred duty of the women of this country to secure to themselves their sacred right to the elective franchise." Thus, the women's movement established itself at Seneca Falls *ideologically*. They had established goals, and as the Civil War era began, sought their achievement.

The suffragettes, as they were now called, gained political acumen first in the abolitionist crusade and then in post-war Reconstruction in the movement to ensure black emancipation. The suffragettes had tied their cause to that of blacks. They demanded the right to vote for all citizens, white and black, male and female, as a *natural right*. They were to be sorely disappointed and disillusioned by antebellum politics when former male abolitionist leaders called for freedom for black men first and counseled "patience" to the feminists. Elizabeth Cady Stanton and Susan B. Anthony were outraged by this paternalistic discrimination, and called for the vote, now! But success was not to be theirs. Significantly, the first successes for the emerging woman was not to be in the realm of politics.

One of the reasons that suffragettes did not enjoy political success in the antebellum period was that their movement split, dividing talents and resources, over the issue of tactics. In May 1869, Elizabeth Cady Stanton and Susan B. Anthony formed the National Woman's Suffrage Association (NWSA) and were committed to securing the vote through a national constitutional amendment. Lucy Stone and Julia Ward Howe, author of the "Battle Hymn of the Republic," formed the rival group, the American Woman's Suffrage Association (AWSA) and were content to proceed one state at a time and were dedicated to promoting the right to vote for women through state referendums and amendments to state constitutions. The suffrage campaign crept on slowly between 1865 and 1890. Wyoming, in the process of drafting its new constitution in 1869 to change its status from territory to state, was first to grant women equal suffrage. Wyoming was followed by Colorado (1893) and Utah and Idaho (1896). The western states appeared to be more liberal; the eastern and southern states more hesitant to remove women from their "pedestal" and subject them to the "crassness" of the political arena as typically the polling places at the turn of the century were still set up in saloons. The suffragettes voiced their views: "It is only the poltroon, the misguided fool, and the man with a sixteenth-century mind who opposes their [women's] entrance into the political arena," an activist was quoted as saying in *The Nashville Tennessean.* "Woman Suffrage can make the Statue of Liberty look 10 miles taller to every despairing victim of Old-World conditions," heralded another in the *Philadelphia Public Ledger.* But females were not of one mind as *The Woman Patriot,* the magazine of the anti-suffragettes would write: "The suffragists are bringing us to the culmination of a decadence which has been steadily indicated by race suicide, divorce, breakup of the home, and federalism, all of which conditions are found chiefly in primitive society." As the ideological controversy raged, one female supporter said simply, "We couldn't make a worse mess of it than the men, and we might do better." Susan B. Anthony actually voted in the election of 1872 hoping to make her illegal action a test case. Her case did not reach the Supreme Court because the high court ruled in *Minor* v. *Happersett* that the Constitution did not convey the privilege of voting to all citizens; women were specifically denied the opportunity to exercise full citizenship rights. To correct this social situation, the so-called "Anthony Amendment" was introduced into Congress by Senator Aaron A. Sargent of California in 1878. The amendment read: "The right of citizens of the United States to vote shall not be denied or abridged by the United States or by any state on account of sex." The amendment was either defeated annually or lay dormant until 1914 when it again was seriously re-introduced. Realizing the folly of a movement divided, the NWSA and the ASWA rejoined political forces in 1890 with Elizabeth Cady Stanton as president of the renamed National American Woman Suffrage Association.*

The suffrage movement throughout the nineteenth century was predominately a middle-class, white, Anglo-Saxon Protestant movement. Black and working-class women wanted equality too but held different priorities, as they sought first the basics such as security of person, a living wage, livable shelter, and food for their families. Their concerns were essentially *economic,* although philosophically they supported the middle-class feminist

---

*Stanton served as the NAWSA president from 1890-1892. She was followed by Susan B. Anthony (1892-1900), Carrie Chapman Catt (1900-1904), Anna Howard Shaw (1904-1915) and Carrie Chapman Catt (1915-1920).

drive for political voting rights. But a poor woman, especially a poor black woman, could not afford the luxury of time off from work to march in suffrage parades, listen to speakers, or plot strategy at afternoon teas. Significantly, the female socialists, believing society could only be transformed through economic reallocations of property and the redistribution of the means of production into the hands of the state, were usually *not* active suffragists. Although they too supported the demand for the vote, they believed woman's place could only be elevated by dramatically altering the capitalistic structure and the nuclear family which was its microcosm. Charlotte Perkins Gilman, author of *Women and Economics* (1898) proved to be an important exception to this idea that socialists were usually not suffragists. Gilman was perhaps the most original thinker in both the socialist and feminist movements in America. She argued that since society had already taken over many important former functions of the family, such as educating children and nursing the sick, society (the state) should continue to enlarge its functions. Thus, she called for communal laundries, kitchens, and nurseries staffed by professionals. Women, freed from household drudgeries, would be liberated for more useful functions. Her ideas were never extremely popular with the American suffragists, but she was widely read in Britain and Scandinavia where cooperative schemes were more widely praised. In spite of Gilman's contributions, the suffragists were typically WASP reformers, working within the political system to reform it, not essentially challenge it. They believed that votes for women would actually strengthen the American family, which they desired to preserve intact.

Most feminists accepted the traditional view of sex roles in both the nineteenth and early twentieth centuries. Feminists supported marriage and motherhood, did not equate domesticity with slavery, and generally wanted simply to enlarge their proper sphere though it was still centered in the home. They supported Anthony Comstock's crusade against obscenity in Boston; they encouraged the formation in 1895 of the American Puritan Alliance dedicated to suppressing prostitution and the "vulgarisms" of red-light districts. They turned thumbs down on such social experiments as "free love," trial marriage, and companionate marriage. These more liberal ideas were associated with either anarchism or communism and were shunned by the more middle of the road, middle-class, matronly, WASP reformer.

And too there were the *antis*. The antifeminists and the antisuffragettes accused the reformers of violating biblical teachings which pronounced women as inferior to men. They stated that the reformers were brazenly inciting men to rape as they stood on street corners and entered barbershops and saloons to make their reforming harangues. The antis believed that talking politics within the domestic circle "would make every home a hell on earth." "The antis," stated Leonard Pitt in *We Americans* (1976), "were impressively organized." Their support came from "liquor interests who feared the feminists would bring about Prohibition. The wives of prominent men, like the wife of General Sherman, lent their voices to the antifeminist cause. Both the Protestant and Catholic clergy also supported the antis. Industrialists, who saw their authority challenged by the feminist pressure for factory legislation, supported them too. . . . In the 1890s the anti-feminists formed a national organization called Associations Opposed to the Extension of Suffrage for Women, which had the support of former President Cleveland." But the feminist reformer, if she was to be successful, believed she had to select carefully a middle ground between the radicals and the ultra-conservative antis. In *moderation*, she sought the broadest base possible.

What social conditions had allowed the reformer to emerge? Aileen S. Kraditor in *Up from the Pedestal* (1970) suggests " . . . the growth of industry made the United States a magnet for Irish immigration in the Forties (1840s) providing the middle-class women with abundant domestic help, which in turn gave them leisure for self-education and reform activities." Too, near the end of the century, women themselves were deciding to have fewer children, as Illinois frontierswoman Mary Austin explained in *Earth Horizon: Autobiography:* "The pioneer stress was over" and with it had ended "the day of the large families, families of from a dozen to fifteen." Lois Banner interpreted this as a "yearning of these women for leisure, for culture, and for some world outside the home." British observer Denis Brogan wrote in *American Character* (1944) that America's technology had liberated the American woman and would continue to do so as "the American woman entered into a more abundant life." Viewing the effects of the Industrial Revolution, he stated: " . . . to the daughter of the effects of the pioneer woman came the sewing machine, an effective system of heating, good oil lamps, running water in cities, anesthetics so lifesaving in childbirth, and the economic margin to spend on luxuries."

In addition to foreign immigration, the decision for fewer children, and improved technology, we must add perhaps the most vital liberating force in the history of the emerging woman—education. It was in the realm of education rather than politics that the American woman enjoyed her first successes. The eastern women's colleges like Vassar and Smith were founded partly because the major male institutions such as Harvard, Princeton, and Yale had refused to become coeducational. Oberlin College, in Ohio, had been the first college to admit women in 1833, despite complaints that "they'll be educatin' cows next." Coeducation appeared first in the West and Midwest, "but it is incorrect," states Lois Banner, "to conclude from this evidence, as many historians do, that it was a democratic 'frontier' spirit alone that brought about coeducation in the West. No doubt Western statesmen were proud of their 'pioneer' women, but outspoken women— and male allies—were present, too, to put pressure on facilities, administrations and state legislatures." Banner stresses the importance of *individual* feminine accomplishment and activism. Significantly, she points out, the New Woman by the 1890s had new role models, new heroines, with which to identify such as Elizabeth Blackwell, the first licensed female doctor, and Arabella Mansfield, the first practicing female lawyer in America. Woman's proper sphere was becoming greatly enlarged by the social framework of immigration, industrialization, and education certainly, but it was the American woman *herself* who acted upon these new opportunities.

How did American women handle their new freedoms and opportunities? The answer has something to say about why women continued to be more and more successful and their success more and more accepted as proper in the sense of normative behavior. Women handled their successes *conservatively;* successful professional women were not ribald activists. This essential conservative nature is perhaps best expressed by Elizabeth Blackwell (1821-1910) when she said upon receiving her medical degree, "I cannot sympathize fully with an anti-man movement. I have too much kindness, aid, and just recognition from men to make such attitudes of women otherwise than painful. . . . " But even though the new heroines were not radicals but essentially competent conservatives who strove to carve out a professional niche, the old prejudices would die hard. The Columbian College of Law, now George Washington University, as late as 1887, according to Karen Meyer Wilcox's article "Women Lawyers in the United States, 1870-1900" (1973), refused to admit women on the grounds that "women had not the mentality to study law." But by the turn of the century seven out of ten colleges had become coeducational and America's colleges and universities had graduated 7,500 women doctors, 3,000 ministers and 1,000 lawyers. Women at Cornell even had their own funds for athletics and the ladies crew team in 1896 lobbied for "a bathhouse of their own."

Other social fronts were open to women between 1870 and 1890. Divorce, although far from respectable, increased from approximately eleven thousand in 1870 to over fifty-five thousand in 1900. By 1900, women in the majority of states legally claimed and controlled their own personal property and were granted rightful guardianship over their children upon their husband's death. The Victorian monarch was being forced to give way to a benevolent despotism and even to consider marriage as a true partnership although the old quip still was popular that "husband and wife are but one, and the husband is that one." Many new job opportunities opened for women. In 1870 there was no such thing as a telephone; by 1900 there were 19,000 female operators, "hello girls" as they were called. In American business, the bursting growth of technology and industrial expansion had created an avalanche of paperwork. An ingenious machine, the typewriter, was invented to meet the need. In 1870 there had been but seven stenographers in all of America; by 1900 there were over 100,000 "lady typewriters" as they were called. Women moved up through the ranks of industry into bookkeeping and accounting, merchandising and supervisory positions. Clothing factories, expanded during the Civil War to mass produce soldiers' uniforms, were employing 1.45 million people at the turn of the century and most were women. By 1890 there were 3.7 million women in the United States labor force. These new opportunities for the professional and working classes permitted women, quite realistically quipped the editors of *This Fabulous Century,* "the luxury of choosing a $15.00-a-week job of their own or a $12.00-a-week husband."

And what of the new social amusements and leisure time activities of women between 1870 and 1890? In the 1870s a lady might attend the horse races; in the 1880s a baseball game, minstrel show, vaudeville or even a burlesque. She read *Godey's Lady's Book.* After 1889, she might prefer the new *Ladies Home Journal.* She might have ridden on a cable car in San Francisco for the first time in 1873, soon to be followed by possible experiences on the electric trolley. She took to cycling in the 1880s and might have enjoyed touring with her beaux or husband in the tandem tricycles or quadricycles. Even Mrs. Frances E. Willard, the leader of the Women's Christian Temperance Union, took cycling lessons in 1892, recounted the editors of *This Fabulous Century 1870-1900,* "to encourage those sinful menfolk to foresake saloons for the wholesale pleasures of the high road."

Speaking of the pleasures of the "high road" a real life heroine, journalist "Nellie Bly" (born Elizabeth Cochran), was dispatched around the world in 1890 by Joseph Pulitzer, editor of the New York *World.* The world watched as courageous Nellie flashed around the globe racing against the 80-day record set by Phileas Fogg, the central character in Jules Verne's novel *Around the World in Eighty Days.* Traveling by junk, sampan, ricksha and donkey, fearless Nellie circumvented the globe in 72 days, 6 hours, 11 minutes and 14 seconds. A victory was marked for Pulitzer's sensationalism, advancing technology, and significantly for the idea of woman as a *winner.* The old Victorian pruderies had broken down. The New Woman, fun-loving, athletic, competently entering the marketplace, was the new breed. American men seemed to enjoy the new relaxing social changes too, tired as they were of the extravagant posturing of Victorian etiquette. Men appreciated the New Woman. Diamond Jim Brady epitomized the new change in spirit as he said: "Hell, I'm Rich. It's time I had some fun." And more often than not the New Woman was asked to come along and share the fun of America in high times.

While more Americans worshiped the Gibson girl, foreign observers were more critical of the image the American woman projected. Irish playwright George Bernard Shaw, visiting the United States in 1907, was quoted by the editors of *This Fabulous Century* as saying: "Every American woman explains that she is an absolute exception and is not like any other American woman. But they are all exactly the same. The only thing to be said for them is they are usually very well dressed and extraordinarily good looking." Many foreign observers noted that American men wanted their women to be dazzling ornaments, "but not so bright and sassy that they wandered from their place in the home." Beauty not brains, viewed Shaw, was the American female's greatest asset. Perhaps due to his Fabian politics he found this artificial image of the American female disgusting. Many women pandered to the egos of their men; where was their individual identity? Would she lose her feminity if she became a person in her own right? Shaw didn't think so and urged her toward autonomy.

Historically, the early period of the feminist movement from the 1870s to 1890, is the period in which women claimed the right to political equality using the "justice" argument. Equality was a natural right. After 1890, and after the reunification of the suffrage movement into the NAWSA, the argument for equality and woman's autonomy changed to the argument of "expediency." The expediency argument, which linked the vote for women with social reform, enabled women to capitalize on the Progressive political momentum and, ultimately, women's suffrage became part of the political Progressive platform. Aileen Kraditor believes women were really saying to men, "*double your political power* by enfranchising us." This argument would become exceedingly effective.

"Give women the vote and they will reform society" proved a powerful propelling force for feminism at the turn of the century as the American woman proved she could combine freedom and responsibility. The Woman's Christian Temperance Union (WCTU), founded in 1874 to press for laws forbidding the sale and consumption of liquor, had broadened its base since the hatchet-swinging days of Carrie Nation. By the 1890s under the leadership of Frances Willard the WCTU lobbied for industrial legislation such as child labor laws, safety inspections in factories, adult education, reformatories for juvenile delinquents, and the abolition of prostitution. The General Federation of Women's Clubs, founded in 1893, lobbied for the fifty-four-hour workweek for working women, pressed for the Pure Food and Drug Act and circulated pamphlets and lobbied congressmen in support of the National Child Labor Bill. The Consumers' League was formed in 1890 originally to improve working conditions for saleswomen in department stores through consumer boycotts. The Women's Trade Union League (WTUL) was founded in 1903 at a convention of the American Federation of Labor. The goals of the WTUL were to organize and educate middle-class and especially working-class women to improve labor conditions and press for higher wages, fringe benefits such as health insurance, and safe working conditions. As Lois Banner remarked: " . . . the Women's Trade Union League consistently remained an amalgam of the workers and the well-to-do," and this represented a significant expansion of the feminists' political base. This alliance faced its first real political test in 1909 when the shirtwaist makers, mostly women, went out on strike in New York. Lasting thirteen weeks in a bitter cold winter, the strike proved women had spunk and spirit and more—they led an increasingly cohesive political bloc. The moderates within the women's movement took up the cause of the working-class women even more strongly after the Triangle Fire in New York in 1911 in which 146 female garment workers burned to death. For someone like a scrubwoman, unionization offered job security, regular pay, and a sense of common cause and companionship with individuals formerly seen as rivals. But unionization of women was difficult. Women came from many diverse immigrant backgrounds, speaking many languages. Many women chose to work part-time or only during special seasons, and the female work force was relatively unstable as many women entered the labor market only briefly before marriage. There also existed all the attendant problems of nativism and racial prejudice that the reformers had to seek to eradicate or minimize. Female union leaders such as Rose Schneiderman, the first national president of the WTUL, really had been forced to organize when male-dominated unions such as the craft-oriented American Federation of Labor refused women membership. Even though the constitution of the AFL specifically outlawed sex discrimination, Theresa Wolfson in *The Woman Worker and the Trade Unions* (1926) quoted a member of the International Association of Machinists as saying: "There are few real machinists. A machinist is born and not made. One must have a feeling for machines and women haven't got that." But in fairness to the AFL, that seemingly closed men's shop did support the WTUL with some funding at a time when the average man still believed the proper place for *his* woman was in the home. As economic conditions improved for men, and they had less reason to fear competition from women, the former bias against admitting women to full membership would decline. And too, sometimes women union leaders undercut their own ground. For example, even socialist Elizabeth Gurley Flynn thought that working women needed "special legislation" and that a true equal rights amendment would be against their best interests. Lois Banner makes this point: "It is ironic that in an age of enlightenment about women, an age that in its best moments tried to see women as independent human beings, special legislation campaigns were waged on behalf of two groups within the population: women and children." The best example of "special legislation" which passed was a minimum wage law (*Muller* v. *Oregon*) in 1908. Louis Brandeis successfully argued before the Supreme Court that "besides anatomical and physiological differences, physicians are agreed that women are in general weaker than men in muscular strength and in nervous energy." Women were therefore allowed shorter working hours than men. Modern feminists realize women cannot have it both ways as the feminists of the Progressive period attempted to do, and sometimes successfully.

One of the chief reasons that women were successful politically during the Progressive period was that their reforming efforts were very often related to their accepted social sphere—that of the home, the nurturing of children, and care for the aged, sick and, disadvantaged. Nowhere can this dovetailing of urge to reform and political acceptance of it be seen more clearly than in the institution of the settlement house and in the energies of social workers. Jane Addams at Hull House and Lillian Wald at Henry Street were merely the most visible of the early social workers; many others especially feminist college graduates followed their leadership.

"Faced after college with a choice between marrying, making their way in professional and graduate schools that still discriminated against women, or taking low-status positions as schoolteachers or nurses," wrote Lois Banner, "they responded with typical American ingenuity: they invented their own profession by founding houses in the midst of urban slums where they would live and provide social services to the poor." Banner said social work, at the time, was considered "respectable," even "glamorous." Moreover, it blended perfectly with the old ideal that women were dedicated to service and were by nature nurturing. It was a new, innovative, and liberal solution within a socially acceptable though conservative framework. Their accomplishments were many. They were instrumental in the founding of the Children's Bureau and the drafting of the child labor laws; they offered advisory services to women in regard to child care, nutrition, personal hygiene, taught courses in homemaking and domestic skills for immigrant women, offered visiting nurse services, established nurseries and kindergartens for children of working mothers, investigated employment agencies, fought for better housing in slum neighborhoods, acculturated newly arrived immigrants, and in some cities the settlement houses financed legal aid groups committed to helping women obtain divorce, alimony, rightful wages, and child custody. The settlement house leadership supported the birth control crusade of Margaret Sanger and believed an open discussion of sex would help control both prostitution and veneral disease, not to mention unwanted pregnancies. Socially, there was hardly a single area of public welfare that crusading women did not touch in one way or another. "Mother" was still the most important pivot of the American family, but women everywhere saw also new successful heroines—the working woman, the settlement worker, the female unionist, the muckraking journalist, and the suffragette who seemed able to combine many roles simultaneously. Mass media reinforced the idea of "women outside the home" assuming new successful roles, so long as the home was properly cared for first. A woman's sphere was not seen as being *changed* so much as it had been *enlarged*.

How did the American woman's leisure time pursuits reflect her enlarged but *relatively unchanged* proper sphere? Smaller families and technical innovations in the home allowed her more time for herself. She might spend hours with the "wishbook"—the catalogue published by Sears Roebuck, which in 1905 offered among other things 150 versions of the shirtwaist dress, the trademark of the 1890 Gibson girl. In 1907 there was even a peek-a-boo shirtwaist in embroidered eyelet that exposed one's arms seductively, and increasingly, skirts were rakishly going higher to give men a peek at the ankle and slightly beyond. Health continued to be a theme with the "health skirt" advertised for walking, and simpler, easier to wear and care for clothing was demanded by the professional and working–class female alike. As men were reading Horatio Alger stories of the rags-to-riches theme at the turn of the century, women were still bound by the eternal theme that love and romance conquered all. Romantic novels provided the palpitations and fantasies of amorous embraces that real life could never really measure up to. Indeed the etiquette books of the period reflected the old blue-nosed pruderies, suggesting that even holding hands during courtship was taboo. Every girl's dream was still the passionate white knight, yet the *Ladies Home Journal* (March, 1908) counseled to "keep healthy hours, to think sound thoughts, breathe pure air, to dress with loveliness, to strive to be a type of warm, chaste girlishness—these, are all . . . a preparation for Love's coming."

The American home had moved beyond pioneer simplicity. It was now standardly equipped with a wood-burning stove (available through Sears for $17.48), a bread toaster, an ice cream freezer, an iron, wooden ice box, coffee grinder, and enameled teapot. Sears' wishbook even offered a live palm plant delivered for 59c, not to mention the fantastic array of furnishings for the parlor such as an organ, a Turkish leather couch, a stereoscope and 500 slides, a glass bordeau lamp, and grandfather's clocks. Such was the influence of the Sears wishbook upon the family, particularly women, that a clergyman once sent Sears this unsolicited note, quoted in *This Fabulous Century, 1900-1910:* "A little child in one of my church schools was asked the other day, What was the Tenth Commandment? The reply was, 'Thou shalt not covet.' When asked what covet meant, she replied, 'Not to want other folks' things, but to get a Sears Roebuck catalog and buy for yourself'."

One clear indication that women had more money to spend on themselves was the enormous number of concoctions made for her personal toilette. She could buy cold cream, a hair-waving iron, a satin-lined glove box, tortoise shell hairpins, perfumes, and even the world famous La Dore's Bust Food, "unrivaled for its purity, perfume, elegance and effect," cited the chuckling writers of *This Fabulous Century, 1900-1910.* "It is unsurpassed for developing the bust, arms and neck, making a plump, full, rounded bosom, . . . a smooth skin, which before was scrawny, flat and flabby."

The emerging woman enjoyed her new freedoms, but from the list of items especially marketed for her use alone, it appears she still very much wanted to remain a woman; she certainly was not aspiring to become a man. Her sphere had *enlarged* but remained basically unchanged as society still believed the proper place for a woman was in the home. The central question that George Bernard Shaw had pondered still remained: Could American society allow a woman autonomy as a woman? Did women not have the right to be judged, not simply as women, but as Americans?

Shaw would have been pleased by the antics of Alice Roosevelt, the President's haughty and naughty darling whose image infatuated most Americans between 1900-1910. Alice Roosevelt stood midway between the Gibson girl and the Flapper, and she represented the drive of the American female toward greater autonomy. She sought an identity in her own right, apart from that of being the "President's daughter." T. R. himself once said: "I can do one of two things. I can be President of the

United States, or I can control Alice. I cannot possibly do both." Harrison Fisher, writer for the *Ladies Home Journal* in February 1913, described his own feminine ideal: "She is gentle, she is shy; But there's mischief in her eye, She's a flirt." And so the public applauded and joked about the new freedoms for women and their new darling. Alice toured Europe, danced till dawn in Paris nightclubs, smoked openly, and once aboard ship jumped into a swimming pool fully clothed with a congressman. She was an excellent poker player, could tell a smutty joke or two, and in Honolulu she danced the "lascivious" hula. And while she startled, she also enchanted. Americans, men and women, loved the "New" New Woman. She was freer, more relaxed and laughed at convention. She was in tune with America's coming of age, a time when it was beginning to feel confident, dynamic and pulsating with new energies. The American male was not threatened by the "New" New Woman and was relaxed with the new state of companionship. He was even getting used to the idea that maybe a woman should vote.

World War I proved to be the last step toward securing the vote for women. The dormant amendment which would enfranchise women was reintroduced on March 19, 1914, after a massive campaign waged by Alice Paul, President of the National Woman's Party in conjunction with the National American Woman Suffrage Association led by Carrie Chapman Catt. Five hundred thousand names had been affixed to petitions asking Congress to reconsider the Anthony Amendment, but it was defeated until 1918. When America declared war in April 1917, women's organizations, although still disenfranchised, joined the war effort. Despite the arguments of the pacifists, the feminists believed that again by working in support of the system, they would triumph in the end. And triumph they did. Women's groups bolstered morale; they staffed the Red Cross; they sold war bonds; they nursed the wounded overseas; they knitted socks and made clothing to help the boys "over there in Europe." The Suffrage Association raised $200,000 to contribute to a hospital in France servicing America's wounded. Women became auto mechanics, telegraph messengers; the iron and steel industry in America employed 40,000 women in 1918, a threefold increase over 1914. Working within the system paid off. President Wilson, in a special address to the Senate in 1918, said it was inconsistent for the country to wage war for democracy overseas but to bar women from voting at home. He urged adoption of the Anthony Amendment: "I tell you plainly that this measure which I urge upon you is vital to the winning of the war and to the energies alike of preparation and battle." Congress approved the equal suffrage amendment in June 1919 and the states, after Tennessee was the thirty-sixth state to accept it, made it legal just a few months before the election of 1920. Seventy-two years had elapsed since Elizabeth Cady Stanton proposed the idea at the Seneca Falls conference. What had produced the suffrage victory? Eleanor Flexner in *Century of Struggle* gave equal congratulations to the NAWSA led by Carrie Chapman Catt and to the efforts of the Women's Party led by Alice Paul. Jane Addams, on the other hand, felt that major credit for victory should not be awarded to the suffrage leaders, but to the "war psychology" of the moment. Wherever the laurels should be placed, women had won the vote and secured the prohibition amendment in 1919 which had long been the goal of the WCTU. The majority of the organizers were elated with their accomplishments, as Elizabeth Gurley Flynn described women to be "united" in common cause and spirit in 1920. This sentiment was soon to prove illusionary. Almost immediately after the war, the women's movement, fragmented again over tactics and feminism, was to take very divergent directions once their original symbol, the vote, had been won. After 1920 both progressivism and feminism seemed passé, conservativism was in. Americans tired of crusades, were about to "slide into a bath of nostalgia," as Alistair Cooke said, "for the good old days before the war and Wilsonian internationalism."

Initially in 1920, the women's movement had broken apart when Carrie Chapman Catt denounced the "militancy" of Alice Paul. The NAWSA had been formally disbanded, and it had been assumed that the Women's Party would be its natural successor, but the party led by Paul seemed too aggressive for the times. Hence, a new moderate group sprang up, the League of Women Voters which was dedicated to "social feminism," largely the old ideals of the progressive reformers. The league first successfully challenged laws which had prohibited women from serving on juries or holding public office and then they had become committed to "educating women for proper citizenship," which meant teaching women about politics and how to exercise their right to vote. In the postwar period, the Women's Trade Union League and the Consumer's League, led ably by Francis Perkins, remained strong. But the women's movement was fragmented by too many leaders. Some women worked for social feminism, some for a new cause, pacifism. Carrie Chapman Catt established the National Conference on the Cause and Cure of War, while Jane Addams became involved in the Women's International League for Peace and Freedom (WILPF). On the periphery of social feminism and pacifism, the activists, led by the Women's Party and Alice Paul, centered its efforts on attaining an Equal Rights amendment (ERA) which would, they believed, be the surest way of ending many state and national laws that discriminated against women. The amendment was simple: "Men and women shall have equal rights throughout the United States and every place subject to its jurisdiction." It was first introduced into Congress in 1923. It failed to muster much support, and the moderate League of Women Voters actually opposed its passage. *Degrees* of feminism would remain but as a movement feminism had all but been eclipsed by the new pastimes of the Jazz Age. The young woman of the twenties was interested in fun and freedom; her generation was one of "flaming youth," as the *Ladies Home Journal* called it in 1921. The Flapper was the new model of the 1920s as the Gibson girl had personified the 1890s. John Held, Jr., drew the original "flapper" for *The New Yorker* magazine and, like the Gibson drawings, the Held flapper images reigned as the new symbols for feminine America. Everyone loved the Flapper, with her bobbed hair, her nips on a hip flask, her long cigarette holder, her rolled stockings, her rouge on the cheeks and *knees,* and how she could dance the Charleston! The *Ladies Home Journal* glorified her as "independent, bright-eyed, alert, alive." She also personified society's expectations, as the Flapper, after her fling, was destined, she believed, to marry and have a family.

William H. Chafe in *Women and Equality* (1977) summarized what had happened to the feminist movement of the 1890s through 1920: the "enact-ment of women suffrage brought few of the changes envisioned by the proponents." The definition of woman's place *had not changed* when she received the right to vote. Her proper sphere was still related to the home, children, the family. The New Woman of the 1920s, the flapper, like the Gibson girl before her, seemed to be having more fun, freedom, leisure and economic opportunity, but she certainly was not considered an equal of man. Sex role stereotyping remained constant, with the basic options avail-able to both sexes relatively unchanged. The postsuffrage generation continued in overwhelming numbers to be *homemakers.* A change in legal status for women had not produced an altered cultural status. The female of the 1920s had not overcome woman's greatest difficulty—the profound sex-role conditioning that was an integral part of their upbringing or socialization.

The decade of the 1920s wanted its women soft and pliant and condoned aggressiveness only in sex and sports. A new symbol to rival that of the flapper in the 1920s was the symbol of the Beauty Queen. Inaugurated in 1920 in Atlantic City as a promotional scheme to lengthen the summer tourist season, the "Miss America" pageant continued the image of the virgin woman reigning from a pedestal. Like the Gibson girl and flapper, she sought her ultimate fulfillment in marriage and family. One of the basic reasons why this imagery was so acceptable to so many was that the American "home" was glamorized as never before. In the era which gloried that "the business of America is business," every woman was told through the media and advertising that she was entitled to an automobile, radio, washing machine, vacuum cleaner and, a "total electric kitchen." This was her *true* liberation; with her new leisure she could be a better mother and more beau-tiful wife. Helena Rubinstein and Elizabeth Arden made fortunes catering to the cult of youth and beauty. The old styled feminist was at best now portrayed as a frump in low heels and horn-rimmed glasses and at worst as an anarchist or communist. Times had changed. The first great wave of feminism in American history had ended when women won the vote. Feminism as a national movement would not attract regiments of young committed women again until the decade of the 1960s.

Hence, the emergence of the New Woman from the 1870s through the 1920s was but a *beginning.* Women had gained experience in politics, were better educated, had entered some professions in limited numbers, engaged in sports and were generally considered to be convivial companions of men, but they were *not considered equal*. As the goals of feminism remained divergent and diffuse throughout the 1920s, women found themselves in a curious state of *ambiguity*. They knew they were not equal, but they were not sure they really wanted to be. Sex-role conditioning had taught them to remain subordinate while the great American ideal of equality beckoned them onward to its achievement. This ambiguity of condition for the woman of the 1920s is the background for the Women's Liberation movement of today. Modern feminism seeks to have American women achieve an identity and an autonomy which has been lacking in the Feminine experience. Modern women are posing significant questions, which were also concerns of the earlier feminists. They ask, Can the basic stereotypical role of women as homemakers in America be changed? And, if sex-role orientations were changed through new socialization patterns, would this break up the American nuclear family? Most provocatively, women are asking *can* a woman be the equal of a man? *Should* she be the equal of a man? These issues are but a few of the general concerns passed on to our generation from the 1890s-1920s era. They suggest the history of the emergence of the American woman is as yet incomplete. The sequel to this story of feminism through the 1920s will prove as interesting but will be more controversial and perhaps thereby more liberating.

Suggested Readings

The best scholarly overview of the total emergence experience of women which includes the suffrage movement is Lois Banner's *Women in Modern America* (Harcourt, Brace, 1974). There are numerous volumes of selected readings dealing with the political and social emergence of women and two of the best are Aileen S. Kraditor's *Up from the Pedestal* (Quadrangle Books, 1970), and Miriam Schneir's *Feminism: The Essential Historical Writings* (Vintage, 1972). Among the best books for the specific time period covered in this essay, the 1890s through the 1920s, the following are recommended: Peter N. Sterns, *Modernization of Women in the Nineteenth Century,* (Forum Press, 1979), Susan Hartmann, *The Paradox of Women's Progress, 1820-1920,* (Forum Press, 1979), and Aileen S. Kraditor's *The Ideas of the Woman Suffrage Movement, 1890-1920.* Two other recent books, equally readable but slightly larger in the time period attempted to be covered are Ross E. Paulson's *Women's Suffrage and Prohibition* (Scott, Foresman, 1973) and June Sochen's *Herstory. A Woman's View of American History* (Alfred Publishing Co., 1974).

To give "women's history" a complimentary perspective there are several excellent volumes written by male contributors such as William L. O'Neill's *Everyone Was Brave* (Quadrangle, 1969) and his *Divorce in the Progressive Era* (Watts, 1973). As insightful and cogent as the O'Neill books, are William Chafe's *The American Woman: Her Changing Social, Economic and Political Roles, 1920-1970* (Oxford University Press, 1974) and his recent *Women and Equality, Changing Patterns in American Culture* (Oxford, 1977). The Chafe volumes are especially analytical in relation to the traditional norms and role expectations of women and how both men and women tend to continue through all historical periods to reinforce these socially internalized values and display normative behaviors based on sex role stereotyping.

Beyond these recent interpretive books, the events of the woman's movement must be read through the eyes and words of the "insiders," those who took part in the panoply of historical moments and have come down to us as the activists or the inspirationalists. Among the best of the "insiders" volumes are: Eleanor Flexner's *Century of Struggle* (Cambridge, 1959), Jane Addams' *Twenty Years at Hull House* (Macmillan, 1910). Charlotte Perkins Gilman, *Women and Economics* (1898; reprinted 1966), Elizabeth Cady Stanton et al., *History of Woman Suffrage,* six volumes, (New York, 1881, 1922), Elizabeth Gurley Flynn, *I Speak My Own Piece,* (Masses and Mainstream, 1955), Mary Jones, *The Autobiography of Mother Jones,* edited by Mary Field Parton (Chicago, C.H. Kerr, 1925), Emma Goldman, *Living My Life,* 2 volumes (Alfred A. Knopf, 1931), Margaret Sanger, *Margaret Sanger: An Autobiography* (Dover, 1938, reprinted 1971) and Mabel Dodge Luhan, *Intimate Memories* (Harcourt, Brace, Javonovich, 1936). An excellent article which deals with many of these interesting personalities is Jill Conway's,

"Women Reformers and American Culture, 1870-1930," *Journal of Social History,* V, (Winter, 1971-72), 164-77.

Several regional studies are of significance, especially Anne Firor Scott's *The Southern Lady: From Pedestal to Politics, 1830-1930* (University of Chicago Press, 1972). Another regional study which certainly adds color and flare is Dee Brown's *The Gentle Tamers: Women of the Old Wild West* (Bantam, 1974). Viewing the South as a distinct region, are two other important articles in relation to women in this period: Benjamin Quarles, "Frederick Douglass and the Women's Rights Movement, *Journal of Negro History,* XXV, (January, 1940), pages 35-44, and Anne Firor Scott's "The 'New Woman' in the New South," *South Atlantic Quarterly,* LXI (Autumn, 1962), pages 473-83. Special studies which deal with black women and other disadvantaged groups of women are Gerda Lerner's *Black Women in White America* and by the same author, a look at a "disadvantaged" group of women at the top of society in the South in *The Grimké Sisters from South Carolina: Rebels Against Slavery* (Boston, 1967).

No list of volumes about women or women's movements could be complete without a reference to the excellent Time-Life publication *This Fabulous Century* which does visually for the changing experiences of woman what no book can ever tell; this collection contains fascinating photos of the Gibson girl cycling to the antics of the flapper and beyond. It is an excellent photographic supplement.

Lou Gehrig, Babe Ruth, and Tony Lazzeri were the three big hitters in the famous Murderer's Row lineup, along with Bob Meusel (not shown here). These four Yankee hitters each had over 100 runs batted in with 544 total runs batted collectively. The 1927 Yankees team symbolized power and excitement. (New York Yankees Baseball Club)

Sports in the Twenties

Douglas A. Noverr
Lawrence E. Ziewacz

Flashy, flamboyant, fabulous—the age of Fitzgerald, flappers, speakeasies, the "It Girl," gangsters, rum-running, Lindy's flight, a time of booming optimism and stunning feats of individual achievement—such is the popular image of the "Roaring Twenties." Recent scholarship has demonstrated that not all participated and shared in the economic prosperity or indulged in zany feats such as goldfish swallowing. Yet undeniably the decade was one of tremendous change, excitement, and accomplishment.

Sporting events and sport heroes provided much of the excitement and glamor of the age. A glittering galaxy of stars such as Babe Ruth, Red Grange, Bobby Jones, Helen Wills, and Jack Dempsey to name just a few, by their splendid physical exploits and achievements, earned for the decade the title, "the Golden Age of Sport." As John Betts has stated in his work, *America's Sporting Heritage, 1850-1950*, "More than in any previous era, entertainers, actors, musicians, aviators, and athletes were in the limelight. In a decade dedicated largely to escapism, and general levity, sports gained the publicity which made it one of America's foremost social institutions."

Not only did Americans swarm in huge throngs to arenas to cheer their heroes on, but they also became participants. Preston Slosson, writing on the twenties in his work *The Great Crusade and After*, stated that "next to the sport of business, the American enjoyed most the business of sport." In 1928 it was estimated that almost one-fourth of the national income was spent for leisure activities, and of that amount, about $200 million purchased sporting goods and equipment.

Golf was an especially popular pastime. By 1924 there were 89 municipal golf courses in the nation for public play. By 1928, the investment in golf totaled over $2 billion, and created jobs for 3000 instructors, a half million caddies, and over 100,000 assorted workers.

Much important business was transacted in a foursome on the links or afterwards while reviving from strenuous play by sipping cool refreshments in the pleasant confines of the 19th hole. The country club became a social institution that reflected society's need for status and separation of the classes by means of recreational and social activities. So deeply had golf and the spirit of play pervaded culture that when President Harding was criticized for spending his leisure time on the golf links, the *Literary Digest* felt compelled to publish an article in its September 17, 1921, issue entitled, "Sports That Helped Our Presidents Make History." The article asserted the following conclusion:

> When will we learn that we the people lose if the President gives all his time to the office of chief executive? He must get away from the Capitol and the White House and his official self and obtain a perspective of his job and the Nation's needs. He can't do this by sitting in any chair and hovering over any desk. So paradoxically it often happens that a President at play is really and truly a President at work. . . . He plays today that he may be a better executive tomorrow and on each tomorrow's morrow.

Sports attendance figures attested to the popularity of mass spectator sports in the twenties. The following examples aptly illustrate this popularity. On July 2, 1921, 81,000 fight fans jammed "Boyle's Thirty Acres" near Jersey City to witness the Dempsey-Carpentier fight and provided the first million dollar gate in ring history. In 1913 the World Series attracted 150,000 customers and gate receipts of $325,980. In the 1926 World Series between the St. Louis Cardinals and the New York Yankees, total attendance was 328,501, and the gate receipts were over $1,200,000, a record not surpassed until 1936. College football in the fall of 1927 saw 30 million rabid fans push their way through turnstiles, bringing $50 million. Certainly the term, "Golden Decade," as the figures indicate, reflected more than a description of record-breaking athletic feats.

Why did the twenties foster such an upsurge in sporting interest and produce so many great athletes? No single reason will suffice, but many factors contributed to bring about the "Golden Age" of sports.

First of all, the nation was weary of war and eager to return to normalcy. Yet the nation's optimism in the future was undaunted. The war for democracy had been won, the economy was booming, and there was a chicken in every pot—or so it seemed. The *New York Times* in 1919 verified that America was war weary by commenting that "the Nation, released from years of gloom and depression, is expressing the reaction of plunging into sport."

Secondly, the army experience of millions of Americans had introduced them to many sports. *The Scientific American* in its February 8, 1919, issue published an article entitled, "How Uncle Sam Has Created an Army of Athletes." The article described how personal combat like wrestling helped to "develop the fighting instincts." While in the service, four million men and women were trained in such sports as football, baseball, basketball, soccer, boxing, track and field, and winter sports as thousands of sports-proficient service personnel served as recreation directors and instructors. The army virtually transformed boxing from a "forbidden sport" to one of great popularity and undoubtedly created many future fans for the great Dempsey fights of the twenties. The army also promoted intercamp sports rivalries to keep up morale. In a football game between Camps Grant and Custer held in Chicago in the fall of 1918, the gate receipts totaled $40,000. With the promotion of football on such a large scale, future fans of Army-Navy football games—depending on the branch of their service—were virtually guaranteed.

Thirdly, sports provided an outlet for the exaltation of the human spirit and individual achievement in a nation undergoing monumental changes. No longer was there a frontier to provide challenges and rewards for individual endeavors. America was now becoming an urban rather than a rural society, with its cities teeming with thousands of people crowded together in faceless, amorphous masses. But according to Roderick Nash, sports provided "living testimony of the power of courage, strength, and honor of the self-reliant, rugged individual who seemed on the verge of becoming irrelevant as the covered wagon." Thus for many Americans, sports in the twenties represented, as Roderick Nash has stated in his work *The Nervous Generation*, the following symbolism:

> The American sports fan regarded the playing field as a surrogate frontier; the athletic hero was the twentieth-century equivalent of the pathfinder or pioneer. In athletic competition, as on the frontier, people believed, men confronted tangible obstacles and overcame them with talent and deter-mination. The action in each case was clean and direct; the goals, whether clearing forests or cleaning the bases, easily perceived and immensely satisfying. Victory was the result of superior ability. The sports arena like the frontier was pregnant with opportunity for the individual.

Fourthly, the technological revolution clearly influenced social patterns. New machines increased productivity and reduced the work week from sixty to forty-eight hours. The automobile made Americans more mobile and more accessible to recreational opportunities and leisure pastimes. Under these influences, the "gospel of work which stressed the value of labor and frowned upon the pursuit of pleasure" had seemingly given way to the leisure ethic. The president of Colgate University openly lamented the pervasiveness of this spirit of play which preoccupied Americans during the twenties when he declared, "To call this a land of labor is to impute last century's epithet to us, for now it is the land of leisure."

Fifthly, sport received support from organized religion. In many cultures, from the times of the Greeks and the Olympics to our present day, religion and sports have been closely associated. Many clerics, worried about the potential corruption of youth by the lurid enticement offered by urban living, eagerly advocated youth involvement in sports as a good means of instilling Christian virtues, as well as developing healthy bodies. In an article entitled "Sports as a Religious Factor," published in the *Literary Digest* in 1921, the author found that it was "the religion of healthy mindedness that is going to save us from the perils of mere denominationalism and the futility of otherworldliness." He also declared that: "If every Christian were a sportsman, we should have a healthier atmosphere in all our churches. We should be less parochial in our outlook and less given to that pettiness of mind which has so often hindered the work of God among the young." He concluded by noting the following:

> To get our boys and girls out into the open spaces, to guide them along lines of noble comradeship, to fill them with respect for the body in its needs—this is surely to open up another channel along which the Gospel may flow into heart and mind.

Another article, published in the *Literary Digest* in 1924 and entitled "Muscular Christianity," extolled the feats of ministers and ministerial students. The Scot parson, Eric Liddel, was depicted as one who "literally strives to run the straight race by God's good grace." Hal Cuthill, a ministerial student at Boston University and the 1920 Baxter mile winner, was described as "the most prominent representative of the muscular school of Christianity in modern times." The *Digest* quoted Cuthill as having made the following observation with regard to religion and sport:

> Athletics and religion are of mutual benefit. Clean athletics keep young men from crooked paths. And running is the cleanest of all sports. A man may cover up a yellow streak in football or baseball but it is bound to show up on a cinder path.

On the question of Sunday sports, some fundamentalist ministers such as the Reverend J. Frank Norris, known as the "Texas Cyclone," opposed participation on the Sabbath, declaring that "it is unthinkable and blasphemous that any form of sport should be as important as prayer. It is impossible to believe that Jesus would endorse sports on the holy day of his resurrection." More ministers, however, were of the opinion of Bishop W. T. Manning of New York, who believed that there was "nothing wrong with sport and recreation being indulged in on the Lord's Day since 'they have just as important a place in our lives as our prayers'." Similarly, Dr. Albert C. Duffenbeck, editor of the *Christian Register*, declared that "if the Church will tell them to play and build up their bodies, I believe the people will, under proper instructions, come to the sanctuary to pray and build up their souls."

Finally, the expansion of sports publicity and technology greatly popularized sporting events and helped to immortalize sports heroes. Such outstanding journalists as Heywood Broun, Ring Lardner, Westbrook Pegler, and the incomparable Grantland Rice, who in one column managed to etch forever the nation's memory of the 1924 Notre Dame backfield, brilliantly chronicled the exploits of the stars of the playing fields and tactfully ignored their flaws.

The use of sports stars in advertising promotion provided a successful introduction of many new products to the customers. Sports publicists and promoters utilized advertising techniques to promote similarly the reputations of athletic heroes. As one commentator has stated: "The same arts of publicity which made bathtubs, face creams and vacuum cleaners universal were employed to sell sporting goods and the same press agenting which helped make the reputation of a grand opera star or a politician was also at the service of a pugilist."

The impact of newspapers was greater in the twenties because illiteracy had been reduced and newspaper circulation had increased. In 1899, 15 million copies were sold, but by 1919, 33 million were sold. As newspaper circulation increased, the newspapers expanded their sports coverage and the number of pages devoted to sporting news. For example, in 1890, sports totaled four percent of a Muncie, Indiana, newspaper's news content, but by 1923 sports accounted for 16 percent of the news content.

So complete was the public's addiction to sporting news that a *Dallas News* reporter covering the 1920 presidential election made the following observation:

> Ohio has two contenders for the presidency of the United States and one contender for the baseball championship of the world. Ask anyone in the State today who's going to win and they'll answer 'Cleveland.' It would never occur to anyone to think that the questioner might be referring to Ohioan Cox or Ohioan Harding and the trifling matter of the country's presidency.

Of course, the Cleveland Indians won the American League in 1920 by two games over its Midwestern rival, the Chicago White Sox, and went on to defeat Brooklyn in the World Series, five games to two games.

Another example of the importance of sport news was illustrated in 1928 when "the debarrment of the tennis champion W. T. Tilden from the amateur ranks drove from the front pages a presidential campaign, the assassination of the Mexican president elect, the mysterious death of a Belgian millionaire, and the search for lost aviators in the Arctic."

Perhaps the greatest communication development to popularize sports coverage was the radio. In 1930, over 12 million Americans responded affirmatively to a census question: Do you own a radio set? Ten years earlier that question need not have been asked.

As early as August 20, 1920, WWJ of Detroit broadcast the results of the

World Series. In 1921 Pittsburgh's KDKA carried an account of the Johnny Ray-Johnny Dundee fight in April of that year and followed that in July with the broadcast of the Jack Dempsey-Georges Carpentier fight. Five years later, on September 23, 1926, NBC carried the Jack Dempsey-Gene Tunney fight nationwide while WGY of Schenectady broadcast the bout by short wave to England and South America. In 1925 WMAQ of Chicago was broadcasting home baseball games, and in 1926 the first World Series was broadcast. By the late 1920s, most major athletic contests were being carried by radio. As one sport analyst noted: "Sportscasting had no crawling or creeping stages. It jumped down from the obstetrical table, kicked its heels in the air and started out to do a job."

Thus the popularity of sports in the twenties stemmed from many sources, and in a sense, provided a cultural unity to a diverse and variegated society which lacked many of the factors that contribute to a feeling of national identity. Let us now turn our attention to a discussion of specific sports. The three mass spectator sports of greatest importance in the twenties were baseball, college football, and boxing. Each will be examined individually in some detail to show their increasing popularity, mass appeal, and the changes within the sports that reflected broader cultural and social changes.

Baseball

Baseball developed as the nation's most popular sport because of the talent that developed in the 1920s. The public needed heroes and celebrities who could be lionized and idolized, but they also wanted excitement. By its nature, baseball is a slow-moving, deliberate game—a lazy spring and summer ritual punctuated more by pauses and delays than by sustained action. But baseball changed dramatically in the 1920s as it became more explosive and offensive in nature. Babe Ruth's patented towering home runs jumped off a bat that swung as mightily in a round tripper clout as it did in a glorious strikeout. Ruth hit balls out of parks that before had been seemingly home-run proof, and the outfield fences took on a new meaning and symbolism. The fences were obstacles for Ruth and other power hitters to conquer, and the baseballs sent sailing into the bleachers were prized beyond value. Baseball parks became places of explosive excitement as hitting became dominant. The National League saw only 138 home runs in 1918, but in 1929, 460 home runs were hit. In 1927 Babe Ruth hit 60 home runs, with Gehrig hitting 47. In all, 439 home runs were hit in the American League that year.

But home runs were not the only excitement. The 1920s saw the development of great hitters like George Sisler of the St. Louis Browns, who in 1920 had a record 257 hits, with 122 runs batted in, and a .407 average which he upped to .420 in 1922. Rogers Hornsby led the National League in hitting for six consecutive years (1920-1925), hitting over .400 in three of those years. His average of .424 in 1924 established a record unsurpassed. In the American League, three players hit over .400 in the 1920s: George Sisler in 1920 and 1922, Ty Cobb in 1922, and Harry Heilmann in 1923. In addition, the number of players with more than 100 RBI's jumped dramatically in the period from 1920-1929, as in the National League, 63 players had over 100 RBI's, and 79 in the American League surpassed the same figure. By contrast there were only ten players in the National League who had one hundred or more RBI's in the period from 1910-1919 and seventeen in the American League for the same period.

The numbers of players with 200 or more hits in a season showed the same dramatic increase. In the National League from 1910-1920 there were only two players who attained 200 or more hits, and thirteen in the American League. In the period from 1920-1929 in the National League 50 players had 200 or more hits (12 players in 1929) and 52 players in the American League. Between 1910 and 1919 there had been 32 no-hitters in the major leagues, with seven pitched in 1917, but from 1919-1929 there were only nine no-hitters pitched, with three years when no no-hitters occurred.

Team batting averages also reflected the increase in hitting. The 1921 Detroit Tigers averaged .316 as a team (including pitchers) with Heilmann hitting .389. The Cleveland Indians averaged .308 the same years, and four other teams had team batting averages of over .300 during the 1920s. This incredible increase in hitting added excitement and drama to baseball, putting men on base, providing for dramatic rallies, and scoring runs. Even the fans for the sixth place Cardinals, who had a 65-89 won-lost record in 1924, could rejoice in the hitting exploits of Rogers Hornsby's .424 average as he captured his fifth consecutive National League batting title with a league leading 227 hits with 82 extra base hits that year.

The hitting talent in the major leagues during the 1920s was remarkably spread out, and a team like the Detroit Tigers, which did not even have a .500 won-lost record for the decade, had a remarkable hitter like Harry Heilmann who won four American League batting titles and hit .403 in 1923.

While all this hitting influenced pitchers' earned run averages, the excitement which dominated baseball in the 1920s was also generated by star pitchers. Although rules, changed in the 1920s, eliminated much of the doctoring of the ball to the pitcher's advantage, spitball pitchers continued to flourish. Urban Shocker of the St. Louis Browns had four straight twenty-game seasons from 1920-1923, winning 27 games in 1921. Stanley Covelski, a spitballer pitching for Cleveland, had four straight seasons from 1918-1921 when he won 22 or more games. But the favorites of the fans were the fastball pitchers like Grover Cleveland Alexander, who won 15 or more games in seven years during the twenties and three times won 29 or more games; Walter Johnson, who won 23 games in 1924 and 20 in 1925; Carl Mays, who had three 20-game or better seasons in the 1920s; and later Lefty Grove, who after winning 20 games in 1927, had seven straight seasons of winning twenty games or more.

The fans wanted to see power pitching against power hitting, such as the famed Yankees' "Murderer's Row" of 1927 or the remarkable hitting teams of the Detroit Tigers in the late 1920s. Baseball provided the stuff of drama—dramatic confrontations of talent, baseball savvy, power, and personalities. This conflict has always provided the universal, day-to-day appeal of baseball, and in the twenties pitchers had to learn to rely more on speed, variety of pitches, and knowledge of batters to curb the aggressive and explosive hitting of the period. The game became more sophisticated and skillful, and this was not lost on fans. The towering Ruth home runs which shot on a line up and out of the park were dramatic, but the excitement took diverse forms.

For example, Walter Johnson's appearance in relief in the seventh game of the 1924 World Series, after failing in two previous games in the Series, with his six innings of shutout pitching providing the Senators with the Series' win over the Giants, was probably the most dramatic moment of baseball in the 1920s. Johnson was one of the most loved and respected pitchers of the period, and after seventeen seasons toiling with the Washington Senators (including eleven seasons when he won 20 or more games), Johnson experienced the joy of World Series victory over a team which had appeared in four straight Series and won world championships in 1921 and 1922.

The World Series in the 1920s provided the apex of baseball excitement. Two teams created dynasties for themselves in this period. The New York Giants won four straight National League pennants from 1921-1924 and experienced World Series victories over the Yankees in 1921 and 1922, losing to the Yanks in the Series in 1923 and to the Senators in 1925. The Yankees won three straight league championships twice in the decade, 1921-1923 and 1926-1928. They swept the World Series in 1927 and 1928. Baseball became associated with New York City, and with the Polo Grounds as both the 1921 and 1922 Series were played there. Yankee Stadium, "the house that Ruth built" and filled, opened in 1923, costing two million dollars. Other National League cities shared the pennant after 1925 with the Pittsburgh Pirates winning in 1925 and 1927 and the St. Louis Cardinals in 1926 and 1928, the Chicago Cubs winning in 1929. The Pirates won the World Series in 1925 and the St. Louis Cardinals won it in 1926, so the teams in the hinterland proved that the Gothamites could be challenged. In 1924, 1925, and 1926 the World Series went seven games each time with the seventh game being decided by scores of 4-3, 9-7, and 3-2. Each time the World Series was played, it received more and more press and radio coverage, especially since the Series was played in New York City seven out of the ten years of the period from 1920-1929.

Another reason for baseball's popularity in the 1920s was its dynamic qualities and its equally dynamic personalities on and off the field. Babe Ruth was known to be intemperate and lusty, although his positive popular image was carefully guarded by the press. On the field he had the skills and power to overshadow his private excesses and indiscretions. He personified what people wanted for themselves in their own lives. They wanted public success, but they also wanted freedom to pursue their own private desires and pleasures. If they could do the job, then what did it matter how they conducted their private lives?

Ruth also possessed that boastful pride and insouciance that the public admired. He was casual but confident, accessible yet aloof (a king or sultan), excessive in his pleasure yet hard working, earning his high salaries honestly. Ruth also struggled with physical problems and injuries, overcoming them and even overcoming his own self-indulgence which brought him fines and suspensions. Ruth even fought a battle with Commissioner Landis, asserting the freedom of the baseball player and banking on his star status and fan appeal to carry him through. He also battled with his manager, Miller Huggins, yet Ruth's love of the game always brought him back to the role of the disciplined athlete. He dared pitchers to try to strike him out, and to Ruth a walk (he was walked 2,056 times in his career) was a triumph over an adversary pitcher. He was power personified, a personality that belonged with royalty and the rich, but he never forgot his common origins or his popular appeal. He was the man who forged his own success on raw talent and remarkable reflexes. He made headlines and created stories, and he represented the spirit of a culture that sought excitement, hoopla, and even sensationalism. Even more than that, Ruth represented the struggle for individual freedom as he fought those who controlled his career or as he fought his own limitations to gain success.

Other baseball players, like Ruth, also provided colorful images and reputations. Rogers Hornsby (called Rajah) fought the same battles against authority, first against Sam Breadon over Hornsby's salary as the Cardinals' manager and later with Judge Landis over the divestment of Hornsby's stock in the Cardinals team after Hornsby was traded to the Giants. Hornsby was also a cocky and self-confident individual who used profane language and was blunt in his comments. He also answered his critics with his bat. Ruth and Hornsby both had a rawness to them that to their fans signified honesty, directness, and energy. They both deeply loved the game and swallowed their pride when necessary to remain part of the sport. They were men who played a boy's game, but in the 1920s they made baseball a truly professional sport and big business.

Baseball became an increasingly urbanized sport with the minor leagues providing the connection to the rural parts of America. In New York City there were three teams, and together they attracted almost 26 million people in attendance at baseball games in the period from 1920-1929. The Yankees drew over a million attendance eight out of ten years in that period, falling below that mark only in 1925 and 1929 (years they finished second). The Dodgers averaged 664,861 attendance a year during the twenties, and the Giants' average attendance was 863,550. The only other city that could begin to match New York City's influence on baseball was

Chicago (with two clubs), where about 14.5 million people attended baseball games from 1920-1929, with the Cubs drawing over a million three years in a row from 1927-1929. The Pittsburgh Pirates, who figured in two World Series (1925 and 1927), drew almost 6.5 million fans from 1920-1929, while the Detroit Tigers (who finished second only once in the decade) drew over 7.5 million in attendance. Baseball, then, became big business, but it also provided a "green space" in urban areas which connected city people with their forsaken rural origins.

Baseball stars were newsworthy celebrities to the adults and children who looked on them as scions of character and virtue. Many of the players were rural country boys who had come to the big city to play, and many were sorely tested by the temptations and corruptions of big city life (alcohol, sex, gambling, and other forms of dissolution), which threatened character and endangered careers that depended upon physical conditioning. Thus, baseball players were a source of moral drama. People could vicariously enjoy their success, for in many ways the careers of the baseball players represented the collective lives of society in the 1920s written large. Fans sided with the ball players in their struggles against ownership, the management, the Commissioner. The ball player's struggle for success and stability within the system symbolized the increasing complexity of modern life. Baseball players were local heroes, reflecting urban and even regional pride.

During the 1920s baseball became increasingly more professional as great hitters and great teams became a central focus of the game. Statistics grew in significance as the ballparks became places of excitement and drama. Baseball games provided both competition and contemplation. As baseball was a game in transition in the 1920s to a big business sport with high salaried stars, so was American society with its orientation to production, consumption, and business corporations with concentrations of talent. Afternoons of baseball provided a break in the workday world as people of all social and economic levels sought out the confines of a stadium to enjoy one of the most democratic sports in a society becoming increasingly stratified.

College Football

If baseball reminded people of the past, then certainly college football was the contemporary game during the twenties. A violent game of groups playing under tension and time limitations, football reflected the conflicts of the new urban society.

College football almost never received a chance to achieve the prominence that it did. In 1905 eighteen players at various levels of the game were killed and 159 injured. Alarmed by these statistics, Pesident Theodore Roosevelt called a football conference to emphasize the need to eradicate brutality and dangerous practices in the game. Subsequently, an American Football Rules Committee was formed to introduce changes and modifications in the game. By 19i0 mass plays such as the flying wedge had been outlawed—as well as Pudge Heffelfinger's famous counter action to the wedge, a jump into the leading man of the wedge, feet first. With more liberal offensive rules including less restrictions on the use of the forward pass, the game became a more wide-open affair.

From about one hundred players playing the game in 1889, the number of players involved in 1926 numbered over 200,000. During the earlier period, Walter Camp could select his All-American list from players at Yale, Harvard, and Princeton, but during the twenties the center of football power had shifted to the Midwest and West. California built a stadium which held 80,000 spectators while Ohio State, Illinois, and Michigan erected stands accommodating at least 70,000. On Saturdays, the stadiums teemed with boisterous spectators, many who had never been to college but who were caught up with the pageantry, color, and spectacle of the bands, the crowds, and the exploits conducted on the field.

College football in the twenties also reflected the democratic spirit, both in terms of teams and individuals. For example, as some scholars have noted, "a Notre Dame victory was important in the twenties, in a way a Yale or Harvard victory never was, and no Irish or Polish boy on the team could escape the symbolism." Also, college football proved that the small could still smite the mighty. Tiny Centre College of Kentucky, nicknamed the Praying Colonels, on October 29, 1921, under the leadership of their outstanding quarterback, "Bo" McMillin who raced 23 yards on a reverse, beat mighty Harvard 6-0. Harvard had not suffered a defeat in football since 1916 and had gone unbeaten in seven of its previous seasons.

The most outstanding football player of the decade undoubtedly was Red Grange, halfback for the University of Illinois from 1923-1925. In his total career Grange played in 237 games, carried the ball 4,013 times for an average of slightly over eight yards per carry, producing 531 touchdowns. Son of the police chief of Wheaton, Illinois, and without a mother since he was five, Red earned such titles as the "Wheaton Iceman" and the "Galloping Ghost" for his backfield heroics. His greatest day on the gridiron came at home in 1924 against Michigan, the Big Ten Conference favorite. Grange took the opening kickoff and raced 95 yards for a touchdown. The next three times he was given the ball, he streaked for touchdowns of 67, 56, and 44 yards. Removed by his coach, Bob Zuppke, after the first twelve minutes, he went back into the game in the third quarter. Grange responded with a twelve-yard touchdown run and passed for another. The final score was 39-14 in favor of Illinois. Grange had rambled for 402 yards and had five touchdowns.

Grange somewhat tarnished his reputation by signing a professional contract with George Halas and the Chicago Bears twenty-four hours after his last collegiate game. On December 6, 1925, 73,651 spectators crowded the Polo Grounds in New York to see Grange and the Bears play the Giants. For the next ten years Grange starred in the National Football League and helped to establish a firm foundation for the sport. Unfortunately, Grange never received his "sheepskin" from Illinois.

Knute Rockne and Notre Dame Football

For millions, however, football during the 1920s meant following the exploits of the "Fighting Irish" of Notre Dame. From 1920-1930 Notre Dame sported a fantastic record of 96 wins, 12 losses and 3 ties. The architect of this football dynasty was Knute Rockne, a football player himself at Notre Dame from 1911-1913 who had helped popularize the use of the forward pass.

Notre Dame teams caught the public's attention because they represented a national team, since its players came from all areas of the country and were of many ethnic origins, thus giving millions of "subway alumni" a chance to identify with a college team. Of course, Notre Dame's "razzle dazzle" tactics and the emotional and colorful personality of Rockne, whose impassioned half-time exhortations such as his "win one for the Gipper" speech became legendary, provided much of the "mass appeal."

Perhaps no better example of the impact of the written word upon sport and college football could be given than the immortalizing of the Notre Dame backfield of 1922, 1923, and 1924 by the outstanding sports journalist of the twenties, Grantland Rice, when he labeled them the Four Horsemen. These players established outstanding records, climaxing their careers with an unbeaten record their senior year and a 27-10 Rose Bowl win over Stanford. Other teams perhaps have been more powerful—as it was, the backfield averaged only about 163 pounds—and it was probably not even the best Notre Dame team ever, but it became the best known. Rice, after witnessing Notre Dame's 13-7 victory over Army in 1924, stamped immortality upon them when he wrote the following words:

> Outlined against a blue-grey October sky, the Four Horsemen rode again. In dramatic lore they are known as Famine, Pestilence, Destruction and Death. These are only aliases. Their real names are Stuhldreher, Miller, Crowley, and Layden. They formed the crest of the South Bend Cyclone before which another fighting Army football team was swept over the precipice at the Polo Grounds yesterday afternoon as 55,000 spectators peered down on the bewildering panorama spread on the green plain below.

A publicist from South Bend quickly published photographs of the backfield attired in football gear and mounted on horses. The public loved it, and as time passed their exploits and deeds became even more heroic. Notre Dame teams symbolized the collective team effort, and even their being a "Catholic power" was overlooked by a nation looking for invincible and memorable sports heroes.

The new emphasis on college football may have pleased alumni and fans but many academics rebelled against the presence of poorly qualified student athletes and against the funds allocated to athletic facilities when many academic departments were sorely underfunded. According to one story prevalent in the twenties, the following incident was all too common on college campuses. The college dean, seeking to establish the eligibility of an All-American tackle, asked him what was the sum of eight and six. The All-American pondered awhile and then replied, "thirteen." Instantly the head coach commented, "Aw Dean, give him another chance. He only missed by two."

Heywood Broun, one of the outstanding sports writers of the day, in a column in *Forum* in 1928 thought all the "petty bickering and suspicious pointing" could be ended by making football "frankly professional." He concluded by ironically stating:

> Think of the sentiment which might grow up around some veteran who held the post of fullback at Yale for twenty years and when the inevitable diminution of his powers set in, he could be fullback emeritus.

College football in the twenties had indeed become big-time, and with it came the problems of maintaining both academic and athletic excellence which still plague universities today.

The Ring

Perhaps no hero gained more print during the 1920s and more clearly reflected the tensions of that decade than did Jack Dempsey. In eight years of fighting, from 1919-1926, he garnered over $10 million for his efforts. Expertly managed by Tex Rickard, a master of public relations, Dempsey drew national attention to himself on July 2, 1919, when he literally pulverized the gigantic but aging champion, Jess Willard, who threw in the towel at the end of the third round.

In his article "Jack Dempsey: An American Hero in the 1920s" (*Journal of Popular Culture*, 1974) Randy Roberts comments that:

> ... a popular hero, helps to perpetuate certain collective values and to nourish and maintain certain socially necessary sentiments. Thus the popular hero served a dual function: he both reflects the psychology of a society at a given time and acts to reinforce necessary social values.

Roberts contends that the press perceived in Dempsey's victory over Willard a reverification of old American virtues and saw him as a "stable force" in times of race riots and Red Scares. Furthermore, Roberts argues that Dempsey's subsequent fights continued to mirror the tensions that plagued American society in the twenties. For example, Dempsey's victory over Georges Carpentier in 1921, which was the first to be broadcast by radio, reflected lingering war tensions. Carpentier was a war hero and a foreigner while Dempsey, who had a deferment during the war, was regarded by many as a draft dodger. However, Dempsey flattened Carpentier in four rounds and the press reported that they were "weeping in the cottages of France." The fact of the matter was that most Frenchmen were not aware of the existence of either fighter.

In Dempsey's fight against the Argentine Luis Angel Firpo ("the Wild Bull of the Pampas") held on September 14, 1923, the press ballyhooed it as the "Nordic race against the Latin." Before 82,000 fans, Dempsey flattened Firpo seven times in the first round but was awkwardly knocked out of the ring by Firpo in the same round before vanquishing him for the count in the next round. Dempsey's victory was touted in the press as a "Dempsey corollary to the Monroe Doctrine" and a "bold reaffirmation of Americanism." Dempsey was popular because he provided wildly dramatic fights in which his hammerlike punching and vicious attacks on his opponents created wild mass excitement. Out of the ring Dempsey was known as a dedicated family man, and he made international news when he made a tour of Europe in 1925 with his wife, motion picture star Estelle Taylor.

Dempsey lost his title defense to a clean-cut, "All-American type," Gene Tunney. In his rematch with Tunney in 1927 which brought $2,658,000 in gate receipts and almost 105,000 spectators, Dempsey was victimized by a long count. He stood over Tunney for several precious seconds after having decked him before retreating to a neutral corner. Tunney was able to recover and defeat Dempsey.

Tunney never captured the attention of the American public. Early in his career he had been caught by the press with a book of Shakespeare, and in an age which reflected a conflict between "high brows" and "low brows," and a distrust of the educated by the general public, Tunney did not represent the popular image of an American hero. The public was more sympathetic to Dempsey, who even in losing, fit the American image. "I lost to a good man, an American—a man who speaks the English language. I have no alibis." The public liked humbleness in its heroes, and when Dempsey departed, the popularity of boxing declined significantly. But in the 1920s Dempsey bouts provided big events which captured the popular imagination as the matches took on national significance.

Tennis

Golf, tennis, and polo had remained rich men's games until the twenties. Because of its expense, polo remained a wealthy man's pursuit, but the other two became widely popularized during the twenties. Tennis owed its popularity to the efforts of William Tilden III and Helen Wills.

Tilden was a Californian whose smashing serve, all around court brilliance, and sense of theatrics brought million dollar gates. From 1920-29 Tilden was the number one ranked player in the nation. During that time he won the American National title seven times, the Wimbledon three times, and seventeen of twenty U.S. Davis Cup singles matches. Tilden's chief rival was "little" Bill Johnston, whom Tilden defeated seven times at Forest

Hills in bitter and furious matches. Not only was he a competent player, but Tilden also possessed a sense of drama and artistry that thrilled the crowds.

Helen Wills, known as "Little Miss Poker Face" and "O Helen," was the premiere American female tennis player of the decade. She was national champion seven times between 1923-1931. She also won Wimbledon eight times beginning in 1927. According to one chronicler, Wills was the epitome of the American idol for she:

> . . . neither drank nor smoked nor kept late hours. She didn't douse herself with perfume, . . . have her hair frizzled in beauty salons. She was 100 percent clean, soap and water-virginal, American girl.

And the American public loved her for it.

Golf

Golf was popularized in the twenties by two men with contrasting personalities—Robert "Bobby" Tyne Jones and Walter Hagen. At fourteen Jones was playing in major tournaments. Between 1923-1930 he won thirteen national championships. In 1930 he completed the Grand Slam by winning the British Open, the British Amateur, the U.S. Open, and the U.S. Amateur, and then promptly retired. To the end, he remained a rarity who was a "genuine amateur" and who "loved golf for the fun of it."

Just the opposite was Walter Hagen, a free spirit and a supremely confident golfer who won eleven national and international titles. Among his championships were the U.S. Open (two times), the British Open (four times) and the PGA (five times).

Hagen was brash, outspoken, and colorful. Grantland Rice characterized him as "golf's super salesman" who "basked in the roar of the crowd." In match play against Bobby Jones in 1926 in two 36-hole matches, Hagen won 12 and 11. According to his friends Hagen lived by the following philosophy:

> Don't worry, Don't hurry. You're here on a short visit. Be sure to smell the flowers.

Undoubtedly such words struck a familiar chord in the hearts of those who became his fans.

Swimming

Swimming's two major stars during the twenties were Gertrude Ederle and Johnny Weismuller. Ederle was an eighteen-year-old daughter of an "Amsterdam Avenue liverwurst purveyor." On August 6, 1926 she became the first woman to swim the English Channel. Only five males had previously accomplished her feat and the fastest time had been sixteen hours and thirty-three minutes. Gertrude had covered the distance in fourteen hours and thirty-one minutes, breaking the record by two hours. On her return home she was treated to a ticker tape parade through New York City. Although she was never able to capitalize commercially on her fame, Ederle's performance certainly was an outstanding example of women's ability to achieve stellar athletic performances.

Johnny Weismuller was the Babe Ruth of swimming. By 1929, Weismuller held every freestyle world record from 100 yards to a half mile. He possessed five Olympic gold medals, and as a professional he won every freestyle race he participated in. At 6'3", Weismuller was dark and handsome and a star who remained "unspoiled" by his accomplishments. He was later able to parlay his athletic feats into an acting career, portraying for many years Tarzan in the movies and swimming across set lagoons rather than swimming pools.

Basketball

The original Celtics, formed in 1918, brought basketball into the limelight during the twenties. Led by Nat Holman, the Red Grange of basketball, the Celtics' exciting play so captured the public that they drew 23,000 for a game in 1922 in Cleveland. Playing 150 games a year, in an eleven-year span the Celtics posted 1,320 victories and 66 losses. In 1926 the Celtics joined the American Basketball League founded by George P. Marshall. The Celtics proved to be too successful and, in 1928 for the good of the league, they were disbanded. Despite this action the league folded in 1929.

Track and Field

Track and field during the twenties was dominated by the Phantom Finn, Paavo Nurmi in the distances and Charlie Paddock in the sprints. Nurmi won four gold medals in the 1924 Olympics. Arriving in the U.S. in 1925, he set or broke thirty-nine records and became the first runner to break the nine-minute barrier in the two mile.

Paddock blazed to victories in the sprints in the period 1920-24. In 1921 and 1924 he was the national 100 yard dash champion and the 220 yard champion in 1920, 1921, and 1924. In 1920 he was the 100 meter Olympic champion. Known for his flying leap at the tape, Paddock earned the title as the "world's fastest human" in the twenties.

Conclusion

Americans participated in many other sports and cheered for many other heroes during the twenties. Yet those discussed represent the sports with the greatest spectator appeal and which featured the heroes who appealed to the public the most. In an era when the nation was seeking escape from the memory of war and expressed a nostalgic longing for the past, athletics provided entertainment and a reaffirmation that the qualities which made America great could still be witnessed vicariously on the playing fields of the nation. Sports fans showered adulation on record breakers and identified with winners who prevailed by individualism, raw talent, and opportunism. Sports provided a focus for the energies of the period as millions of fans sought to share in the excitement generated by sporting events.

Suggested Readings

The best general introduction to American sports history is John Betts, *America's Sporting Heritage: 1850-1950* (Reading, Mass., 1974). John Durant and Otto Bettman, *Pictorial History of American Sport* (Toronto, 1952) provides an excellent section of text and pictures on the twenties. Will Grimsley (ed.) *A Century of Sports* (Maplewood, N.J., 1971), a volume compiled by the AP sports staff, is useful but not detailed. Roderick Nash, *The Nervous Generation: American Thought, 1917-1930* (Chicago, 1970); Frederick Lewis Allen, *Only Yesterday* (New York, 1931); Preston Slosson, *The Great Crusade and After, 1914-1928* are three general works on the twenties which provide valuable information and commentary on sports in that decade. Frederick W. Cozens and Florence Scovil Stumpf, *Sports in American Life* (Chicago, 1953) contains a useful analysis of the role of media and sports. Robert H. Boyle, *Sport-Mirror of American Life* (Boston, 1963) contains information on the cultural impact of sports. Paul Gallico's, *The Golden People* (Garden City, N.Y.) is the best work on sportsmen of the twenties although Allison Danzig and Peter Brandwein (eds.) *Sport's Golden Age* (New York, 1948) and Grantland Rice's *The Tumult and the Shouting: My Life In Sport* (New York, 1963) are useful. David Q. Voigt's *America Through Baseball* (Chicago, 1976) is indispensable for understanding baseball's cultural impact on American society. For good general histories see Voigt's *American Baseball: From the Commissioners to Continental Expansion* (University of Oklahoma Press, 1970) and Lee Allen's *The American League Story* (Hill and Wang, 1962) and *The National League Story* (Hill and Wang, 1961). Two excellent articles on baseball and its role which admirably supplement Voigt are Richard C. Crepeau, "Urban and Rural Images in Baseball," *Journal of Popular Culture* (1967) and Murray Ross, "Football Red and Baseball Green" *Chicago Review* (1971). Allison Danzig's *Oh How They Played the Game: The Early Days of Football and Heroes Who Made It Great* (New York, 1971) provides much factual information on early football while David Riesman and Reuel Denney's article "Football in America: A Study in Culture Diffusion," *American Quarterly* (1951) provides a cultural analysis of the game. An excellent analysis of the role of Jack Dempsey in the decade is Randy Roberts, "Jack Dempsey: An American Hero in the 1920s," *Journal of Popular Culture* (1974). Allison Danzig and Peter Schwed, *The Fireside Book of Tennis* (New York, 1972) contains much factual information on the sport. Guy Lewis, "Sport, Youth, Culture and Conventionality, 1920-1970," *Journal of Sport History* (1977) gives a nice synthesis of the long-range impact of sport on America in the years indicated.

Business and the Mass Mind

Ted C. Hinckley

"Man belongs to God alone: man's only purpose in life is to enhance God's glory and do God's will, and every variety of human activity, every sort of human conduct, presumably unpleasing to God, must be discouraged if not suppressed." To many a seventeenth-century New England colonist this declaration was axiomatic. Contrast this belief with that of a New Englander in the White House three centuries later, "The chief business of the American people is business." Professors and preachers may grit their teeth over President Calvin Coolidge's boast, but for the mass of their students and parishioners is not their chief preoccupation an unquenchable consumption of business' goods and services?

By 1900 western farmers commonly referred to the Sears Roebuck catalog as the "Bible." Concurrently within America's industrial cities the weathered stone churches of Lincoln's day were overshadowed by glistening steel skyscrapers, the "temples of American business." In 1913 the tallest of Manhattan's temples, the just-finished forty-two floor Woolworth Building, was quickly christened a "Cathedral of Commerce." Critics damned the edifice as "an outrageous display of wealth." It may have been that, yet trillions of free-will offerings had built F. W. Woolworth's cathedral, the St. Paul's to over 600 mini-cathedrals dotted from coast to coast. These "five and dime stores" had enabled Woolworth to amass a fortune estimated to be worth between sixty and seventy million dollars. Millions of buyers who rarely paid more than a dime for any single purchase had made it possible.

By the 1950s, the Lord's day had become shoppers' day. Churches still opened their doors on Sunday (now locked during the week to prevent public pillage), but a diminishing number of citizens still meditated over

$^$265

Order Your Ford Runabout Now!

Each spring the demand for Ford Runabouts is far in excess of the immediate supply.

Fast in traffic, easy to park and fitted with ample luggage space, the Ford Runabout is especially adapted for the work of salesmen and others who must conserve time and energy in making their daily calls.

If you do not wish to pay cash for your car, you can arrange for a small payment down and easy terms on the balance. Or you can buy on the Ford Weekly Purchase Plan.

Ford Motor Company

Detroit, Michigan

See the Nearest Authorized Ford Dealer

Ford

CARS · TRUCKS · TRACTORS

ethical questions and what God wished of man. However, for tens of millions of Americans, a dollar sign had long since supplanted Christ's cross. To win redemption, our "Now Generation" joins a swelling throng of consumers worshiping dazzling wares at the local shopping mall mecca. To state that these votaries of mammon have eschewed all matters of mind and spirit is grossly simplistic. Albeit, our generation's marketplace exaltation of the flesh, be that source of gratification metal, electronic, or plastic, is undeniable. And not only do Americans live more luxuriously—those who doubt this need only examine a 1900 Montgomery Ward catalog—Americans also live longer and possess unequaled civil-social freedoms. Yet strangely, contentment continues to elude the mass of citizens.

For a sociologist to compare the 1890 living-working standards with those of today can be instructive. Donald Russell quite rightly warns his fellow historians they risk losing their credibility if they attempt to interpret the past from the present. "History's enduring value lies in the interpretation of the present from the past." Some scholars ignore the steadily rising quality of life across nineteenth-century America, focusing, rather, on "the terrible human cost extracted by American industrialization." Others agonize over the "tragic human cost extracted by the American automobile industry," as though Detroit were primarily guilty for our highway slaughter. Such lopsided generalizations may only magnify misunderstanding. Yet, as canards, they do illustrate an important point.

Any author reviewing the history of American business must assume that a large number of his readers will approach his comments with an anti-business perspective. Business, even more than education and government, remains a convenient public scapegoat. Then there are those observers who insist that American business has been *the* elementary component in providing us with our homes, clothing, processed food, and much which enlivens our leisure time. A growing number of political scientists now speculate whether authentic democracy can survive without a significant degree of relatively free business enterprise. Fairness requires at least a consideration of pro-business historian John Chamberlain's opinions. "Business . . . is both a *process* that cuts across class lines, and a system wherein production and individual effort are geared to consumer and public need." Chamberlain in fact believes that "the history of American business becomes in the broadest sense the history of a people."

Producers, sellers, and buyers, and that's business, have blossomed in these United States as nowhere else in history. To be sure, Sybaris and Rome were famous for their hedonistic consumption, while the commercial aggressiveness of thirteenth-century Venice and seventeenth-century Holland became equally notorious. Today the international impact of America's mass production, mass marketing, and mass consumption is without parallel. The Soviet Union may refuse to admit Big Mac, but the face of Colonel Sanders and the whirr of IBM computers will greet you on six of the continents. Yet these foreign merchandising triumphs pale when compared with the volume of our domestic consumption. America is now so rich that merely the waste from our food production, that is, our garbage, could fill the New Orleans Superdome from floor to ceiling twice a day, including weekends and holidays.

Maybe any discussion of business and the mass society should begin with garbage. Among the fundamental factors creating American business, none has been more vital than the country's capacity to feed not only the burgeoning population at home but to employ this prodigious agricultural surplus in a rewarding overseas trade. Nature's generosity to these United States has been overwhelming. A moderate climate, fertile soil, abundant flora and fauna, even a remarkable built-in system of waterways—such a "new Eden" invited development. Exploitation was what it got.

Millions of Europeans crossed the Atlantic to obtain not only a more comfortable physical existence but a freer, more creative way of life. As these "new men" utilized what Walter Prescott Webb so aptly described as "a gigantic windfall," powerful latent psychological forces were unleashed. Another historian, David Potter, has probed these varied human reactions in his *People of Plenty*. America's callous wastefulness was accompanied by a more attractive national characteristic: a popular belief that an expanding public consumption was socially desirable. Too many Europeans had contended that the mass of society should accept an existence that was "nasty, brutish and short;" none but the well-born should aspire to live comfortably. In "the land of the free" such an assumption was intolerable.

Like Aladdin agog at his fabled magic lamp, Mississippi Valley settlers hardly believed what they beheld. Nineteenth-century German immigrants wrote to Bavarian relatives, "This land is rich. Just one day's wages here will buy a fertile acre. You may call me liar, but the sum you annually relinquish to use another man's land can here buy you your own farm, and it will be double the extent of your present leased plot." Nor did this exciting expanding equalitarianism confine itself to independent farmers. Ultimately Nature's bounty would affect every segment of national life from the treatment of women to the destruction of slavery. On business the diverse influences of North America's munificent environment proved both profound and pervasive.

It is common knowledge that independent-minded Yankee merchants and manufacturers helped bring on the American Revolution. Too little appreciated is how their "go-ahead," innovative spirit created a breathtaking new marketing philosophy. Unshackled from Europe's class-bound distribution notions, America's optimistic middle class doubled its population every thirty years. During the first half of the nineteenth century the country's equalitarian spirit was dramatically strengthened by the Jacksonian faith in mass capitalism and the mass man's inherent capabilities for self-improvement. Factories and railroads gave birth to what would become mass markets, and that supreme American sales invention, consumer credit, appeared. Europeans thought that the installment plan system instituted by

Cyrus McCormick and Isaac Singer was folly. Merely a small "down payment" and a promise to pay the remainder later promised business bankruptcy. The astonishing acceptance of McCormick's reapers—crucial agricultural weapons in preserving the Union—was matched by mass credit sales of Singer's sewing machines. The latter machine enabled an impecunious first generation immigrant to become president, foreman, and worker of his own tenement flat factory. America's resultant inexpensive food and clothing should be set in balance against the later protests of outraged Populists and Progressives condemning low farm prices and malodorous sweatshops.

Certainly it is wrong to ignore the cruel human costs of nineteenth-century industrialization: long harsh hours laboring in dirty, oft-times dangerous conditions, and wage compensation too frequently not equaling the labor expended. But the post-Civil War urban workers' lot cannot have been too unpleasant. Year after year tens of thousands of European immigrants poured into New York, Philadelphia, Chicago, Cincinnati, Milwaukee, and other swelling metropolitan centers. Nor did this exodus into hundreds of American factories occur because of "foreign ignorance." At century's end for every American youth who abandoned city life for a western homestead, approximately twenty native sons of the soil opted for concrete and asphalt.

The rise of the modern city went hand in glove with the business dynamic. "Steeltown Pittsburgh," despite its ugly sprawl and ubiquitous soot, was a vibrant kaleidoscope of human activity. "Cowtown Kansas City" stank all right, but in contrast to the ennui of life in its surrounding countryside, what a diversity of job opportunities and things to do and merchandise to buy! Within America's major cities the recreational and cultural activities by which one could be entertained or self-advanced were almost limitless.

Worker-consumer, chicken and the egg, consumer-worker, each indispensable for burgeoning business. Auto titan Henry Ford grasped how interdependent, how profitable this commercial corollary, and to the shock of his competitors, introduced the five dollar day in 1914. Much later he played the fool and stubbornly opposed auto-worker unions seeking to attain a similar end. It may well be that a millennium hence, with the detachment which only centuries provide, scholars may designate Henry Ford as the industrialist who most effectively wedded mass production and mass consumption. If they lionize his "humanitarian impulses," old Henry's ghost may rise to haunt them. When his friend, naturalist John Burroughs, once suggested such a noble motive in Ford's presence, the auto maker scoffed; his reaction had been "simply a good business move." Before a Federal Commission, he was equally abrupt. "I give nothing for which I do not receive compensation." Henry was mistaken. Like any historic giant, he gave an immense amount more than he ever received, but whether the benefits of his contribution to society will outweigh the liabilities of our age's auto addiction, only post-petroleum sages can determine. There is no doubting the worldwide publicity he gave to mass production. At his Highland Park plant, Ford's technicians proved Frederick W. Taylor's admonishment that efficient production was the master key to business success. Weaving together interchangeable parts, specializing labor for specific machines, and constantly refining their movable assembly line, Ford's employees produced an entire auto in ninety-three minutes. Ultimately Henry Ford's mass-produced "Tin Lizzie" would facilitate an explosion of mass marketing that even Utopian dreamer Edward Bellamy could hardly have imagined.

For his leadership in organizing corporate gigantism, John D. Rockefeller may be entitled to a similar premier position in the business pantheon. It is no coincidence that while Ford built his enormous organization, supplying Americans with their dream machine, Standard Oil Company became a colossus feeding the flivver's progeny. The disgust which Rockefeller's fellow Americans voiced over his ruthless business policies is common knowledge. Dissatisfied with an 84 percent control of the nation's oil refineries, the Ohio merchant went on to construct a vast horizontally and vertically integrated petroleum empire from the sanctity of his New Jersey headquarters. One historian would have us believe this type of consolidation occurred because "businessmen knew they could do virtually whatever they wished with impunity." Surely this is exaggeration. Rockefeller was no Al Capone, nor even a Jay Gould. Muckraking indictments by Henry Demarest Lloyd, Gustavus Myers, and Ida Tarbell have now been considerably modified. Unfortunately, some authors are deaf to the research of revisionists such as historians Allan Nevins, Harold F. Williamson, and Arnold R. Daum. Such social scientists hear only the furious echoes of those petty capitalists whom Standard Oil swept aside while ignoring what Rockefeller's consolidation usually effected: cheaper and better petroleum products for the consumer. An unblushing Social Darwinist, John D. Rockefeller is easy to dislike; his male heirs would win the grateful smiles engendered by his globe-circling philanthropies. Doubly ironic is how penny-pincher Rockefeller's unceasing war on waste is so often overlooked. Had the meat packers Gustavus F. Swift and Philip D. Armour, who utilized every part of the pig but its squeal, consulted the cold, calculating Rockefeller, he might have devised a means by which even that squeal could have been profitably canned, bottled, or bagged.

Well over a century has transpired since the take off of big business. Scholars therefore have a far better understanding of why by 1900 the United States was able to lead the world in the production of steel, coal, locomotives, electric power, telephones, bathtubs, and fraudulent patent medicines. What wizardry had created this industrial mastery? Already mentioned has been America's abundant resources, its nomadic, acquisitive labor force, the huge internal market forever distending from improved transportation and imaginative marketing systems. Certainly the financial institutions which abetted capital formation were vital. Public acclaim for inventors like Thomas A. Edison also helped. With the epoch of cheap energy vanishing, an electrified-petroleum-driven world cries out for a new "Wizard of Menlo Park." Even less obvious, but of paramount importance to America's industrialization, was the happy hemispheric condition that favored us with two weak contiguous neighbors, thus keeping wasteful military expenditures at a minimum. Quite as beneficial was the generally pro-business attitude at all levels of government and among the citizenry at large. As one Bostonian looking back on pre-Civil War America, commented, "Everybody was at work trying to make money . . . the only real avenue to success."

There really did exist a widespread public faith in the Horatio Alger rags-to-riches figure; Andrew Carnegie was one of them. Most of the others were myth. In part this explains America's reluctance to regulate business even when an avowedly "free enterprise" pursued practices leading to monopoly. The quandary reminds one of today's western world grappling for some means to regulate the amoral power of its multinational corporations, but incapable of doing so because of the multinationals' scale and their newness. Proliferating big business a century ago challenged American leaders everywhere. Leaders in law, government, and indeed business feared the unleashed genie, but few wished to see him back in the bottle. In any age such an econo-political power vacuum invariably attracts hard-driving, cunning, commercial-minded men. Belatedly, laymen and legislators enacted half measures such as the 1890 Sherman Anti-trust Act and the 1914 Clayton Act. Freshly created commissions struggled to check the corporate colossi. Clearly the 1911 partial break up of the Standard Oil Company and the American Tobacco Company signaled that the Supreme Court was not going to sit idle and permit all competition to vanish.

Of course it can be argued that this was closing the barn door after the horse had fled. Only in part is this true. Hundreds of corporate colts had not yet been born, as for example today's vigorous stallions like IBM, Xerox, Zenith, Lockheed, and United Airlines. Although the excesses of John D. Rockefeller's business imperialism deserves our disapprobation, one wearies of casting Rockefeller as the cardinal villain. His contemporary John H. Patterson, builder of the National Cash Register Company, is seldom excoriated, but Patterson's price cutting, corporate spying, bribing of competitor's engineers, and imaginative use of unfair trade practices, may have surpassed Rockefeller's.

Another aspiring Ohioan, Patterson had formerly owned a coal business, when in 1884 he acquired National for $6500. To a store owner a cash-counting machine might make sense, but for his retail clerk, the appearance of a "thief catcher" reflected badly on his integrity. Resentful clerks were known to tamper with the contraption. Patterson overcame this formidable opposition by heavy mail order advertising to owners, backed up by the distribution of actual working models. To intimidate recalcitrant clerk saboteurs, he hired Pinkerton detectives. Maybe it was these early battles that transformed mild-mannered Patterson into such a competitive tiger. In 1895 the National Cash Register Company confronted 158 rivals; fifteen years later 153 had gone to the wall. Here was "survival of the fittest" with a vengeance. Among the predatory tactics which Patterson encouraged was in-plant training on how to defame his competitors' products and quite literally how to damage an adversary's machine should a store proprietor be so careless as to possess a non-National machine. At his Dayton plant, Patterson maintained a competitors' "graveyard," and to speed his rivals' ruin, he produced "knockers" in his own plant which National salesmen passed off as opponents' "poorly built registers." A 1916 United States Department of Justice action publicized Patterson's brutal competitive practices; however, as late as 1940, the Company controlled 90 percent of the cash register business. Tomorrow when you go shopping, note the degree of rivalry in the cash register field. It may improve your day.

As might be surmised, John H. Patterson's drive for domination had a more attractive side. Like Rockefeller, he was relatively frugal in his personal life and poured back most of his profits into the National Cash Register Company. Although a rather domineering captain who ran a taut corporate ship, he introduced profit-sharing among his employees; "all profits in excess of 6 percent on the investment were divided equally between the company and the employees as a group." Curiously, Patterson's unseemly competitive ethics are rarely recalled today, while his skill as an advertiser is celebrated.

Although it discomforts us to include anything so slick, so superficial as advertising as one of the elementary components undergirding industrialization, few would dispute that American business success owes something to advertising. "Yours for health, Lydia E. Pinkham;" "Ask the man who owns one;" "A skin you love to touch;' "The pause that refreshes;" "Reach for a Lucky instead of a sweet." Most of these slogans stir only faint memories today, but in their heyday they were as valuable as the proud name Coca Cola. When we reflect on the universal impact of that trade name, the color, the fizz, even the euphonious sound Coca Cola, we must confess "the power in a name."

H. J. Heinz, son of a Pittsburgh brickmaker, seems to have been among the first businessmen to discern the infinite promotional power in a catchy slogan. When Heinz adopted his "57 Varieties" in 1896, he was already processing more than fifty-seven varieties of food products, but "the poetic cadence of that particular number appealed to him." "57 Varieties" quickly began to appear on his bottles, jars, and cans. From there it moved up to billboards and joined the first electric sign on Broadway, "57" illuminated by 1,200 bulbs. Heinz didn't stop with mere showmanship. He provided his employees hygienic and attractive working facilities, and when other food processors roared in anger at Upton Sinclair's *The Jungle*, Mr. 57 Varieties invited the public to tour his plants. In fact he even sent his son to Washington, D.C., to lobby for the Pure Food Act which aimed to clean up the meat-packing horror described by socialist Sinclair. In 1969, Heinz's corporate heirs dropped "57" from their firm's symbol. It was a wise action for by that time "the number of its food products had grown to more than twenty times that figure."

It is a curious fact that by 1910 the total American advertising expenditure reached 4 percent of the national income, and since then has never substantially topped that sum. But if the percentage didn't change, the quantity did, racing upward alongside the booming twentieth-century economy. The clients of advertising agencies discovered that adroit promotion could create wants that had never before existed. How the advent of radio, movies, mass magazine readership, and predictably the automobile enflamed admen's imagination! By 1929 American business was spending billions of dollars extolling the virtues of soap that was "99 and .44 percent pure," and "the joys (sic) of smoking a clean (sic) cigarette." Little wonder that the famous adman J. Walter Thompson opined that the average consumer had the brain of "a fourteen-year-old."

Johns Hopkins Professor John B. Watson, the father of behavioralist psychology was hardly less impressed by the mass mind. Watson insisted that man possessed only three unconditioned responses, love, fear, and rage, and that everything else could be drilled into man's manipulatable mind. With such a dim opinion of his fellow humans, it probably surprised few that in 1920 Watson abandoned his professorial robes for an adman's career. But then, 1920 was a year when only the most sanguine of earthlings held high hopes for humankind.

Most historians would agree that the First World War, 1914-1918, marked a monumental turning point in the history of Western Civilization. Mass military mobilization had been introduced a century earlier in the wake of the French Revolution. It took the gargantuan appetite of modern industrial war to effect an undreamed of volume of manufacturing and commercial centralization. Europeans soon proved the ghastly capabilities of modern technology: machine guns, poison gas, tanks, guns that fired enormous shells over twenty miles, weapons that simulated fish and the birds of the air. The United States entered the nightmarish blood bath on the Allied side (France, Great Britain, Russia, etc.) in 1917. Notwithstanding the late hour, American business eagerly demonstrated what marvels of production could be achieved "to make the world safe for democracy." For American manufacturers, the increase in physical plant was enormous. "Expenditures for new buildings and equipment rose from $600 million in 1915 to $2.5 billion in 1918." The industry that enjoyed the most spectacular boom was motor vehicles which more than quadrupled its output. Next in order came rubber goods with an increase of 186 percent, due primarily to the need for tires. "The profits for ten steel mills in 1918," according to economic historian George Soule, "ranged between 30 percent and 319 percent on their invested capital." Actually the gains of the average American business were considerably less, and it should never be overlooked that the war boom was largely at the cost of peacetime goods and services. Furthermore, war production was not a steady string of successes. The manufacture of aircraft, only in its infancy, failed badly, particularly in airframe construction. The pell-mell ship construction to overcome German U-boat sinkings also became involved in controversy. Nevertheless, the final figures did speak for themselves. By the end of the war American yards had launched nearly three million tons of shipping.

In one of those painful ironies of history, the "sweet land of liberty" that had gone to war to defeat "autocratic militarism" found the embrace of Mars rather pleasant. While the postwar United States appeared to slip back into a state of "normalcy," the consolidation of national power with industrial power had been made manifest. This unprecedented exercise of national authority "was never legislated by Congress but simply grew up by executive fiat." Big businessmen serving on the War Industries Board directed both national production and distribution. Symbolically, the nation's railroads, historically America's first big industrial corporations, surrendered to actual government ownership. Nor were the brilliant generals of American business unduly hesitant about directing this warborn collectivized economy. Years afterward, Bernard M. Baruch wrote, "Not until World War I . . . did I really come to appreciate how truly total had become the continuity of happenings and forces in the world. With the demand for everything in excess of available supplies, I was forced to weigh the relative importance of the many competing uses for the same things. . . . I often had to decide where the same tonnage of steel would make its greatest contribution—if used to build a destroyer or a merchant ship, if kept at home or sent to a French artillery factory."

In 1919 President Woodrow Wilson looked ahead to the postwar era. "The financial leadership will be ours. The industrial primacy will be ours. The commercial advantage will be ours." Too bad that his father, a Presbyterian minister, could not have added, "And you know, Tommy, pride goeth before a fall." Yet Wilson spoke the truth. As the "war to end wars" ended, the United States alone among the Allied powers emerged stronger than when it entered. No longer a debtor nation, America now held European credits worth over twelve billion. And by 1929 "almost half of the world's industrial production was located in the United States."

During the 1920s the golden age of American business peaked. "Never before," declared the *Wall Street Journal*, "here or anywhere else has a government been so completely fused with business." In 1926 *Nation's Business* boasted, "There is no doubt that the American businessman is the foremost hero of the American public today." To President Coolidge "The man who builds a factory builds a temple, the man who works there worships there." What did he worship? "Machinery is the new Messiah," replied the Flivver King. In the past to achieve fame it had been deemed necessary for a man to develop and dominate his own corporate fief. Now it became increasingly fashionable to gain status as a corporate executive, a highly skilled, often technically trained manager. Given the vast diversity and size of many a business behemoth, there was no other solution. However, as Thomas C. Cochran, today's most distinguished business historian, has observed, "Good organization men were probably less aggressive risk takers, less relentless in the quest for profits than the owner managers of smaller enterprises." In other words, the professionalization of management se-cured increased corporate stability, but at the cost of institutional dynamism. Stabilization-become-ossification could not be discerned until the 1960s; then the dismal response of American automakers to an invasion of German "Beetles" made it patent.

Although the career executive won growing acceptance following World War I, 1920s citizens were fascinated by his antithesis, the stock ma-nipulator, a plunger who risked other people's savings on a simply stagger-ing scale. The "utilities king" Samuel Insull, and the Van Sweringen bro-thers Otis and Martin, "monarchs of the railroads," these and too many other brilliant pyramid builders became household names. There were other "captains of finance" with greater scruple for the firms they com-manded. California-born Amadeo Peter Giannini was one of them. Gian-nini's reasonable loans to fellow Italian-Americans in San Francisco, busi-nessmen and workers alike, paid off. Attracted to the idea of chain banking, he had by 1929, 453 branches extending up and down the Golden State. It is not being maudlin to say he really did care about "the little man." With the Great Crash, Insull entered a Chicago jail, while Giannini's West Coast Bank of Italy became Bank of America. By the 1960s, it was the world's larg-est bank.

Manufacturing businesses that roared ahead during the twenties were municipal construction, home appliances, and just about everything related to keeping America's dream machine rolling. Wholly new industries that had not existed before 1914 mushroomed. "Light metals like aluminum and magnesium experienced a meteoric rise," recalls William E. Leuchten-burg in his sobering *The Perils of Prosperity*. "American factories turned out a host of new products—cigarette lighters, oil furnaces, wrist watches, antifreeze fluids, reinforced concrete, paint sprayers, book matches, dry ice, Pyrex glass for cooking untensils, and panchromatic motion-picture film." Refrigerators, radios, revolutionary improvements in the common person's transportation appeared to be spiking the guns of labor radicals. Even more remarkable, actual labor productivity rose to the point where "a per-son living in 1929 produced about four times as much as his father or grandfather living in 1865."

Most businessmen seem to have been as stunned by the 1929 stock market debacle as the typical private citizen. Shortly before the collapse, a confident entrepreneurial leader cabled Bernard Baruch, the general business situ-ation is "like a weathervane pointing into a gale of prosperity." At least he was right about a gale. When the storm ended, Franklin D. Roosevelt en-tered upon the longest White House lease in American history, and as he propounded in his 1933 inaugural address, "The money changers have fled from their high seats in the temple of our civilization."

A year later Matthew Josephson came out with his book *The Robber Barons*. Men who had only a few years before been praised as "industrial statesmen" were now despicable robber barons whose commercial principalities had been acquired by theft and extortion. Josephson's timing could not have been more perfect. The fact that his book stopped with Theodore Roosevelt's attack on "the malefactors of great wealth" did not matter; big business was inherently evil in any age. Had not Professor Vernon L. Parrington, and especially Thorstein Veblen's *The Theory of the Leisure Class*, demonstrated how vulgar, how predatory were America's rich? To the forgotten man, battered and bruised by the depression decade, the answer to that question was easy. By the mid-thirties, after the findings of a congressional investigation of World War I business profiteering hit the headlines, "Merchants of death" was added to the charge of "conspicuous consumption" and "purblind greed."

Unions had begun the thirties in sorry shape. Rent by jurisdictional battles with their membership sagging and tired old men running things, observers wondered if the thirteen million unemployed spelled the end of America's labor movement. As it transpired, Roosevelt's New Deal, fresh administrators in both the unions and business, and a latent sense of national fairness revitalized collective bargaining. At the time, business, both big and small, viewed the pragmatic F.D.R. as "a dangerous threat to American capitalism." How curious indeed that today's New Left historians damn Roosevelt for perpetuating capitalism! Space does not permit an analysis of the causes and cures of the nation's worst business collapse. Huge doses of federal money, heretofore a medicine restricted to wartime, did not cure "Mr. Depression," but did alleviate the disaster's most ominous aspects. Unduly frightened by F.D.R.'s "reckless experimenting," the business community suffered such a loss of confidence that it could not bring its own spending for investment purposes up to the levels of the 1920s. Robert L. Heilbroner specifies another fundamental why in why prosperity eluded America during the thirties: *"The New Deal did not spend nearly enough!"*

Any such restraint quickly disappeared with the onrush of World War II and the mind-boggling credit investment in America's "Arsenal of Democracy." Taxpayers might heatedly argue how to solve the depression riddle, however, when it came to crushing the Axis powers, especially after Japan's "Day of Infamy," virtual unanimity existed. In 1940 the nation's Gross National Product had been approximately one hundred billion dollars; just five war years later it had risen to three times that sum. To be sure, consumer prices were about 28 percent higher in 1945, but unemployment had vanished; so had the byproducts: gloomy bread lines, bitter strikes, and the frenzied polemics from the right and left. Of the wartime heroes lauded for the "stupendous success of America's mobilization miracles," none got a more favorable press than those businessmen who filled the Arsenal of Democracy. Gone was the image of the selfish, greedy plutocrat; in his place was democracy's savior.

Although no halos were ever seen circling the likes of Henry J. Kaiser, Charles E. Sorenson, Andrew Jackson Higgins, and J. H. Kindelberger, their public reception was second only to that of a touring air ace who had zapped twenty Messerschmitts. Unlike the sorry record of 1917-1918, the American aircraft industry rushed out 300,000 military planes, only a few of them were poorly designed, and almost all were tough flying weapons. On the ground, 86,000 tanks roared forth, while at sea the United States launched a multi-ocean navy whose tonnage will probably never again be equaled. The author recalls participating in a Navy Air strike against the Japanese Kure Naval Base in which close to a thousand carrier aircraft participated. To the best of his knowledge, not a single Japanese plane rose to contest this mass aerial assault.

Muscular unions emerging from the depression doldrums made certain that millions of defense workers got their fair share of the amazingly prosperous wartime conversion. With millions in the armed forces, every laboring man could at last find work. So could millions of his wives, sisters, and daughters—"Rosie the Riveter" became their proud identification. And it didn't stop there. High school students lucky enough to reside near one of the literally thousands of war-spawned manufacturing plants—hundreds upon hundreds were located in backyard garages—secured part-time employment, and not at the minimum wage of twenty-five cents an hour, but sixty-five and more. "Even after goods were skimmed off to fill military needs, most people were better off during the war than ever before," is the conclusion of Richard Polenberg. In fact, so great was the explosion of America's economy that "at the peak of the war effort in 1944, the total of all goods and services available to civilians was actually larger than it had been in 1940."

During the conflict the *Saturday Evening Post* had snappishly reminded enemy Yamamoto, "Your people are giving their lives in useless sacrifice. Ours are fighting for a glorious future of mass employment, mass production and mass distribution and ownership." Cynical readers whose memory stretched back to an impoverished pre-Pearl Harbor America, probably muttered a few well chosen expletives at such gush. "Anybody with any common sense knew that a wartime binge had to be followed by a depression hangover" was how one citizen summarized reality. Yet unbelievably, the *Post's* prediction came true. Since 1945 the mass man has enjoyed sustained employment. And by the 1960s an amazing number of neo-Rosies were accompanying him to mill and office; "they didn't want his job, only his boss's." As early as 1947, businessman William Levitt had commenced the first of his Levittowns, and "the tracts" began to engulf prairie, shore, and slope from the Atlantic to the Pacific. In the mid-1950s, two hundred dollars down enabled Californians to become "home owners." America's famous mass market now included mass housing.

What happened to the predicted crash of 1948, or 1955, and then 1960? Thankfully none of them hit. Sadly it was the Cold War (turned hot after the outbreak of the Korean War in 1950) and America's militarization which in considerable measure kept big business and the mass man robust. Albeit, America's economy continued to laugh at pessimists. By 1952 the average work week was down to forty hours, yet the actual output of goods and services broke one new record after another. In 1970 the GNP topped one trillion dollars. During the previous decade, and alarmed at the Yankees' commercial triumphs, a French businessman-intellectual, Jean-Jacque Servan-Schreiber, warned his countrymen, "The American challenge is not ruthless, like so many Europe has known in her history, but it may be more dramatic. . . . Its weapons are the use and systematic perfection of all the instruments of reason."

Would reason prevail? It is unquestionable that lacking reason America's high standard of living could never have been won, the dynamics of big business and the mass society notwithstanding. Historian Robert Sobel sees business leaders as willing to live within the post-New Deal confines of the government-business nexus. "Relatively free from dogma (in actions if not in words), and able to adapt to changing technologies and techniques, the American businessman . . . has become more willing than most to challenge the established norms of his society, and more adaptable to the changing needs of the national and world environments than not only his predecessors, but most of his contemporaries as well."

How about the mass consumer society—could it exhibit reason in its economic attitudes, or would this "the first large nation in history to become economically and emotionally middle class" kill the goose that laid the golden egg? Certainly America's business bellows could not escape a frightening responsibility for how it blew on the forever hot public appetite seeking more and more goods and services. Historian John Brooks believes, "the growth of the giant corporations into supergiants . . . to be the single economic change that has had the farthest reaching effects over the past quarter century." Three-quarters of a century ago, America's super rich liked to decorate their mansions with suits of armor—it heightened their identity with Old World aristocracy. In 1968 the Sears catalog—a fascinating instrument for gauging both public taste and the taste-makers— offered its readers a suit of armor of Toledo steel, "true in weight and scale to the original." No "dollar day special" this item, but sent prepaid for $1600. Yes, indeed, the people's Bible had come quite a way. But to repeat: Had reason accompanied the people's capacity to consume?

Suggested Readings

The authors and books mentioned in this essay represent but fragments of a far larger bibliographic mosaic dealing with American business and the mass mind. For a single narrative listing of sources germane to this topic, readers will find the bibliography in Daniel Boorstin, *The Americans: The Democratic Experience* (1973) invaluable. Those who feel a need for the pictorial and a popularly written summary will enjoy Alex Groner, *The American Heritage History of American Business and Industry* (1972).

Both Walter Prescott Webb, *The Great Frontier* (1952), and David M. Potter, *People of Plenty* (1954), speculate how natural abundance affected those who settled North America. Roger Burlingame's readable *Machines That Built America* (1953) details the machines that exploited this legacy. The role of businessmen in the new nation's commercial growth is traced by Douglass C. North, *The Economic Growth of the United States, 1790-1865* (1966). For the post-Civil War years, see Harold G. Vatter, *The Drive to Industrial Maturity: The U. S. Economy 1869-1914* (1976), and the decades since, Robert Sobel, *The Age of Giant Corporations: A Microeconomic History of American Business 1914-1970* (1972). Long the dean of American economic historians, Edward C. Kirkland wrote a solidly-packed, balanced account in his *Industry Comes of Age: Business, Labor, and Public Policy 1860-1897* (1961). His successor, Thomas C. Cochran, continues to compile fresh and more analytical business history while bringing it forward to our own epoch. Cochran's *The American Business System: A Historical Perspective 1900-1955* (1957), and his *Business in American Life: A History* (1972), surely confirm the universality of John Q. Public's commercial mindedness.

For the rise of automobile manufacturing in the United States, Alfred D. Chandler, Jr., *Giant Enterprise: Ford, General Motors, and the Automobile Industry, Sources and Readings* (1964) and John B. Rae, *The American Automobile, A Brief History* (1965) are both excellent. An important study on the might of the huge corporations and their social consequences is John Kenneth Galbraith's *The New Industrial State* (1967). How American business helped defeat Germany in the First World War and explode the dynamic 1920s is recounted in George Soule, *Prosperity Decade, 1917-1929* (1951). Describing how comfortably homefront Americans fought the Second World War are Richard Polenberg, *War and Society: The United States 1914-1945* (1972) and John Morton Blum, *V Was for Victory* (1976). Mira Walkins, *The Emergence of Multinational Enterprise: American Business Abroad from the Colonial Era to 1914* (1970) bravely launches American business history onto a world stage.

Section III
World War II to the Present

Modern American culture is a mixture of old and new. Changing technology has led to the arrival of a new culture with its emphasis on videorecorders and computers. Other aspects of modern culture clearly reveal its evolutionary nature and how it has changed throughout American history. Two of the essays in this section reveal the new, while two others reveal that evolutionary nature. Ray Lenarcic focuses upon the role of the American Indian in American society and the movement toward militancy. His essay shows the early activism of Indian leaders and then traces government policy in the twentieth century. He sees them attempting to bring about change through organizations and direct action. Much of his essay deals with the birth of the modern Indian movement known as Red Power. Jim Williams presents a critique of television as a reflection of American society. He points out the close relationship between television and social change. The role of the Federal Communications Commission and its leadership in television regulation is described; the essay concludes with a detailed evaluation of television in general. Tom Heiting shows the application of new technology to space travel in his essay on the race in space. Initially he describes the pioneers of space travel, then he details the government's path to the moon. Finally Warren Johnson discovers the origins of ecology in the conservation movement. In his essay he describes the origins of conservation and the role of Theodore Roosevelt in its early years. The transformation from conservation to ecology was a logical one that occurred by the 1960s.

The Moon of Red Cherries

A Brief History of Indian Activism in the United States

R. J. Lenarcic

The Moon of Red Cherries was a glorious time. The days were long and warmed by the sun's hot rays. The buffalo were as plentiful as the stars in a clear night sky. When the warriors had finished the hunt, they put on the paint of war. It was now time to test their manhood, to count the coup, and for the older men, a time to show the young how to lead. The Moon of Red Cherries was a glorious time. The warriors were proud and strong and FREE.

The end of World War II was accompanied by numerous and significant changes for the United States of America. New blood had been pumped into the nation's economy and with it the specter which had haunted the country for fifteen years seemingly disappeared. The devastated nations of Europe which had formerly dominated world affairs conceded supremacy to an American nation which had enjoyed the luxury of fighting the war on other people's soil. Britannia no longer ruled the waves; France, Germany, and Italy were shells of their former selves; and Russia had paid dearly in manpower and money for her victory. The many benefits deriving from our economic and political superiority helped raise the standard of living of millions of Americans. And yet, despite the general prosperity, one segment of the population actually found conditions as bad and in some cases worse than during the Depression. The haunting specter alluded to previously had not disappeared after all. It continued to hover over more than 200 reservations and urban ghetto areas occupied by American Indians.

American Indian Movement leader Russell Means (left) and United States Assistant Attorney General Kent Frizzell sign an agreement at Wounded Knee, South Dakota, ending the 37-day confrontation between armed Indian militants occupying the town and federal agents. (Religious News Service Photo)

That Indian people would be on the outside looking in was nothing new. For over three centuries American Indians had been locked in an oftentimes violent struggle with the white man. Between the early seventeenth and late nineteenth centuries, the native peoples were forced to resort to militant means for coping with the problem.

The problem, simply stated, was the repeated aggression on the part of land-hungry English colonists. First in Virginia, then in New England, and again in New York, in the Ohio River Valley, Georgia, California, the Great Plains and Arizona, the inexorable crush of white humanity would force the Indians from their homelands until, when the guns at last fell silent in 1890 at Wounded Knee, only some 50 million acres remained in their hands.

Initially, the English colonists were forced by the nature of their circum-stances to assume a passive relationship with the native people. Faced with starvation in both Virginia and Plymouth, the colonists depended heavily on the natives for survival, but as the Europeans' numbers grew and as they learned to master the environment, the relationship changed. The factors causing Opechancanough's War in Virginia in 1622 would recur again and again; only the names and places would change. With the tobacco crop requiring a great deal of land, the English were forced deeper and deeper into the Piedmont. The natives, the Powhatan Confederacy of Pocahontas fame, soon found themselves sandwiched between the English and hostile inland nations. In their efforts to resist further white encroachment, they fought two wars. In both cases after gaining the advantage, the Indians couldn't sustain the momentum and eventually succumbed to the superior numbers and technology of the enemy. In 1649, the victors imposed an apartheid-like system on the vanquished, a system which relegated the Native Americans to an existence on the other side of an imaginary line. Thus, the pattern of encroachment, resistance, and a militarily enforced segregation had been established by the middle of the seventeenth century.

The list is long and distinguished of Indian leaders who led their people in a series of valiant efforts to preserve their territorial and cultural integrity in the face of the recurring pattern described previously. Metacom, or King Philip, a Wampanoag chief, led his nation and its Naragansett ally in a futile effort to stem the tide of Massachusetts Bay Puritan advances. Following his defeat in 1676, New England's "Indian problem" had been resolved for the most part. During the period from 1701 to 1756, the Mohawks, led by the indefatigable Joseph Brant, joined with the five other nations which comprised the powerful Iroquois Confederacy in playing off Europe's two most formidable kingdoms, France and England. Brant later displayed his leadership abilities during the Revolutionary War. Even after he and his British allies had been defeated and the Confederacy irreparably dam-aged by war-induced divisiveness, Brant continued to fight for his people's rights from a new home base in Canada.

Another early activist, the Ottawa chieftain Pontiac, led a rare alliance of Native Americans in the Ohio River Valley. Pontiac's War lasted from 1763 to 1765. As the others before it and those to come later, Pontiac's effort succeeded only in temporarily forestalling the loss of millions of acres of land to white settlers. In fact, by 1812 only a few nations had maintained their independence in what is presently the American Midwest. That year produced what essentially represented the final act of resistance in that region. The imaginative and sensitive Shawnee leader, Tecumseh, led his people against the American government in a conflict which began before but eventually merged with the War of 1812. Originally, the Shawnee leader wanted to forge a Pan-Indian alliance which would pressure Washington into granting territorial integrity for Ohio River Valley Indians. Tecumseh's efforts were especially important in light of the government's new Indian policy. (The removal policy was designed to move Indians east of the Mississippi to territory west of the same river.)

Unfortunately, Tecumseh was frustrated in his attempt to realize a dream which even today has meaning for Indian people. Intra-tribal differences and intensely democratic traditions which had surfaced in the past to prevent Indian nations from presenting a united front against the white men once again combined to impede Tecumseh's progress. When attacks against his people by William Henry Harrison, leader of the American forces, culminated in the burning of his main village, Tippecanoe, Tecumseh and his brother The Prophet joined the British in fighting against the United States in the War of 1812. As the war wound down and British aid diminished, Tecumseh's forces were driven out of the United States and into Canada. There, at the Battle of Thames, the valiant leader was slain. His Pan-Indian objectives and willingness to fight for his people's future make Tecumseh a model for the young activists of the present, who will be discussed later.

By 1835 millions of acres east of the Mississippi River had been cleared of the native people. Only in the deep South did there remain any large concentrations of Indians. In what may be considered one of the blackest pages in American history, the federal government passed legislation aimed at removing these few enclaves. The Removal Act of 1830 appropriated $500,000 for the purpose of rounding up and transporting west some 100,000 Native Americans, the vast majority of whom were members of the Five Civilized Tribes (Creek, Cherokee, Chickasaw, Choctaw and Seminole). In the process of achieving this objective, the governments in Washington, D.C., and Georgia broke previous treaties and defied the Supreme Court (*Worcester* v. *Georgia,* 1832). In addition, the United States Senate ratified a fraudulent treaty (Echota, 1835) despite strong criticism raised by the famous Henry Clay. As a result of this "treaty" some 17,000 Cherokee people were forcibly incarcerated in makeshift concentration camps constructed in Georgia, Tennessee, and North Carolina.

The removal of these Native Americans was especially disturbing when one considers that most of them had attempted to comply with the government's previous policy of assimilation. The Cherokee, for example, had implemented a bi-cameral legislature, maintained a multimillion dollar plantation economy, accepted Christianity as an alternative to their traditional faith, developed an alphabet as a result of the genius Sequoyah, and constructed several schools throughout the reservation. Cherokee rights had been guaranteed by treaty and reaffirmed by the highest court of the land, and yet the American government during the presidencies of Andrew Jackson and Martin Van Buren succeeded in removing them west of the Mississippi. Despite the courageous efforts of the Cherokee leader, John Ross, the Native Americans of the Southeast were removed in a series of migrations between 1835 and 1842. Ross actively sought a redress of his nation's grievances by working within the system, appealing personally to the President and the Supreme Court. As a reward for his efforts Ross and his people were forced to endure a trek labeled by historian Grant Foreman as the "Trail of Tears." The six-month trip to Arkansas Territory resulted in over 4000 deaths, including Ross' wife. During their eight-year ordeal in the 1830s, the Cherokee as a group did not at any time militarily resist either the federal or Georgian governments. Just as Tecumseh would serve as a model for Indian leaders of the future, so too would John Ross, especially in his attempt to achieve certain objectives via legal means.

While Ross was pursuing a nonviolent path, the great Seminole leader Osceola resorted to much more violent measures in attempting to resist his nation's removal. The Second Seminole War (1835-42) brought the curtain down on the removal period. The victory had cost the American government approximately $50 million, together with over 1500 dead boys in blue, and earned it a reputation for deceitfulness. Osceola had been captured after meeting with army officers under a white flag and subsequently jailed. His death shortly after his imprisonment was a major factor in his nation's defeat. With the exception of a few hundred men, women, and children who took refuge deep in the Everglades, the Seminole nation joined the others west of the Mississippi.

The removal policy introduced during Jefferson's administration had attempted to resolve the Indian problem by permanently separating the two races. The Mississippi River was to provide the natural barrier to that effect. But no sooner had the objectives of the policy been realized at an incredible cost, than white Americans started penetrating the trans-Mississippi region. Manifest destiny, the Gold Rush, Mexican War, slavery issue, population boom, and European immigration accounted for the great exodus westward.

The period of this great thrust westward, 1845 to 1890, found the American west carved up into cattle, oil, sheep, and mining empires. The once virgin prairie was now partitioned by barbed-wire fences and crisscrossed by railroad tracks. Fields of wheat now grew where buffalo had grazed. The incredible riches which lay west of the Mississippi were there for the taking. The lone impediments to this wealth were the militant, nomadic Indian nations whose acts of resistance later would be romanticized in books, paintings, and movies.

The American government's policy in the west was fairly simple on paper. The various tribes would be rounded up, forcibly if need be, and placed on reservations where they could be "detribalized," in effect transformed into English-speaking, Christian farmers. The successful application of this policy proved to be far from simple. The government failed to appropriate enough money to support adequately the chain of forts which were to be the focal points of "Operation Roundup." In addition, the quality of the western troops left much to be desired as the rates of desertion and problems with alcoholism indicated. And finally, the nomads of the plains proved to be a much more formidable force than had been anticipated. First one great leader, then another would emerge to inspire the Sioux, Cheyenne, Arapaho, Comanche, Kiowa, Blackfeet, Shoshone and others. The names of these men ring in infamy for many Americans who have been led to believe by the media and the schools that the Indians were the antagonists. In reality, the red men were the true freedom fighters, struggling in the face of incredible odds to preserve their life-styles. Red Cloud, Black Kettle, Satank, Crazy Horse, Sitting Bull, Quanah Parker and their legions were not interested in doing "women's work" or attending church or living in two-story wooden frame houses. Consequently, for nearly half a century during the moon of red cherries, the warriors put on the paint of war, mounted their charges and rode off to defend their threatened way of life.

By the late 1880s the American government finally achieved its objectives regarding the Indians of the west. The wanton slaughter of the buffalo, prohibition of the sun dance religion, playing off of Indian against Indian, superior manpower of the enemy, and breaking of most of the "sacred" treaties, more than compensated for the red man's valor. One by one the tribes gathered at the various forts, surrendered their weapons and awaited removal to their new, militarily occupied homes. The suppression of the Nez Perce and their brilliant spokesman, Chief Joseph, in 1877 and the Apache and their notorious leader, Geronimo, in 1884 brought to an end what had been deemed the Indian Wars. Aside from a few sporadic and minor outbreaks of hostility and the overly-sensationalized Battle of Wounded Knee, the Native Americans of the west resigned themselves to their fate. Their warrior leaders, either dead or too disheartened to resist any further, quietly disappeared from the American scene.

Between 1890 and 1945 the Indian population lived a virtually isolated existence on their reservations as government officials began to introduce programs intended to prepare the natives for their new lives. The government's main weapon in effecting the hoped for change was education. Unfortunately its efforts in that area failed for two main reasons. First, many Indians were not interested in becoming white men, and secondly, the system they employed to educate Indian youths proved to be counterproductive. By arbitrarily ripping away young children from their homes and subjecting them to the rigorous, punitive discipline of the boarding school, the government managed to produce more psychological problems than well-adjusted, ready-for-assimilation graduates. Those few who successfully endured the ordeal learned that the failure of the system at large to educate whites about Native Americans resulted in the latter's eventual failure to secure employment following graduation. Those who returned home found themselves either shunned as traitors or incapable of resisting the temptation to return to the old ways. In either case, the original purpose of their education, assimilating the graduates or sending them home to teach the "new ways" to others, was not accomplished. Jim Thorpe, the phenomenally gifted athlete who attended Carlisle Indian School, gave many whites the impression that Indian boarding schools were working miracles with the "heathen." Tragically, for every Jim Thorpe there were countless others who wandered about aimlessly, marginal men and women unaccepted by either the white or red societies, finding solace in the bottle or the grave.

For those lucky enough to escape the horrors of boarding school, another form of "rehabilitation" awaited them. In an effort to sever all relationships between the Indian and his past, the government attempted to change the red man's means of subsistence. By turning him into a land-owning farmer, the government could realize two objectives. First, as productive farmers the Indians would not have to depend on government aid, thus saving the government a large amount of money. Secondly, by adapting to an individualistically-oriented life, the Indians' ties to their community-oriented past lives would be broken and their conversion into "red white men" facilitated.

In 1887 Congress introduced legislation aimed at realizing the above goals. The Dawes Act, as it came to be known, included in its provisions the allotment of as many as 160 acres of land for each Indian living on a reservation.* The allotment was inalienable and was to be held in trust for a period of twenty-five years. After that period, the allottee would be given full title to the land. The allottee was also granted citizen status, something unallotted Indians wouldn't be provided until 1924. The land left over after all allotments were parcelled out would be purchased by the American government and sold on the open market. Tragically, the allotment policy, like the removal and reservation policies before it, failed to achieve its objectives. If anything, the plight of the Indians west of the Mississippi worsened.** Those few Native Americans left in the East who had long experienced the hardships resulting from white control would hardly have been surprised at what befell their western brothers.

There were several flaws in the allotment-detribalization policy. First, the recipients of the government's benevolence had no choice in receiving the allotments. Despite the protests of several tribal leaders who did not want

---

*Initially not all western reservation Indians were included in the allotments. However, by the second decade of the twentieth century, the act had blanket application.
**In the 1920s the Osage nation's oil property was worth an estimated $20 million per year. During the same decade the Osage were defrauded of most of this land by whites who resorted to murder and terror to achieve their ends.

allotment for their nations, they were forced to accept or else the government threatened to take the land by other, less favorable, means. Then,
thousands of the allottees literally had their land "ripped off" by unscrupulous individuals who appear to have surfaced past and present,
whenever Native Americans either struck it rich, as in the case of the Osage,
or attained land, as in the case of the allottees. Don Berthrong, in his article
"The American Indian: From Pacifism to Activism," provides a classic example of how the latter were victimized. Note in the following the complicity
of the U.S. Congress.

> In 1902, Congress in its annual Indian Appropriation Act inserted a section
> which permitted an allotted Indian who had inherited land from a deceased
> relative to sell that acreage under the supervision of the Secretary of the
> Interior. Thousands of acres of allotments were sold under the 1902 legis-
> lation, generally known as the Dead Indian Land Act in western states and
> territories. Allotments located near the edges of growing western cities were in
> particular demand by real estate groups who purchased the land at prices
> usually paid for agricultural land but far less than when the land was sold as city
> lots. Indian Agents and Superintendents rationalized the sale of the inherited
> land by maintaining that the proceeds could be invested by the Indian in
> improving his own allotment with a house, by seeing that the Indian purchased
> agricultural machinery to increase his income, and by stocking his allotment's
> pasture with cattle or hogs. Local merchants anticipated the sale of the in-
> herited land. Months or sometimes years before the allotment was actually
> sold, the merchants sold the Indian wagons, teams, farm implements, house-
> hold goods, clothing, and little luxuries at vastly inflated prices. When the
> allotment was sold, the bill with interest was presented to the Indian who
> previously had signed a mortgage for the chattel property received from the
> merchant. Since the Indian often did not have sufficient funds to cover the
> principal and interest demanded, the latter running as high as forty percent
> annually, the merchant foreclosed on the property still possessed by the
> Indian. In the end, the Indian had neither his newly acquired wagons, teams,
> or implements nor his inherited land.

By the time the Dawes Act was repealed, Native Americans had been
"slickered" out of more than eighty million acres of land. This occurred
despite the fact that a government agency, the Bureau of Indian Affairs, had
been responsible for protecting Indian interests since 1824. Its record then
and now is a national disgrace. Those Indians who tried to work the land
often failed for lack of know-how or investment capital or because of the
inheritancy policy.

When an allottee died, his land was divided among his heirs. After two
generations, some allotments had been divided up into thirty or more
parcels. Many allottees had leased their land at ridiculously low prices to
cattle ranchers or land speculators. While the latter grew rich, the farmer
remained poverty stricken. The fact that the most popular form of employment for a native American during this period was either as a member
of the circus or reservation police force is indicative of the success of the
allotment policy.

In 1934 the Indian Reorganization Act was passed and with it the repeal of the Dawes Act. The IRA halted the further allotment of Indian land and extended the trust period on restricted land. Then Commissioner of Indian Affairs, John Collier, had provided the impetus for the writing and passage of the act. The Depression had magnified the severe problems already affecting Indian people, and the IRA was enacted to soften that blow and to rectify several other serious problems which had resulted from the Dawes Act.

Among the programs introduced in behalf of Indian people either directly or indirectly (e.g. 1934 Johnson-O'Malley Act) as a result of the IRA were the Bureau of Indian Affairs funding for the public schooling of Indian children, a revitalization of Indian culture as exemplified by the lifting of longtime bans on old dances and the peyote religion, the involvement of Indian personnel in government programs designed to improve the national economy (e.g. public building projects, relief funds), and political self-determination for those reservations interested in such.

Shortly after Collier's resignation, the last benefit derived from that "positive period" of red-white relations was implemented. The Indian Claims Commission, established in 1946, was empowered to hold hearings and if it so determined, redress those grievances resulting from any frauds, abrogation of treaties or other injustices perpetrated against Native American people by the United States Government. It seemed that Indian people were at last going to get their day in court.

Unfortunately, the Commission has failed to live up to its expectations. Since its inception, the Commission has heard over 300 claims (in excess of 1000 have been filed). Between the period 1946 and 1959 the Commission awarded aggrieved parties a little over $17 million despite the fact that they had requested over $125 million. Another example of the Commission's questionable value may be noted in the following comments offered by Peter Collier in his article, "The Red Man's Burden."

> In the California claims award of 1964, the Indians were given 47 cents an acre, based on the land's fair market value in 1851. The total sum, $29 million, less "offsets" for the BIA's services over the years, still has not been distributed (1970). When it is, the per capita payout will come to about $600, and the poorest Indians in the state will have to go off welfare to spend it.

The frugality implied in the above and the snail's pace at which the claims are handled indicate that to date the Commission has had little significant impact insofar as the Indian's economic well-being is concerned.*

At any rate, Collier's dream of improving everything from the Indian's life expectancy to his self-image was shattered within ten years of the IRA's passage. The reasons for the above were varied. Ironically, many Indian leaders were against the program because they were not interested in re-

---

*The Commission has recently been dissolved. At the time this book was written, it was in operation.

turning to the old ways. The government's detribalization efforts had apparently been partially successful. The BIA helped delay the implementation of several reforms for various reservations, apparently in resentment of the IRA's challenge to its formerly absolute authority over Indian people. As an example, the IRA was not applied at New Mexico's San Carlos Agency until 1946. The final death blows to Collier's dreams were administered by the Depression and World War II. Funds were simply unavailable for the purpose of capitalizing the innovative programs which Collier had hoped would improve the Indian's economic future, and the war had created further instability on the reservations by moving large numbers of people to the cities or into the armed services. Collier's idealistic goals would have been difficult to realize even during times of peace and prosperity. During the 1930s and 1940s they did not have a chance.

One might wonder why, throughout this period, some great Indian leader or leaders did not emerge to defend his people's interests. Other than Collier, a white man, there were no great spokesmen on behalf of Indian rights from 1887 to the end of World War II. There are, however, very good reasons that Indian leadership was lacking. The first generation of "reservation" Indians were caught up in a culture shock situation which confused the old values with the new. The same situation had occurred earlier among the Virginia Indians in the seventeenth century, Iroquois in the late eighteenth century, and Ohio River Valley natives during the middle of the nineteenth century. It seemed as though their freedom-less existences in restricted areas where they were deprived of their century-old ways of worship and means of subsistence had destroyed their will to resist. Over the years future generations would develop as a result a "reservation mentality." Born amidst poverty and despair, in an environment where alcoholism, suicide, short life expectancies, and unemployment were commonplace, most young Indians developed a "what-the-hell's-the-difference" attitude which only served to perpetuate the vicious cycle which had been set in motion when the old ways were forced to give way to the new. The isolated, deprived existences on the reservation were nevertheless preferable to life off them. In the cities or small villages which provided a rare alternative to reservation life, the Native Americans found a lonelier and equally deprived life awaited them. At least on the reservation Indians enjoyed the comfort of starving together. The militant activists of the previous centuries had been great press. The depressed, passive figures who graced the isolation period were the reverse—un-newsworthy. As a result, the American Indian and Forgotten American became synonymous terms by the mid-twentieth century.

Thus, between 1887 and 1945 the majority of Native Americans led leaderless, subdued lives in sub-standard housing on the reservations or in the cities. The life expectancy on the former was forty-four years; unemployment varied from 40 to 80 percent; infant mortality rates were the highest in the nation; and average educational achievement was sixth grade or less. The ominous social problems which flourish in such squalid environments, alcoholism, suicide, crime, and broken families, added to the Indian's plight. Thus statistics of despair, together with Indian experiences during World War II, produced a powder-keg situation which, like the state of the European continent in 1914, required but a spark to ignite.

As mentioned at the beginning of this chapter, the prosperity produced by the war did very little to change for the better the conditions described in the previous paragraph. While the war had not changed for the better the quality of life on reservations, it affected drastically the lives of some reservation residents. Their experiences would help usher in a new age for Indian people, an age which would bring with it the rebirth of the warriors.

During the war, over 100,000 Indians contributed to the American war effort in various civilian capacities, while another 25,000 served with honor in the armed forces. Representing nearly one-third of the country's Indian population, the civilians' experience meant a higher standard of living, a better education for their children, improved housing, and, as a result of all of these, an improved self-image. For the soldiers, a sense of helping to preserve democratic institutions against the fascist menace and an opportunity to display the courage of their forebears had been provided by the war. In both cases, the return to the reservations was incredibly traumatic. For those civilians having tasted the good life, the poverty-stricken reservations were unbearable. The good money, housing, and education were suddenly gone, and as a result, their self-images were again shattered. For the soldier, the thought of having put his life on the line for the preservation of the reservation system with all of its horrors was equally disillusioning. The tragedy of the returning veteran is best epitomized by the saga of Ira Hayes. A Pima Indian who enlisted in the Marines, Hayes distinguished himself on Iwo Jima and was one of five men who helped raise the flag atop Mount Suribachi. After the war, he returned to the Pima Reservation. Incapable of coping with a life devoid of meaning and depressed by the circumstances of reservation existence, Hayes sought an escape through the bottle. The hell which had become his life came to an end when he drowned in two inches of water in an irrigation ditch.

Many Indians chose to follow Ira Hayes' example by turning to alcohol as an escape from reality. And like Hayes, many died for their efforts. Others chose a different route. Taking advantage of the G.I. Bill, several hundred Indians sought to continue their education, establishing a precedent which would play an integral role in the development of post-war Indian activism. The future leaders would use their knowledge of the white man's ways to organize a sophisticated program for resolving their many problems. As important as the quest for additional education was the formation of the National Congress of American Indians. Organized by a group of young Indian intellectuals in November 1944, the NCAI represented the first large-scale effort to unify Indian nations for the purpose of influencing state and Federal decisions affecting red people. Determined to move slowly and to work within the system in the tradition of John Ross, the NCAI leadership in the late 1940s and throughout the fifties was oftentimes willing to take two steps backward in order to take one step forward. Regardless of its conservative approach, the NCAI was significant in that it existed at all. The void which had characterized Indian leadership for over half a century had now begun to be filled. The warriors were about to return.

The most serious problem confronting the NCAI and Indian people in the 1950s was the Federal government's new policy of termination. Frustrated by the failure of past policies, the government was persuaded to accept the argument of Truman's Commissioner of Indian Affairs, Dillon Meyer, that the Indians would be better off under state control. In accordance with Meyer's recommendation, Congress adopted House Concurrent Resolution 108 which stated that it was "the policy of Congress . . . to make Indians . . . subject to the same laws and entitled to the same privileges and responsibilities as . . . other citizens . . . and to end their status as wards of the United States, and to grant them all of the rights and privileges pertaining to American citizenship."

While HCR 108 sounded encouraging, like its predecessor the Dawes Act, the termination bill was a smoke screen behind which lurked the evil of exploitation. Two of the nations to be terminated in the 1950s reflected the folly of the government's latest policy. Prior to 1953 the Menominees of Wisconsin had managed a fairly profitable logging industry which took advantage of the rich timberland on their reservation. With termination, each Menominee received $2,200 and, as is the case with most people who enjoy a sudden windfall, the money was spent very quickly. Without the federal government to fall back on and deprived of the capital essential for operating their logging industry, the Menominee soon lapsed into an abominable state of poverty. They had been sold a bill of goods by the government but had not been prepared to deal with their "new" life. The Menominee's plight became so bad that by 1966 the federal government had to allocate over a million dollars to guarantee the nation at least a minimal existence. Recently, the Menominee were restored to a wardship status. They had come full circle since 1954.

A similar fate awaited the Klamath of Oregon. Tempted by the large amount of money ($44,000) each person would receive, the Klamaths turned over most of their 700,000 acres of rich timberland to the government. Like their Menominee brothers, the Klamath ran through their money very quickly, helped along by amoral white businessmen who charged the Indians outrageous prices for their products. The Klamath had exchanged their economic future, the forests, for a pittance. Hunger and despair now became their constant companions.

As the real purpose and after-effects of termination became known to the other Indian nations, their voices of protest reached crescendo proportions by the late 1950s. The efforts of the NCAI and the many individuals who stood up and were counted in opposition to termination paid dividends when in September of 1958, President Eisenhower's Secretary of the Interior, Fred A. Scaton, announced that the termination policy would be abandoned. In its place a self-determination policy similar to the IRA but with much greater financial backing would be attempted. Despite the change, most Indians were hesitant to celebrate. New policies had come and gone but the miseries of reservation life remained. A lot of significant changes had to occur before the champagne corks were popped.

While the government was struggling to come to terms with the Indian problem, two important events took place which presaged the appearance of a new, more militant Indian organization. In 1954 at Sante Fe, a group of college students led by a Navajo named Herb Blatchford met to discuss the various problems posed by the government's attempt to use education as a means for getting them to reject their Indianness and ultimately merge with the great American mainstream. Three generations after the Dawes Act the government was still trying to destroy the Indian's uniqueness, his sense of identity. Although the conference did not produce any monumental results, it did serve as the beginning of an Indian youth movement which would lead to a drastic change in the methods employed by Indians in dealing with their many problems. Also, those attending the meeting agreed that their education should be continued, but instead of rejecting their Indianness they would seek to reinforce it by maintaining a close relationship with the older reservation leaders. While the rest of America's youth was entering a period when rejecting the advice of elders would become fashionable, these Native American youths were pursuing the opposite route. Perhaps more important than avoiding the generation gap, the youths at Sante Fe had ignited the spark for what would become a raging cause celebre during the next two decades—they had paved the way for the movement to be known as tribal nationalism. In short, the Sante Fe conference had brought together the nucleus of the new warriors of the 1960s and seventies.

The other event involved the efforts of one man to help resolve the problems plaguing his people. Wallace "Mad Bear" Anderson, a Tuscarora merchant seaman, devised some rather innovative tactics in challenging the white power structure. In 1957 he led the Mohawk Nation in its refusal to pay New York State income tax. The Mohawks considered themselves a sovereign nation and hence beyond the jurisdiction of the state. Organizing some four hundred Indian supporters, he led them into a courtroom where the group tore up summonses which had been issued for failure to pay the taxes. In 1958 on his home reservation, Mad Bear successfully led the Tuscaroras in their attempt to prevent the construction of a reservoir on their land. Among the tactics employed in this venture were the harassment of workers, deflating of tires, fisticuffs, and the firing of guns over heads of company officials. Later Mad Bear led a delegation of the Iroquois Nation to Cuba where he asked Fidel Castro to sponsor its admission to the United Nations as a sovereign state. Castro refused but the public's attention was now focused on the fact that some Indian nations were no longer willing to shuffle along to the tunes played by pipers they now deemed as their "colonial masters."

As Day pointed out in his article entitled, "The Emergence of Indian Activism," Anderson's tactics "fall into a clear pattern of using various laws and old treaty agreements to challenge existing white efforts to encroach upon Indian rights and land. Mad Bear's protests are marked by a certain sense of wit combined with impeccable logic with regard to the legal status of his activities and a stubborn, if passive, resistance. In many cases he successfully puts the Establishment on in an essentially nonviolent way while at the same time gaining unsurpassed publicity, sympathy, and support and achieving the protection of legal victories and altered government policy."

Thus, as the 1950s came to an end, many Indian people were beginning to see some light at the end of the tunnel. The calamitous termination bill had been repudiated, the NCAI had survived the decade intact, and government efforts to educate Indians had begun to bear fruit, albeit not in the form that the government had intended. What is more, the prototype of the new warrior had at last emerged. Mad Bear Anderson's essentially nonviolent civil disobedience tactics would serve as models for the collective actions of the new breed of Indian spawned by the turbulent 1960s.

Despite these glimmers of hope, Indian people everywhere continued to suffer from the effects of poverty. Despite the NCAI and Mad Bear, divisiveness and indifference continued to preclude the unity of action indispensable for Indian progress. Despite claims to the contrary, the Bureau of Indian Affairs continued to fail in meeting its responsibilities to Native American people. The new warriors would have ample reasons to don their warpaint. Spurred on by the memories of Philip and Pontiac, Tecumseh and Chief Joseph, they were about to make the American public remember the "Forgotten American."

In 1960 Sol Tax, the noted University of Chicago anthropologist, sponsored the Chicago Conference. This meeting was attended by the largest number of modern-day Indians ever to gather independent of the BIA or other government agencies. Their purpose in meeting was to consider what direction they would take in the future to deal with the multitude of problems presently facing them. As the meeting dragged on, it became apparent that there was no consensus in that regard. Views expressed ranged from maintaining a close relationship with white society to the complete severing of relationships with whites in the name of tribal nationalism.

In attendance at the conference was a group of young, college-educated Indians who had not been formally invited. Nevertheless, the group, which included Herb Blatchford, Mel Thom, and Clyde Warrior of Sante Fe Conference fame, formed a caucus and voiced their views. Some members actually became chairpersons of numerous conference committees. Disgruntled by the rhetoric and past failures of other organizations, the NCAI included, the youth caucus expressed articulately its belief that affirmative action had to be taken if any significant changes for the betterment of

Indian people could be made. Their exuberance and logic deeply influenced the others in attendance; so much so that when the meeting terminated, a declaration of purpose was issued reflecting *their* viewpoints.

The Declaration of Indian Purpose was one of the most important documents ever conceived by Indian people. Its effects continue to be felt today, and it can be likened in impact to our own Declaration of Independence and France's Declaration of the Rights of Man. The document called for a unity of action on the part of all Indian nations and insisted that these nations be allowed the right of self-government. The statement reasserted the philosophy of tribal nationalism inherent in Mad Bear Anderson's actions in the late fifties, and also demanded that Indian nations be guaranteed complete autonomy in the protection of their land rights. This demand is especially noteworthy in light of some recent developments which will be discussed later. Finally, one declaration encouraged the government to provide Indians with the opportunity to determine their economic destiny and to preserve their cultural heritage. Indian nations now had a tangible battle plan to follow, and the decade of the sixties would find many of them attempting to put it into action.

The young Turks who had been so influential at Chicago met again a year later in Gallup, New Mexico. There they formed the National Indian Youth Council. The Council's function was twofold: first, to aid Indian people in understanding the meaning of tribal nationalism, and second, to develop the strategies necessary to realize the goals established at Chicago. Mel Thom, the first president of the NIYC, signaled what was to come when he stated that unless Indian people "rise up in unison and take what is (theirs) by force," they faced extermination. Thom and the others believed that theirs was a "war for survival."

The first battle waged by the NIYC took place in March of 1964. The battlefield was Washington State and the issue an old and emotional one, Indian fishing rights. The previous year, Washington's Supreme Court decided to restrict the commercial fishing activities of a number of coastal tribes. The Court's action was considered in violation of Indian treaty rights and the victimized tribes called in the NIYC to organize a "fish-in." The tactics employed by the NIYC and their Yakima, Spokane, Colville and Makah allies involved collective, nonviolent action which included soliciting good lawyers to aid jailed Indians and participating in symbolic war dances held on the steps of the State Capitol building.

The confrontation in Washington State over fishing rights continued throughout the sixties and into the early seventies until in 1974, Federal Judge George Boldt recognized the "economic rights of 25 Puget Sound Tribes under treaties enacted in the 1950s to secure their lands from white settlers." (*New York Times Magazine*, Feb. 11, 1979). The judge also ruled that said treaties guaranteed today's Indians the opportunity to take half of the harvestable catch of Pacific salmon. The aggressive efforts of the "new warriors" paid dividends in this instance, although opponents of the

Indians led by Congressman John Cunningham are attempting to negate Judge Boldt's decision. Cunningham has introduced a bill to revive the hated termination policy of the fifties. It is difficult to believe that representatives of the federal government continue to deprive Indians of those few rights, those few million acres of land to which they presently cling.

Buoyed by their success in Washington State, the NIYC became involved throughout the sixties in a number of confrontations with the white power structure. They took on Secretary of the Interior Stuart Udall in April 1966 at Sante Fe when he made proposals which reflected the government's paternalistic attitudes toward Indian people. The meeting drew the more moderate NCAI and NIYC closer together as both realized that despite promises to the contrary, the government's policy of neglect had not really changed at all.

In 1967 the NCAI and NIYC submitted for publication the "Resolution of the 30 Tribes" which reaffirmed the principles and objectives of the 1960 Chicago Conference, especially the goal of tribal nationalism. Claiming that because Indian tribes had been referred to as nations by both the government and courts throughout American history, the modern-day tribes deserved to be treated as such. Furthermore, in keeping with past treaty obligations, these nations deserved "foreign aid" from the United States in order to develop their resources. Even though the government rejected the resolutions, many Indians today remain committed to the philosophy inherent within them.

The end of the sixties saw the NIYC and supporters take their most militant action to date. Disgruntled with the government's lack of response to its nonviolent attempts at change and unwilling to pursue totally a "work-within-the-system" policy, the young warriors answered NIYC leader Mel Thom's call to "take what is ours by force" by occupying Alcatraz Island on November 20, 1969. The Indians' objectives in taking the island included establishing an Indian Studies Center where tribal history and culture would be taught. Although their nineteen-month occupation failed to achieve their immediate objectives, the Indians did attract national attention. In addition, Alcatraz symbolized a new concept for Native American people everywhere, the concept of Red Power. The aggressiveness demonstrated by the takeover presaged events to come in the seventies just as Mad Bear Anderson's civil disobedience at the end of the fifties signaled more of the same on a broader scale in the sixties.

Before leaving the decade, it must be mentioned that, in addition to civil disobedience and militant confrontations, another means of informing both Indians and the general public of the Indian's plight appeared. Vine Deloria, Jr.'s book, *Custer Died for Your Sins,* was published in 1969. It provided readers with a satirical, poignant analysis of Indian life in this country, past and present. Pulling no punches, the Yankton Sioux lawyer was critical of both white and red leadership. While suggesting that the NCAI and NIYC had not been all that effective, Deloria did intimate that a new organization, the American Indian Movement, held forth the real hope for the Indians' future.

Just as the 1950s had been dominated by the NCAI and the sixties by the NIYC, the seventies has been the decade of the American Indian Movement. Conceived in the red ghetto of Minneapolis, Minnesota, in July 1968, AIM was dedicated to combating "injustices inflicted on Indians by a hostile, white world." The movement's leaders, Dennis Banks and Clyde Bellecourt, initially intended to concentrate their efforts on the resolution of problems affecting urban Indians like those in Minneapolis. The urban Indian has been truly the Forgotten American. Most of the energy of organizations like NCAI and NIYC has been spent on behalf of reservation Indians and, subsequently, tribal nationalism. The latter had definite reservation connotations since within the boundaries of most reservations are homogeneous groupings identified as tribes. During the post World War II period thousands of Indians sought refuge in such large cities as New York, Minneapolis, Chicago, Los Angeles, and San Francisco. The doors they found open during the war were suddenly closed, and the majority of these urban dwellers soon found themselves in a worse state than ever before. Not only were conditions there as bad as their former homes, but the federal aid which had eased the pangs of poverty on the reservations was not available to them. Insofar as aid is concerned, an Indian is an Indian only as long as he or she resides on a reservation.

The programs introduced by AIM in Minneapolis provided Indians with legal and health services, educational alternatives to the BIA contract schools which AIM denounced as failures, and opportunities through advisory councils to deal with such problems as crime, suicide, and alcoholism. Suicide is an especially tragic problem as indicated by the Indians' twenty out of 100,000 rate. That figure might even be higher if the accusation that many Indian suicides are written off by white officials as "accidents" is valid. Thus, during the early stages of its existence, AIM provided some valuable services.

In 1973 AIM became involved in a number of nationally publicized violent confrontations which reflected the organization's interest in expanding its operation beyond Minneapolis' red ghetto, and, in the process, earned AIM a bad reputation. Dissatisfied with the NCAI and NIYC, AIM believed a more militant stand on behalf of Indian rights was necessary. A new type of contemporary warrior now emerged. Much like their ancestors, these men were prepared to put their lives on the line in defense of their beliefs. Banks, the Bellecourt brothers, and perhaps their most famous spokesman, Russell Means, went "on the warpath," seeking out as they did, Indians who had been victimized by what they deemed the white man's double standard of justice. The word was sent throughout the reservations and red ghettos of America that AIM would be available to help any Indian people seeking aid.

The best known AIM exploit of the seventies was the takeover of the Pine Ridge Sioux Reservation hamlet of Wounded Knee. Wounded Knee was the site of an infamous "battle" which, as mentioned earlier, rang down the curtain on America's Indian Wars. Following earlier violent confrontations between themselves and white law-enforcement officials in Custer and Rapid City, South Dakota,* AIM decided that the time was ripe for a show of force which hopefully would shock the American people into realizing the tragic plight of not only the Sioux, but all Indians. AIM believed that the after-effects of the shock would take the form of a public outrage which would in turn pressure the federal government into taking decisive action to resolve Indian problems.

For three months AIM and its supporters held out against a combined force of federal marshalls and FBI agents. Shots were exchanged on several occasions but casualties were remarkably low. After lengthy negotiations, the siege was lifted with AIM surrendering its weapons and dispersing, and the government promising first to study then act upon the Indians' demands. AIM had insisted that the government recognize Indian nations as independent and that the Senate Foreign Relations Committee review carefully the treaties broken in the past. In addition, AIM demanded an investigation of alleged corruption in the BIA and, directly pertinent to Pine Ridge's Oglala Sioux, the removal of the heavy-handed tribal spokesman, Dick Wilson.

In the months following the siege, the main actions of the government involved rounding up AIM leaders and imprisoning them on a variety of charges. The promises to study and act went unfulfilled. The divide-and-conquer tactics of deceit, tactics employed by the English and American governments for over three centuries, continued to be employed with equal success in the 1970s. Despite lengthy trials, internal dissension spawned, according to AIM officials, by FBI agent provocateurs, and a parting of the ways of some of its original leaders, AIM survived the post-Wounded Knee purge and remains active today. Co-founder Dennis Banks is no longer affiliated with AIM. Instead, he is teaching Native American Religion and Philosophy at D-Q University in California.

While their original objectives for taking over Wounded Knee have gone unrealized, AIM's efforts did produce some positive results. The American public was made aware of the fact that Indians still existed, that their willingness to accept their fate passively had changed, and that their plight was, for this supposed land of plenty, reprehensible. The movement itself gained a large following from within the Indian community, a following which transcended the age and ideological barriers which had hampered the NCAI and NIYC. That AIM was willing to fight for its objectives represented a departure from the philosophies of action of previous Indian organizations. The warriors' reborn image of the AIM leaders had great appeal for thousands of Native Americans who had grown tired of their old cigar-store Indian image.

---

*In both instances AIM was defending the interests of Indians victimized by white injustice and in both cases the injustice was incredibly blatant.

But unfortunately, AIM also had some negative effects. On many reservations it was banned on the grounds that its militant actions had done more harm than good. Despite its good intentions, it added to the divisiveness which has plagued Indian nations for centuries. Most reservations are polarized into two factions. One, the progressives, believe that the red man's best hope in the future lies under continuing BIA control and cooperation with the federal and state governments. The tragic byproducts of termination reminded the progressives of what going it on your own could do. At the other extreme are the traditionalists, the tribal nationalists, with whom AIM affiliated. They believe, as mentioned previously, that only by being guaranteed independent nation status can Indian people avoid the exploitation of the government and escape the vicious cycle presently operating on most reservations. With the NCAI, NIYC and AIM among others seeking the allegiance of Indian people, and given the deep cleavages resulting from the progressive-traditionalist conflict, it is easy to understand why the Indian activists as a whole have failed to achieve many of their objectives. Thus, although AIM had a few positive effects, it has also caused problems by contributing to the divisiveness which remains a major reason why the Indian people live the way they do. One of the latest organizations to emerge is the Council of Energy Resource Tribes (CERT). Founded in 1975, CERT is comprised of twenty-two tribes who control most of the Indians' energy resources. It is too soon to tell how "activistic" it will be and who will assume its leadership.

Today conditions on the reservations have not improved a great deal since Indians were forced to live on them. As reflected in the 1970 Government Census, Indians are at the bottom of the "economic barrel." Their median income per family was $5832 and their per capita income was sixty-one dollars. Forty percent of the Indian population (reservation) was categorized below the "low income" level. While the income figures have probably risen due to inflation, the "low income" classification remains applicable today. Unemployment among Indian people varies from reservation to reservation, but the average has been estimated to be about forty percent. Indians continue to live in sub-standard housing and drop out of school at a high rate. Reservations continue to be a breeding ground for such social evils as alcoholism, crime, and suicide. In the face of all of the above, the Bureau of Indian Affairs continues to make noise about how successful it has been of late in improving the quality of life for all Indian people.

At present, the NCAI and NIYC continue to work actively on behalf of their people. AIM also remains in existence but the government's efforts to disband it have taken much of the wind out of its sails. The loss of Dennis Banks and Russell Means' trouble with the law have combined to weaken further AIM's effectiveness. The inability of these organizations to provide a united front deprives Indian people of the clout essential if the government is to be pressured into helping them realize their goals. This lack of unity is especially critical today in light of the fact that billions, perhaps trillions, of dollars worth of coal lie beneath heretofore worthless, barren Indian lands. In addition to coal, there are also valuable reserves of natural gas, uranium, and oil on the same lands.

The development of these resources has become as controversial an issue as tribal nationalism. On the one hand the vast wealth produced by resource development could bring to an end the economic, educational, and social problems mentioned previously. Resource development would also lay open the "sacred earth," pollute the air and detour vital water routes. Such sacrilege would be unthinkable for a large number of Indians who believe that some things are more important than economic well-being. This problem is compounded by the fact that a bloc of western Congressmen have introduced a bill (H.R. 9054) aimed at depriving Indian nations of control over the resources lying beneath their land. Reminiscent of the Dawes Act nearly a century ago, this legislation would be consistent with the government's past efforts to exploit economically Indian land and resources.*

Perhaps more than ever before there is a need for strong leadership within the Indian community. Since 1945 there has been an "activization" of certain Indian elements and as discussed throughout the chapter, Indian people have a rich warrior tradition to draw upon. The new leader or leaders must grapple with the dilemma of exchanging economic well-being for cultural preservation or vice versa, in addition to having to deal with such older problems as tribal nationalism, BIA and state government incompetence, and the like. Joining in a common cause over two hundred reservations with divergent languages, religions and values, with thousands of urban Indians, many of whom have long since severed relationships with their people, will require a leader or leaders of unusual abilities. Others in the past who have tried to organize a Pan-Indian movement, men like Tecumseh and Joseph Brant, failed in their efforts because, like today, they couldn't convince the other nations that their individual interests had to be subordinated to the interests of the group.

One thing is certain. As long as the nations remain torn apart by dissension, and as long as the activist organizations continue to disagree over principles, that specter referred to at the outset will continue to hover over both reservations and red ghettos. One great warrior remains to be born, and his birth might very well help fulfill Peter Blue Cloud's prophesy in respect to the Indian's future.

---

*CERT's value will be in part determined by how effectively it deals with the dilemma described previously.

Tomorrow

We have wept the blood of countless ages as each of us raised high the lance of hate . . .

Now let us dry our tears and learn the dance and chant of the life cycle.

Tomorrow dances behind the sun in sacred promise of things to come for all children not yet born,

for ours is the potential of truly lasting beauty born of hope and shaped by deed.

Now let us lay the lance of hate upon this soil.

Suggested Readings

Howard M. Bahr, Bruce A. Chadwick and Robert C. Day, Eds., *Native Americans Today: Sociological Perspectives* (New York, 1972). An excellent study of the educational, economic, political and social problems affecting Native Americans today. One of the few sociological studies dealing with the contemporary Indian scene.

Donald J. Berthrong, "The American Indian: From Pacificism to Activism," *Forums in History Series* (St. Charles, Mo., 1973). A brief but well-written and researched examination of the post-war Indian activist movements, with especially poignant commentary on the Dawes Act and modern educational problems.

Dee Brown, *Bury My Heart at Wounded Knee* (Bantam Books, 1970). Perhaps the finest historical chronicling of Indian-white relations west of the Mississippi; well documented and readable.

Edgar S. Cahn and David W. Hearne, Eds., *Our Brother's Keeper: The Indian in White America* (Washington, D.C., 1969). A comprehensive study of contemporary Indian problems with an emphasis on the inadequacies of the Bureau of Indian Affairs.

Angie Debo, *And Still the Water Runs* (Princeton, New Jersey, 1972). A moving portrayal of the plight of the Cherokee Nation from the late nineteenth century until the Depression.

Vine Deloria, Jr., *Custer Died for Your Sins* (New York, 1969). This Native American's account of his people's plight is both incisive and insightful. A lawyer by profession, Deloria does an outstanding job in differentiating between the black and red minorities and in examining the purposes of the activist organizations.

Mark Kellogg, "Indian Rights—Fighting Back with the White Man's Weapons," *Saturday Review* (Nov. 25, 1978), pages 24-34. This most recent discussion of Indian problems has an outstanding segment devoted to the Navajo Nation and its struggle to cope with the problem of developing its vast natural resources.

T. C. McLuhan, *Touch the Earth* (New York, 1971). An illustrated study of the American Indian which includes statements made by Tecumseh, Black Hawk, Joseph, and other great Indian leaders.

Wendell Oswalt, *This Land Was Theirs* (New York, 1966). An excellent study of several Indian nations, tracing their history from pre-Columbian times until the present.

Monroe E. Price, *Law and the American Indian* (New York, 1973). A detailed study of the American legal system as it pertains to the American Indian. The book complements Felix Cohen's classic, *Handbook of Federal Indian Law*.

Howell Raines, "American Indians: Struggling for Power and Identity," *The New York Times Magazine* (February 11, 1979), pages 21-32; 48-54. An excellent article dealing with such topics as the Council of Energy Resources Tribes (CERT), the Taos, New Mexico, situation, and the Washington State fishing rights issue.

Stan Steiner, *The New Indians* (New York, 1968). A thorough study of the Red Power movement from its inception until the late 1960s.

Stan Steiner and Shirley Hill Witt, Eds., *The Way* (New York, 1972). An anthology of American Indian literature which includes valuable information on the plight of contemporary Indian people.

Robert M. Utley, *Frontier Regulars: The U.S. Army and the Indian (1866-1890)*. An extremely well researched study of the final phase of the Indian Wars. Extensive bibliography included.

Television —
Reflection of Modern America

James C. Williams

The end of the Second World War found most Americans riding a crest of affluence hardly dreamed of in the 1930s. Together individuals and corporations had saved more than $48 billion during the war years, thus stimulating an unexpected postwar economic boom. Most Americans chose to ignore the problems festering under the surface—international instabilities, race relations, persistent poverty, and urban decay. Millions of people moved upward into a middle-class way of life which included ranch-style homes, leisurely weekends, automobiles, boats, trailers, expensive hobbies, air conditioning, and pre-packaged foods. Prominent among new products available to Americans was television.

Originally developed during the 1920s, television was introduced commercially by RCA at the 1939 New York World's Fair. Although the war cut short the new media's growth, RCA rushed TV sets on the market soon after the 1945 Japanese surrender. By late 1948 the Federal Communications Commission had issued 108 station licenses, but wave spectrum interference problems and the lack of continental TV cables and microwave relays slowed television's growth. Nevertheless, the media's popularity was evident. In 1951 cities having TV stations reported movies, nightclubs, and sports events were suffering audience losses. Jukebox and taxi receipts dropped, and radio listening declined substantially. Network radio sponsors were ready to switch to television when American Telephone and Telegraph Company completed nationwide cables and relay stations in 1952. The countdown for TV passed its final stage.

A scramble to open stations followed the solution to interference problems, and by the end of 1952 over nineteen million TV sets were tuned to *I Love Lucy*, Ed Sullivan's *Toast of the Town*, *Arthur Godfrey's Friends*, and the *Philco Television Playhouse*. Of America's homes 46 percent had "the tube," launching a new age in communications media. By the end of the decade almost 90 percent of America's homes had a TV, and by the 1970s New York State courts had ruled that TV—along with tools, pots and pans, and prosthetic devices—was an essential necessity of life and as such beyond the reach of creditors. More homes had a TV than had indoor plumbing, refrigerators, and telephones. Indeed, 45 percent had two or more sets in 1978.

Television has grown so rapidly that there has hardly been time to examine its significance. Critics of the media have generally pointed to its negative impact upon Americans. They have argued that TV made Americans passive; it eroded important differences in regions and social classes; violence on the screen prompted an increase in real world violence; children raised on TV grew up as illiterates; and TV conditioned us to seek simple, formulized solutions for problems. Marshall McLuhan bravely saw TV as a positive force, reshaping the very nature of humankind and making us all inhabitants of a "global village." Now we are beginning to see that television, both as an industry and in its programming, is as much a reflector as it is a conditioner of society. In and behind the flickering images we see are many facets of our urban-industrial world, our political and economic system, our nation's international role, and our values.

The urban-industrial environment in which modern Americans live has profoundly disconnected people from the natural world. We are no longer personally involved with the nuances of nature, its plant and animal life. The steel and concrete architecture of our cities and the repeated sameness of our suburbs has come to stand between us and our primary experiences with nature. Even the rural areas have felt this mediation of experience at secondhand, as single crops replaced the diversity of natural environments. Urban life often has seemed an abstraction, a sort of arbitrary reconstruction of reality. Single-family homes and apartments separated Americans in both social and physical distance from places of work and the decisive political and economic centers of society. Our lives thrust toward mobile, fragmented privatization. "Broadcasting in its applied form," observed Raymond Williams, "was a social product of this distinctive tendency." The central transmitter broadcasting images to domestic sets provided "a whole social intake" to privatized homes. Our use of television accentuated the privatization process even further when individuals within each home switched on their own sets. TV, argues ex-advertising agent Jerry Mander, became the archetypal mediating machine. Its images further interposed between us and the natural world, thereby standardizing, reinforcing, and confirming the validity of the artificial environment created by our urban-industrial society.

In 1944 Leo Lowenthal published "Biographies of Popular Magazines" in a volume entitled *Radio Research*. He observed that biographical articles appearing in *The Saturday Evening Post* and other magazines had shifted between 1901 and 1941 from describing the lives of public figures who succeeded because of hard work and achievement to describing the lives of people who succeeded because of a lucky break. Biographies of industrialists and financiers, immigrant scientists, and prominent politicians gave way to those of boxers, ballplayers, stars and starlets, and a sideshow barker. "Idols of production," he argued, had given way to "idols of consumption." Success was no longer something to be achieved; it happened to these people. No way was left for readers to identify themselves with the great or to emulate their success, except by identifying with them as fellow consumers. Consequently, the biographers carefully noted that after all their fame and fortune these heroes used the same deodorants, soaps, and toothpastes as the readers. America had transformed itself into a consumer society by the end of the Second World War.

Television became the perfect reflection of this new society. By encouraging privatism and artificial reality, discouraging activism for passivity, and adopting radio's method of selling advertising time to pay for programming, it became, as John Kenneth Galbraith suggested in *The New Industrial State* (Second edition, 1971), the main instrument "for the management of consumer demand." Advertising based heavily on the pleasure principle had been the essential part of the consumer economy as early as the 1920s, but not until television had it really worked well. Pushing escapist entertainment, television's single high purpose soon became the capture of huge audiences for the consumption of advertising messages.

In 1955 Revlon, sponsoring *The $64,000 Question*, illustrated television's advertising power. Erik Barnouw describes the event:

> On each program actress Wendy Barrie did stylish commercials for a new Revlon product, Living Lipstick, but in September the Living Lipstick message was suddenly omitted and a commercial for Touch and Glow Liquid Make-up Foundation substituted because, it was explained, Living Lipstick was sold out everywhere. Stores were phoning the factory with desperate pleas for additional shipments. Hal March, master of ceremonies, pleaded with the public to be patient . . . . In January 1956 board chairman Raymond Spector of Hazel Bishop, Inc., explained ruefully to stockholders that the [company's] surprising 1955 [profit] loss was "due to circumstances beyond our control."

In six months Revlon had badly shaken its principal competitor's sales, and following years saw advertisers rushing pell-mell to sponsor programs. By 1975 companies willingly invested up to $120,000 per minute for network messages and that year spent some $4.5 billion on TV advertising. As many as eighty million people watched TV on the average evening, perhaps thirty million watching the same network program and commercial messages.

Television advertising both reflected and furthered the mediated urban environment and also worked toward the revision of many preconsumer society values. Television quickened the American tendency to replace reverence for what is natural with a desire to reprocess it, from hair and body odors to eyelashes. Americans evermore sought bread that was a pleasure to squeeze, refined foods, and diet supplements. The spender, not the saver, was extolled. Dollars measured everything—success, loyalty, affection. "If children do not spend on Mother, on Mother's Day," observed Harry Skornia, "they obviously do not love her." The sexual sell reduced modesty, added Barnouw, and restraint of ego lost standing. "If one does not proclaim oneself 'the greatest,' one is suspected of not being much good." Advertising encouraged self-love and adoration. "The woman caressing her body in shower or bathtub [became] a standard feature of commercials. A woman applying perfume says: 'It's expensive, but I think I'm worth it.' " Perhaps, in the mediated urban world, people were partially right when they said "money buys happiness." If it did, it bought it from only a few sources.

The high cost of network television advertising confined its broadest use to only a few of the 500 largest American corporations. In 1960 the nation's 100 largest advertisers bought 83 percent of the networks' commercial time, and the top twenty-five advertisers accounted for over 50 percent. In 1975 the leading 100 advertisers accounted for 76 percent of network TV advertisements plus 59 percent of the nation's network radio commercials. In fact, these supercorporations paid for over 55 percent of all the advertising media in the country—radio, television, magazines, newspapers, billboards, and direct mailings. Among these advertisers were always the top three automobile manufacturers (Ford, General Motors, and Chrysler), the ten major drug and cosmetic companies (from American Home Products to Gillette and Bristol-Myers), the three major soap and cleanser producers (Procter & Gamble, Colgate-Palmolive, and Unilever), the leading processed food manufacturers (from General Foods and Ralston Purina to Kellogg and Campbell Soups), as well as leading companies in liquor, oil, soft drinks, appliances, retail chains, and telephone equipment and service. The 1970 advertising leader, Procter & Gamble, spent over $128 million on its TV messages, and in 1976 the firm led the nation in overall advertising expenditures, anteing up $445 million. TV advertising, then, reflected not only consumerism but the overall activities of corporate America.

One of those activities, the continued and accelerating worldwide thrust of American business, had been fueled by fears of post World War II depression. The expansion of the American economy via international investments and markets plus the political instabilities perceived in Europe and Asia helped precipitate the Cold War between the United States and the Soviet Union and presented a blueprint for American empire. Television, according to Erik Barnouw, spearheaded the process, serving as "an advance herald for empire."

Whether or not television led in the expansion of American business, military, and political interests abroad, it certainly reflected the international tensions. American fears of Soviet communism had been fostered during the late 1940s by investigations of the House Un-American Activities Committee and in the early 1950s by Senator Joseph McCarthy's accusations that communists had infiltrated the government. Although Edward R. Murrow's *See It Now* (CBS) courageously focused on McCarthyism in 1953 and all the networks carried the 1954 Senate Army-McCarthy hearings so instrumental in McCarthy's political downfall, the TV mainstream remained uncritical of America's struggle with communism. TV news closely followed the worldwide travels of Secretary of State John Foster Dulles, relaying to Americans his speeches about the nation's struggle with Communists and its obligations to liberate captive peoples, reporting the growing number of Cold War alliances America entered into with noncommunist countries.

In 1952 NBC aired the 26-part *Victory at Sea* series, which traced American naval combat during World War II. The series presented an inspiring view of America's role in the world and, according to Peter C. Rollins, fully developed the American "psychology of self-righteous moralism—what some have called 'the Cold War mentality.' " As America struggled with communism in Europe, China, and Korea, *Victory at Sea* reinforced the American notion that "it is our mission to transform the rest of the world into our image. If we become frustrated in our attempts, we are justified in using any power necessary, for we represent the cause of freedom." The series showed our technological superiority and material wealth drown the enemy. American deaths were depicted as worthwhile compared to those of the enemy, and victory was seen as ensured because the American land of liberty and plenty was designed by nature and God. Historian Bernard DeVoto, speaking of the theme of liberation, wrote in *Harper's* magazine in 1954: "We forget too easily; everyone should see the whole series every year. It will be all right with me if Congress sees it twice a year." And columnist Jack O'Brian wrote that the series illustrated that enemies cannot "push the U.S. too far. It might even be a good idea to show *Victory at Sea* to Nikita Krushchev. A very good idea."

The struggle between good and evil came in full force to television with the successful 1955 western *Cheyenne. Lawman* and *Gunsmoke* followed, and by 1957 action, hero-villain dramas overwhelmed the comedy programs which had taken their cue from the early success of *I Love Lucy*. Thirty western series dominated the networks in 1958, complemented by police-crime series including *Dragnet, Highway Patrol, M Squad, Richard Diamond,* and *Perry Mason*. Violent endings and forceful subduing of evil men by heroes was not entirely new. Motion pictures of the 1930s and 1940s established such a tradition because love scenes were severely restricted; however, it was now seen continuously in the home environment. While westerns reinforced the notion that outsiders were not to be trusted by showing communities obliterating "the agents of external dangers," police-crime series showed evil overcome by leaders representing order, authority, and efficiency.

More directly reflecting the Cold War, foreign intrigue series moved the evil persons out of the United States. The programs of the mid-1950s—*Dangerous Assignment, Captain Gallant,* and *A Man Called X*—were followed by others, as references to CIA intrigue in Cuba, Guatemala, Laos, Malaysia, and Indonesia appeared in print. Allen Dulles' book, *The Craft of Intelligence* (1963), and David Wise's *The Invisible Government* (1964) made international clandestine warfare a topic of the times. Amos Burke, the millionaire cop of *Burke's Law,* became Amos Burke the millionaire secret agent, and *The FBI* became primarily concerned with communist agents. For children, *Tarzan* championed emergent nations against communism. *The Man From U.N.C.L.E., The Man Who Never Was, I Spy,* and *Mission: Impossible* all suggested that Americans lived among unscrupulous conspirators, that America's mission was to search out monsters to destroy. The heroes' instructions were always to do anything the enemy might do—lie, steal, cheat, kill—for the end justified the means; might made right. Erik Barnouw points out that the "official lie" was even enshrined at the start of each *Mission: Impossible* episode, when the leader of the Impossible Missions Force received his tape recorded instructions:

> VOICE: As always, should you or any of your IMF be caught or killed, the secretary will disavow any knowledge of your actions. This tape will self-destruct in five seconds . . . . Good luck . . . .

Generally, television seemed to reinforce the notion that God smiled upon Americans. Anthropologist Edmund Carpenter suggests that electronic communications itself freed our spirit, in a sense, from the flesh:

> The moment we pick up a phone, we're nowhere in space, everywhere in spirit. Nixon on TV is everywhere at once. That is St. Augustine's definition of God; a Being whose center is everywhere, whose borders are nowhere.

We had become angelicized. Is it any wonder that TV reflected America's almost religious struggle with the international evils of communism?

When the Cold War turned hot in Vietnam, an eruption of heroic military drama and comedy about other American wars occurred on TV: *Rat Patrol, Combat, Twelve O'Clock High, Hogan's Heroes,* and *McHale's Navy.* Toy advertisements pressented Mattel's Fighting Men and G.I. Joe, with "a ten-inch bazooka that really works" and a gas mask "to add real dimension to your play battles," and Saturday morning cartoons such as *Crusader Rabbit* and *Secret Squirrel* presented imaginary wars and battles against evil forces. News correspondents adopted the language of military handouts which implicitly supported war policies: Viet Cong attacks on South Vietnamese villages were "terrorist attacks" and American mass bombings were described as breaking "the will of the enemy." *Air War in the North,* a 1967 CBS documentary, prompted Michael Arlen to write in the *New Yorker* magazine "that CBS is another branch of the government, or of the military, or of both." When Morley Safer of CBS News appeared with a filmed report about American soldiers burning some 120 Vietnamese huts, the Department of Defense let CBS know it would no longer welcome Safer. Self-censorship became the rule. Canadian TV critic Neil Compton wrote in 1965 that network Vietnam coverage was generally a variation "on the official line," and he noticed that CBS and NBC presidents, Frank Stanton and Robert Kintner, were in frequent touch with Lyndon Johnson.

Networks and advertisers were unwilling to show things that might undermine current government policies, noted Barnouw, so they "thereby gravitated toward its support." Until 1968, when NBC and CBS news telecasts began to suggest the war was a stalemate, "a visitor from another planet watching United States television . . . might have concluded that viewers were being brainwashed by a cunning conspiracy determined to harness the nation—with special attention to its young—for war." Even after 1968, those who protested America's involvement in Vietnam were persistently shown as peaceniks, yippies, and hippies.

In their business activities, the television industry also became involved in America's drive for empire and in the Cold War. The beginning of foreign commercial television in the mid-1950s offered a new market to producers of telefilms. Network and other distributors sold telefilm episodes for as little as $1,000 each, getting foreign buyers and audiences hooked and keeping foreign film-makers out of the market. As the demand for American telefilms increased, prices went up, but Hollywood and New York safely became the world centers for production, attracting foreign actors and directors such as Lorne Green and Art Hiller. By 1968 one hour shows brought $7,000 per episode from the United Kingdom, $6,000 each from West Germany and Japan, and $4,400 each from France. For the oil countries and others about whom our nation was very sensitive, prices were reduced: $180 for Kuwait, $120 for Saudi Arabia, and $90 for Taiwan. Sales were even made to Eastern European nations, as overall income from the trade increased from $15 million in 1958 to $80 million in 1968. TV became an instrument of worldwide Americanization. *Bonanza* was seen in over eighty countries in 1968 and *The FBI, Mission: Impossible*, and *The Fugitive* were not far behind. Exploitation of cheap foreign labor was also tapped by producers of commercials in 1960. To avoid residual payments to actors and obsolete hair styles and clothing, producers turned to costly but effective animation. Soon animated sequences for some agencies were being completed very cheaply in Japan, Spain, and other countries.

Richard Bunce argues that "the electronic communications system is simply a business adjunct to corporate America." Manufacturers of broadcasting equipment and receivers, both in radio and television, gave impetus to the broadcasting industry. The first network, NBC, was formed cooperatively by RCA, Westinghouse, and General Electric in 1926. Six years later

Westinghouse and G.E. were forced by government antitrust action to give up their control over RCA, but under David Sarnoff's leadership, RCA continued to expand. The company operated two radio networks until 1941, when the government forced it to divest itself of one of them. Selling the NBC-blue network in 1943 to Lifesaver king Edward J. Noble gave birth to ABC. Meanwhile, CBS, founded in 1927 by the Columbia Phonograph Record Company, bought and guided by cigar Magnate William S. Paley, and backed for a while by Paramount Pictures, became a sizable competitor in the industry. Most of the network leaders during the 1930s retained control of the industry during the 1960s, and it was perhaps not surprising that they argued that "real competition" still existed and that network broadcasting was still a "risky and insecure business" in these later years. However, little could shake their secure corporate foundations, and their arguments seemed more rhetoric than reality, reinforcing the somewhat mythical values of free enterprise rather than revealing oligopoly. Indeed, as Harry Skornia argues, "the favorable position of the United States corporation in the minds of most citizens [was] achieved as a result of industry's control of the electronic media."

Indirect corporate access to and influence over national TV audiences illustrates Skornia's point. The networks and owners of stations obviously exerted profound influence on programming, and Richard Bunce showed that many companies, including the networks, owned several TV stations during the 1960s and 1970s. CBS, ABC, NBC, Avco Corporation, and Westinghouse Electric each owned five; Kaiser Industries owned seven; General Tire & Ruibber Company owned four. In addition these companies had many other economic interests. When one watched programs on American space exploration between 1967 and 1971, one watched CBS, RCA (NBC), Westinghouse, General Tire, and Avco. The National Aeronautics and Space Administration assigned each contracts for major research and development or production jobs. It was not surprising that NBC led the networks in TV coverage of the space program, for RCA played a strategic role as a NASA contractor. With few NASA contracts, CBS trailed NBC coverage; ABC, with no contract incentives, devoted barely one-half the program time set aside by NBC for the space program. Similar linkages existed in other areas which might affect programming, such as health care, surveillance and security systems, and mass transit.

The TV industry particularly reflected the military-industrial complex, about whose unwarranted influence and power President Dwight Eisenhower cautioned Americans in 1960. Between 1961 and 1967, RCA received over $2 billion in prime military contracts from the Department of Defense. With the exception of Kaiser and CBS, all the aforementioned corporations appeared among the nation's top 100 military contractors in 1972 and during most of the previous ten years. By producing nuclear naval vessels, helicopter engines, antipersonnel weapons, communications systems, and other military goods, corporations involved in TV broadcasting became deeply a part of the military-industrial complex, its dreams, themes, and taboos. The partnership of the electronic communications industry and the military, for example, dated back to World War I, when the navy needed wireless communications and participated in the creation of RCA. In 1936 a military engineer, David Sarnoff, became the NBC president, and many of his army associates got top positions in the firm's management. Sarnoff worked with the military in World War II, producing programs, and he promoted military-political uses of RCA technology, from its equipment to its propaganda services, until his retirement in 1970.

"The idea that there exists a military-industrial complex," observes Bunce, ". . . is neither novel nor a particularly recent point of view." However, the broadcasting industry and its affiliates "continue to show conspicuous lack of attention for the whole subject of military-corporate relations and policies." In 1968 CBS documentary producer Gene De Poris was removed from research on the subject with the explanation that no such complex existed. Peter Davis, who produced *The Selling of the Pentagon* for CBS in 1971, perhaps the most critical commercial TV program on the subject, was given an indefinite leave of absence from the network the following year. And, in a most celebrated case, Fred Friendly, CBS News president, resigned in 1966 after his superiors decided to carry a rerun of *I Love Lucy* rather than cover the portion of the Senate Hearings on the Vietnam War which would hear critics of government policies.

The federal government's regulatory agency for broadcasters and communications is the Federal Communications Commission. Among its duties is the licensing of TV broadcast stations, including review of new and renewal applications to ensure that stations operate within the convenience and necessity of the public interest. Like the Interstate Commerce Commission which has generally protected big truckers over small and railroads against truckers, like the Civil Aeronautics Board which has a record of refusing new licenses and promoting large air carriers over small, like the Federal Maritime Board which tends to suppress rather than promote competition, Harry Skornia reminds us the FCC has been "capable of regulating the weak but not the strong."

The notion that big business should be regulated by government in the public interest was conceived of before World War I. By the 1920s staffs of the various regulatory agencies had come to associate so closely with the managers of the industries they regulated that they identified with these people and defended them against outsiders. Regulatory agency commissioners, appointed by a succession of Presidents, were generally friends of the industries, often people who did not believe in regulation, and sometimes used the commissioner position as a stepping stone to rise in a particular industry. In essence, the regulatory bodies became captives of private enterprise. The history of the FCC reveals much of what has plagued government efforts to regulate private enterprise.

The parent of the FCC, the Federal Radio Commission, was formed in 1927 and reflected the interests of the young radio industry. In 1934 President Franklin Roosevelt formed the FCC, bringing regulation of telephony, telegraphy, and radio together. The industry lobbied hard and got Congress and the President to base the new FCC law almost entirely on the 1927 one. It placed no restrictions on the networks and later amendments conformed to this precedent. NBC's David Sarnoff argued convincingly that the industry would regulate itself, ensuring presentation of programs which broadly reflected the public interest and limited the time given over to advertisements. The National Association of Broadcasters, today considered one of the most powerful lobbies with the federal government, supported Sarnoff and adopted a code for self-regulation in 1939.

The sort of cooperation between government and industry illustrated in the early stages of broadcast regulation also reflects the new American political-economy born in the 1930s. Labeled "the Broker State" by John Chamberlain in *The American Stakes* (1941), it consists of government action "in an *ad hoc* and piecemeal fashion on behalf of those groups with sufficient political or economic power to obtain assistance." In the case of broadcasting, government handed control of virtually all aspects of commercial broadcasting to the industry. In succeeding years the industry ignored violations of the NAB code, and the FCC built a record of renewing licenses automatically, never denying renewal because of a station's public service performance.

In 1957, for example, contestants on *The $64,000 Question* revealed that the question-answer show was rigged, and a TV quiz show scandal began. A congressional subcommittee held hearings and grand juries probed. Losing contestants instigated law suits which lasted for years, and various other improprieties revealed in the industry and by FCC commissioners prompted the resignation of two commissioners. In the end the industry gave more pronouncements of self-regulation and scrapped big-money quiz shows. As a political peace-offering, David Sarnoff donated time for debates between presidential candidates Richard Nixon and John Kennedy in 1960. Daniel Boorstin suggested in *The Image: A Guide to Pseudoevents in America* (1964) that, like the quiz shows which offered right, simple answers to complex questions, "delivered pithily and without hesitation," the debates were successful in "reducing great national issues to trivial dimensions. With appropriate vulgarity, they might have been called the $400,000 Question (Prize: a $100,000-a-year job for four years)."

In 1963 a sampling of stations by the FCC found 40 percent had been violating the NAB code limiting the amount of time devoted to advertising. FCC Chairman E. William Henry modestly proposed that, since the industry had set up its own code and referred to it proudly, the FCC might logically adopt it as the official guide in renewing licenses. "The industry reaction to this was one of horror and outrage," recounted Erik Barnouw, and a bill was immediately introduced in Congress "forbidding the FCC to take any action to limit commercials." Industry influence led to its quick passage in the House of Representatives, 317-43, the Senate ignored the issue, and the FCC dropped the idea of curbing commercials and adopting the code.

The FCC has seen Congress, which delegates its powers, generally support the broadcasters. Industry influence has been helped by the fact that individual congressmen and senators need access to TV for election and many are owners or part-owners in broadcast properties. Pressure on Congress has kept the FCC budget and staff small. The agency's 1100 people have been barely able to oversee ham and CB radio operation, telephony and telegraphy, not to mention both radio and TV broadcasting. Furthermore, limited staffing has caused the FCC, as it has other regulatory agencies, to turn occasionally to industry for expert assistance and thereby give broadcasters even more influence. In the final analysis the TV industry has been self-regulated and therefore reflected in both its operation and programming the interests and values of the private corporate sector of American life.

Bill Moyers recently observed that commercial TV "sees America as a vast homogeneous society of consumers—as a market, not as a country." While some broadcasters and sponsors may feel they are sincerely involved in public interest work, none can forget their first concern must be business. Erik Barnouw suggests the sponsor, network executive, or station operator "may himself be a lover of nature, and contribute to the Sierra Club and Audubon Society, but in business his eye is on sales and profits." Any ultimate conflict is usually avoided. Consequently, controversial subjects, those which might offend any sizable audience as perceived by the industry, have generally been confined to non-prime time hours, if aired at all.

Courageous sponsors and network executives have been rare, and sometimes their courage has been prompted by less than gallant reasons. In 1951 when Alcoa decided to sponsor Edward R. Murrow's *See It Now* documentaries, the company saw the opportunity as a way to refurbish its tarnished image, acquired by losing a major antitrust battle. When Murrow's attacks on Joseph McCarthy prompted mail running five to four against him, Alcoa held firm, but a year later, in 1955, it withdrew sponsorship. *See It Now* died within three years, lacking a full-time sponsor. In the early 1970s, confrontations between American oil companies and the oil countries led to an embargo, price hikes, and investigations unearthing high-level, international bribery involving the companies. They were then quite willing to begin underwriting public television programs, partly to restore their public image.

An exceptionally brave period for the industry occurred briefly during the presidency of John F. Kennedy. Caught by the Kennedy aura and spirit of "unthinkable thoughts and impossible dreams," network news teams pushed within the industry for expansion. Network news programs were increased to one-half hour in 1963, and *CBS Reports'* "Harvest of Shame," ABC's *Close*

Up series "The Children Were Watching," and NBC's documentary *The Tunnel* represented unprecedented programming dealing with migrant workers, integration, and refugees. But the end of the Kennedy era saw a return to TV as usual, although increased news division budgets and scheduling changes remained. Gulf Oil, which had readily sponsored *The Tunnel* in 1962, was unwilling to sponsor NBC's three-hour Labor Day special on civil rights, and ABC could find no prime-time sponsor for its five-part series on the same subject. ABC finally scheduled its series for late Sunday evenings, following a tradition established in the 1950s for odd hour scheduling of volatile, controversial topics.

Industry executives and sponsors have both sought an ideal of 100 percent acceptability—acceptability by audience and by corporate state. Commercial TV public service advertising reflects this desirability and is guided by the National Advertising Council which maintains a virtual stranglehold over production of such advertisements. The Ad Council had been the industry's answer to meeting the FCC licensing requirement that a certain proportion of public service ads must be aired. Consisting of representatives of advertisers, ad agencies, and the media, the Council carries out ad campaigns for various organizations. It decides which campaigns to undertake and routinely denies access to its services by advocates of anything controversial. Planned Parenthood and the "save the whale" campaign were turned down by the Ad Council, and the National Organization of Women's campaign to remove female stereotypes was initially denied support. Roughly one-third of the Council's annual $500 million expenditures advertise government programs ranging from the Peace Corps to President Gerald Ford's WIN (Whip Inflation Now) campaign. If not supporting government programs, Ad Council campaigns reflect interests of the corporate state. The campaign to end pollution urged viewers to pick up after picnics and stop littering the highways ("People start pollution. People can stop it.") but it made no mention of industrial causes of pollution.

Even the Public Broadcasting Service has not been entirely free to present a full range of public interest programs. Established in the early 1950s when the FCC set aside channels for educational television, National Educational Television (PBS) has always been a beggar. Since the 1950s the Ford Foundation granted it sizable amounts of money, but local stations have had to regularly carry on donation drives. In 1967 Congress underwrote the system, but PBS expenditures still only amounted to five percent of the nation's total TV spending. Budgetary constraints have limited PBS documentary work and resulted in the importation of many British dramas. TV critic Robert Sklar points out that PBS has carried virtually no avantegarde theater, music, film, dance, or video, and the diversity of American ethnic and subcultural life is ignored by PBS as much as by commercial TV.

During the Vietnam War, PBS aired a considerable number of anti-war, anti-establishment programs—*Who Invited Us?*, *Behind the Lines*, *The Great*

American Dream Machine—but it ultimately brought negative political response. In 1972 President Richard Nixon vetoed both a two-year and more modest one-year public TV appropriation. He then made it clear via White House spokesmen that to get his signature on the bill the bulk of federal money would have to go to local stations, not the networks; every federal dollar would have to be matched by two and one-half dollars from other sources; and the system had to deemphasize public affairs programming, leaving it to commercial broadcasters. Fortunately for PBS, oil company funds became available, but dollar matching requirements began a steady PBS pilgrimage to large corporations. By 1975 corporate money supported 40 percent of the system's programming.

Programming itself reflected the values of the corporate state, particularly on commercial TV. Corporate produced technological gadgetry has been ever present in police and spy programs, with special emphasis in science fiction shows. Big, complex technology overwhelmed evil people, whether on earth or in space. *The Six Million Dollar Man* implicitly suggested that "humans may ultimately exercise absolute control of their environment" via technology, and *Star Trek* was committed to technological progress as the solution to our problems. Viewers were also reminded that ours was a society of experts, from detectives and lawyers to teachers and doctors. These cool, unemotional, efficient experts all found their identity in their work. They were the epitome of corporate people, tireless and selfless, completely loyal to their profession and employer, unswerving in their eagerness to help the multitude of souls who lacked their skills. They were the very image of the sort of employee every supercorporation would wish to have.

In addition to reflecting its own interests and avoiding controversy, the TV industry has provided an anesthetic for Americans who live in a world which David Littlejohn described as "messy, unfair, technologically run, out of their grasp, and devoid of much human community." Programs fostered illusions of awareness, understanding, democratic participation, discussion of problems, conversation, order, and control. In doing so they reflected the conventional myths and ideal values of the national society— what Edward Shils has called the "culture of consensus." America's past, as presented in Alistair Cooke's *America: A Personal History of the United States*, the CBS *Bicentennial Minutes* series, and NBC's *Project XX* programs the "Jazz Age" and "Life in the Thirties," reinforced the notions about their history that Americans wanted to hold—America never lost a war, it remained just in God's eyes and was the land of opportunity, plenty, innocence, and piety. In a multitude of programs such as *Happy Days, Little House on the Prairie, Good Times,* and the *Mary Tyler Moore Show*, the real world, too, was befogged but accepted by viewers as what was really happening, because TV presented what Americans wanted to believe and felt they had worked hard to get.

The family has also been presented usually in an ideal way. In the 1950s *The Adventures of Ozzie and Harriet* found their way from radio to TV, offering a "down home" feeling of security, simple pleasures, and middle-class morality. It was just what affluent, suburban America wanted—a sense of timeless importance in the value of family. When the program ended in 1966, it may have reflected the 1960's counter-culture view of the traditional family structure as outdated, irrelevant, and unhealthy; but that very sort of family was reincarnated during the 1970s in *The Waltons*. Anne Roiphe writes "the Walton family is the ideal family as we all wish ours was: the one we would choose to come from; the one we would hope to create." Unlike *The Adventures of Ozzie and Harriet* or its contemporary *Leave It to Beaver*, both shows suggesting real live families, *The Waltons* was set in the 1930s, a time remembered somewhat mistily. Nevertheless, the ideal values of family solidarity, love, and cooperation were the same. The program's producer Lee Rich believed the series succeeded because America was suffering a loss of values: "Many people see ethical qualities in this family that they hope that they can get back to." Even family shows with only one parent, such as *Bonanza* and *The Big Valley*, while they reflected society's slow recognition of the real existence of single-parent families in the late 1960s, reinforced the warmth and security of the traditional, ideal family experience.

Single parents should remind us that males and females coexist in America, and TV has consistently reinforced the traditional sex roles of their existence. Until the 1970s virtually no females starred in continuing prime-time dramatic or situation comedy shows. By 1975 nine or 13 percent of that year's shows starred women or were women-oriented, 63 percent were male-oriented or had male leads, and the rest were general family-oriented shows. A survey by the National Organization of Women in 1972 revealed that of 1200 advertisements in which women appeared 43 percent were engaged in household tasks, 38 percent were adjuncts to men, 17 percent appeared as sex objects, and 0.3 percent were "autonomous people leading independent lives of their own." In drama and soap operas the same survey showed women portrayed only one fourth of all characters, they usually appeared in sexual contexts or romantic or family roles, and two out of three were engaged or married. Another 1975 study of sex roles in cartoons found that animated characters, including animals, were also three-fourths male, girls were subordinate to males as pretty teenagers or housewives, and male occupations compared to female were several times as diverse.

On advertisements women served men gaily, uncomplainingly, singing all the while. Almost all sick adults receiving attention and those receiving food were men, the providers women. Men, on the other hand, protected and defended. They confided only to other men ("My broker is E. F. Hutton, and Hutton says . . ."), and they bought so as not "to leave their family defenseless." Frank Mankiewicz and Joel Swerdlow remind us that "Mom in *The Brady Bunch*, rebuffed by one of her daughters in an offer of help

('Mom, I've got to speak to Dad; this is a math question') . . . , seems to be playing Everywoman." They add that even the invincible Maude at her first day on the job in a real estate office "broke down in tears and stormed out in what could only be called a snit." Motion pictures may have reflected the sexual revolution and feminist movement, but TV hardly did. Under great pressure during the 1970s from the National Gay Task Force and Gay Media Action, some programs included homosexual roles in series, though not overtly; traditional sex roles remained largely unaffected.

Television has reflected cultural change in society very slowly. Throughout most of its existence TV catered to the white middle class, reflecting the race and wealth of its owners and operators and their perceptions. Consequently, black Americans, when they first appeared on the screen in the 1950s, reflected the white stereotype of blacks. *Beulah* presented a black domestic working for a white family, and her friends were the "neighborhood domestic gang." *Amos and Andy* presented a similar white stereotype of the black urban neighborhood. In 1956 NBC undertook *The Nat King Cole Show,* the first black star variety program, but could find no sponsor. They went ahead, supporting it at $20,000 a week, and finally got Rheingold Beer to agree to co-sponsor, a practice uncommon in the 1950s when shows had single sponsors. However, no full sponsor was ever found, so the show died in December 1957. Not until 1966, with Sammy Davis, Jr., did the networks try again.

Indeed, in 1962, eight years after the Supreme Court's desegregation decision in *Brown* v. *Board of Education of Topeka* and many civil rights events, a two-week prime-time survey showed how little TV reflected the existence of blacks in America. Blacks appeared in only eighty-nine of 398.5 hours of viewing. In twenty-seven they were featured as singers, dancers, or musicians. The next highest rating was for news and documentary programs, where appearances were primarily transient and non-weekly. The lowest rating was for drama, where blacks appeared as walk-ons, maids, and in crowds. Gradually blacks got regular series parts during the 1960s—Ossie Davis in *Car 54, Where Are You?* and Bill Cosby in *I Spy*—and Diahann Carroll starred in 1968 as *Julia,* a middle-class black nurse. But opposition had been strong, as suggested by General Motors' 1963 threat to withdraw its sponsorship of an episode of *Bonanza* which introduced a black character. Not until the civil rights movement had subsided in the 1970s did blacks begin to be represented on TV with some measure of regularity.

A similar cultural lag by television existed in its reflection of the youthful counter-culture of the 1960s. At first TV presented the changing life-style in terms of teenie-boppers and hippies in the news. An implication of disgust was plain. In 1967 PBS briefly dipped into the work of underground film and fringe theater, inevitably reflecting subcultures, but commercial TV held back. Then, in 1968, a new look and new sound reflected what Erik Barnouw called a cry for relevance and the political upheavals of the Nixon presidency. Black, brown, and yellow faces appeared with long-haired males and an ethnic mix in clothing, hair styles, and language. Ethnic whites found representation in *Banacek, Colombo, Petrocelli, Kojak, Chico and the Man,* and *Rhoda.* TV seemed to have caught up, and Frank Mankiewicz and Joel Swerdlow suggested that sponsors and networks finally perceived that audiences besides the white middle-class had money to spend.

Some observers feel TV could not have been anything other than it has been. Jerry Mander argues the visual and auditory indistinctness of television, the technology itself, forced concentration on highlighted, action-packed subjects, values of competition inherent in sports and good versus evil themes, and clear-cut behavior. The nuances of slower, subtler rhythms would be lost, and even the news editors, writes Edward Epstein, consciously chopped out the dead wood and dull moments. Other critics, while not slipping into the abyss of technological determinism, have seized the notion of determined technology and argued people have consciously, perhaps conspiratorially aimed television at reinforcing certain values. Since TV has raised no essential questions about the structure of society and has affirmed the *status quo*, suggests Erik Barnouw, "the overwhelming absorption of tens of millions of mid-twentieth-century Americans in football games and struggles against cattle rustlers was a political achievement, in a class with the imperial Roman policy of bread and circuses." Finally, Raymond Williams believes the way TV developed reflected America's own "social and cultural definition" of itself. Our notions of free enterprise and public freedom defined the ownership and use of radio and blazed a trail for television, a continuum of America's tastes and habits from the popular novels of the late nineteenth century through radio-defined programming, and the corporate state's successful rise to power, wealth, and influence defined TV's development and use after World War II.

Since its commercial inception, television has presented Americans with formulized, ritualized programming. It has focused on conventional, national, white mores while emphasizing the special values of networks, sponsors, and other powerful forces of society. It has reflected America's thrust toward a mediated urban environment, her drive toward empire, and the interlock of corporate, political, and military interests. It has generally ignored the ethno-cultural, racial, sectional, and localistic diversities of America; and what it has not presented, or recognized only belatedly, has reflected America's overall conservatism. In doing all this it also presented a vision of reality bathed in happy endings and simplistic, swift, distinct solutions to problems; it focused on the exciting, inspiring, or catastrophic now.

"The 'reality' of television," observed Mankiewicz and Swerdlow, "established a bench mark that the 'reality' of reality cannot hope to reach." Yet 51 percent of Americans in 1976 felt television was more believable than newspapers (22 percent), magazines (9 percent), and radio (7 percent), according to a Roper Organization survey. Furthermore, 70 percent of those polled felt the TV industry's performance was excellent, better than churches, schools, police, and local government. Perhaps they were correct in their assessment, though one would hope Americans had not become metaphorically chained to their TV screens and, like Plato's cave dwellers, blind to the real world behind them, unable to differentiate between shadow and substance.

Suggested Readings

Erik Barnouw's *A History of Broadcasting in the United States*, 3 vols. (New York: Oxford University Press, 1966, 1968, 1970) and his condensation and updating of this trilogy, *Tube of Plenty: The Evolution of American Television* (New York: Oxford University Press, 1975), are indispensable general works on television. An earlier valuable study of television as a social institution is Harry J. Skornia, *Television and Society: An Inquest and Agenda for Improvement* (New York: McGraw-Hill, 1965). Recent important and provocative works are Raymond Williams, *Television: Technology and Cultural Form* (New York: Schoken Books, 1975) and Jerry Mander, *Four Arguments for the Elimination of Television* (New York: William Morrow & Co., 1978). Peter C. Rollins, "Victory at Sea: Cold War Epic," *Journal of Popular Culture*, 6 (Spring, 1973), pages 463-82, is very suggestive of the reflective qualities of television concerning America's overseas involvements; and Herbert I. Schiller, *Mass Communications and American Empire* (Boston: Beacon Press, 1971), discusses the Americanization of the Third World via the airwaves. Richard Bunce, *Television in the Corporate Interest* (New York: Praeger Publishers, 1976) is excellent on the corporate character of TV, and Fred Friendly's *Due to Circumstances Beyond Our Control* (New York: Random House, 1967) records the collision between profit and public interest at CBS which led to his resignation. Erik Barnouw, *The Sponsor: Notes on a Modern Potentate* (New York: Oxford University Press, 1978) is outstanding on the commercial nature of TV, and Paul A. Carter, *The Twenties in America* (2d ed., New York: Thomas Y. Crowell, 1975) integrates Leo Lowenthal's notions into the early development of the consumer society.

An early study suggesting TV is a stronger reinforcer than changer of society is Joseph T. Klapper, *The Social Effects of Mass Communications* (New York: The Free Press, 1960); and more provocative studies include Marshall McLuhan, *Understanding Media: The Extensions of Man* (New York: McGraw-Hill, 1964) and Edmund Carpenter, *Oh, What a Blow That Phantom Gave Me: An Anthropologist in the Electronic World* (New York: Holt, Rinehart & Winston, 1973). Frank Mankiewicz and Joel Swerdlow, *Remote Control: Television and the Manipulation of American Life* (New York: Times Book, 1978) is excellent; and Douglas Cater, *et al.*, *Television as a Social Force: New Approaches to TV Criticism* (New York: Praeger Publishers, 1975), which includes David Littlejohn's "Communicating Ideas by Television," is quite good. Perhaps the best anthology critiquing television is Horace Newcomb, ed., *Television: The Critical View* (New York: Oxford University Press, 1976), which contains Anne Roiphe's incisive "Ma and Pa and John Boy in Mythic America: The Waltons." Edward J. Epstein, *News from Nowhere* (New York: Random House, 1973) is a superb critique of TV news. Important journal articles include Marilyn Diane Fife, "Black Image in American TV: The First

Two Decades," *The Black Scholar,* 6 (November, 1974), pages 7-15; and Richard S. Tedlow, "Intellect on Television: The Quiz Show Scandals of the 1950s," *The American Quarterly,* 28 (Fall, 1976), pages 483-95. Finally, Richard M. Levison's "From Olive Oyl to Sweet Polly Purebread: Sex Role Stereotypes and Televised Cartoons," *Journal of Popular Culture,* 9 (Winter, 1975), pages 561-71, is outstanding among many articles on television in that journal.

Standing on the moon's surface, Apollo 15 astronaut James B. Irwin salutes the American flag during the third excursion the astronauts made outside their lunar lander. (Religious News Service Photo)

The Space Age

Tom Heiting

Today the topics of space and space travel are rapidly becoming an accepted part of the American cultural scene. This trend is the result of a concentrated government program of space development which was initiated in 1957 and lasted until 1975.

Accompanying technical growth of the space age was a media development of considerable visual and literary significance. Words such as "thrust," "satellite," "lunar," "reentry," "astronauts," and "orbital," to mention a few, took on an expanded meaning. The television and movie industries began to produce an increasing number of programs which contributed to the current "Star Wars Syndrome."

The personalities of Obi Wan Kenobe, Luke Skywalker, R2D2, Commander Adama, and Starbuck presently are influencing and indoctrinating the American public toward the next ventures in space. For many, despite some fear and apprehensions, space exploration interests offer a possible escape and a definite relief from the present problems of the country and the world. Suddenly, a new frontier exists! It is a frontier which has attracted the imagination of many citizens of the world, a frontier that will be probed further, explored and discovered in future "yarons."

Space Pioneers, the Accumulation Stage

Thoughts and visions of what existed beyond earth and in the universe have fascinated man since ancient times. The Greek educator Anaxagoras concluded around 465 B.C. that the moon's physical construction could be similar to that of the earth. In 160 B.C., Cicero's *Republic* presented a descriptive account of the size of the universe. Less than two hundred years later, Plutarch wrote about the possibility of mountains and valleys comprising some of the moon's landscape. Lucian of Samosata, an early novelist, wrote two works in A.D. 160 which dealt with traveling to the moon. *A True Story* and *The Flight to the Moon of Idaromenippus* represented scientific fantasies and the use of satire in describing early space ventures.

However, until the seventeenth century a large void existed which tended to keep earth and heaven separated, and this precluded any real concentration on the notion of space travel. It was not until Johannes Kepler, the discoverer of the laws of planetary motion, wrote *A Dream of the Moon* that interest was reawakened. Kepler's work described moon people as serpents who were intelligent and lived in lunar craters.

The scientific revolution of the seventeenth century set the cornerstone for future space research and travel when Issac Newton expounded on his third law of motion in the 1680s. Newton emphasized that action and reaction are always equal and opposite, and that forces acting between two bodies will move both in contrary directions. Newton also inferred that the principle would be applied to man's future encounters in space.

Some two hundred years later, Newton's legacy took on added meaning for a young visionary named Hermann Ganswindt. Born of a distinguished family in Prussia, young Ganswindt enjoyed all the advantages of a quality education. In college he rebelled against a career in law which led to his dismissal from the University of Berlin. By then, the young rebel was addicted to the concept of air travel and he constantly worked on designs of dirigible airships.

Locating in the Berlin area, he vigorously pursued a career as an inventor. It wasn't until he was in his mid-thirties that he began to advance his ideas related to space travel. Ganswindt applied Newton's third law of motion and suggested to often skeptical audiences the possibility of creating a fulcrum and movement in airless space. Included in his ideas were the inventor's designs of a cosmic vehicle to be driven by the thrust of exploding dynamite cartridges.

Frustrated because he was decades ahead of his time, Herman Ganswindt experienced a lifetime of scientific frustration and died in 1935. Future generations and scientists would confirm that Ganswindt's theories formed the basis for modern space travel.

A contemporary of Ganswindt, Konstantin Tsiolkovski was born in Russia in 1857. Reared in an atmosphere of poverty he nevertheless gained an education concentrating in physics. Convinced that air travel would be perfected, the aspiring young physicist often thought of the possibility of interplanetary travel.

Tsiolkovski became a physics teacher in Kaluga, Russia. He was known as the starving scientist who supported his experiments by reducing his diet to only Russian black bread, thereby saving money to purchase laboratory equipment. Konstantin Tsiolkovski spent twenty-five years ex-perimenting with theories and ideas that eventually laid the foundations for all rocket theory.

In 1898, Tsiolkovski wrote a paper entitled *The Exploration of Cosmic Space by Rocket*. Published in 1903, the work outlined the term "cosmic space" as the space between planets which constituted a total vacuum. The Russian also postulated that since the earth's atmosphere did not extend to the moon and other planets, a rocket traveling into space must have an airtight cabin and a continual supply of fresh oxygen. He determined that the major problem of space rocket travel research was propulsion. Since space was a vacuum, the principle of reaction or backward thrust was not feasible. This led the physicist to conclude that a rocket must carry its own retroactive mass. This, he calculated, would require larger rockets than commonly envisioned, and in order to achieve the maximum retroactive capacity, a propellant composed of liquid fuel and liquid oxygen was necessary. It was such a combination that was used in the first successful space rocket ventures; thus, it reconfirmed Konstantin Tsiolkovski's lifetime of patient research.

A few weeks after Tsiolkovski's death, the liquid propellant rocket which he planned, but never produced, became a reality at a test site located in Roswell, New Mexico. The successful scientist who fired the rocket to a height of 7,250 feet was an American named Robert H. Goddard. Despite the fact that this event largely went unnoticed, it marked the real begin-ning of the rocket age.

Goddard was born and raised in Worcester, Massachusetts. In college he studied physics, attended graduate school and earned a Ph.D. His interest in rockets led to his 1913 publication *A Method of Reaching Extreme Altitudes*. Goddard created a sensation in that this book considered the possibility of sending a rocket to the moon.

The publicity and public interest evoked by the book affected Goddard adversely. He was, by nature, a very quiet, unassuming individual who desired to remain in the background researching. The prospect of the news media invading his privacy and peering over his shoulder forced him into semi-seclusion. Goddard didn't feel the need for recognition, but he did require privacy to continue his research.

Naturally Goddard was aware of the historical background of the rocket as a weapon of war. His first real practical experience with rockets was not for the purpose of developing weapons of war but directed toward the use of rockets to fire life-saving lines to ships in distress. From that experience he concluded that the shape of the rockets being used were too blunt and not tapered enough to fully utilize the explosive energy used in firing them.

During World War I, Dr. Goddard was commissioned by the United States Navy to serve as an experimental physicist. He engaged in a wide variety of experiments and made enormous progress in improving the style and design of the rocket's combustion chamber and in laying the foundation for the production of a two-stage rocket.

Because of this wartime progress, Goddard's work became a high priority item, and once again he went to great lengths to ensure his privacy. Funded by the Smithsonian Institution and Guggenheim Foundation, he spent most of the 1920s patiently developing a successful liquid propellant. The continuing inquisitive nature of the press and the local public led Goddard to seek a new testing site location.

By the end of the 1920s, with increased financial assistance, the New England physicist began launching larger scale rockets from his new test sight in Roswell. Continued experimentation and the use of liquid propellants of oxygen and petrol paved the way for a series of successful rocket launchings. Heights of 7,000 feet and maximum speeds of 550 m.p.h. were reached.

With the outbreak of World War II, Goddard went back to work for the U.S. Navy. At the time of his death in 1945, he had laid all of the groundwork for the use of the modern liquid propellant rocket which won both fame and fear as a weapon of the German military forces known as the V2.

During the 1920s and 1930s, research and experimentation with rockets in Germany was uncoordinated and lacking finances. Despite the obstacles, there were outstanding contributors during that era. Hermann Oberth wrote *By Rocket to Interplanetary Space*. His work of the 1920s stressed that science was ready to conquer space. Oberth's publication established him as the founder of the science of astronautics. His career spanned both World Wars and the development of the United States' space program, of which he was a consultant.

Klaus Riedel, Rudolf Nebel, and Willy Ley all played important roles during the 1930s in building rockets that would become the basic prototypes for the German V2. Not only did these scientists work at perfecting a solid structural design, but their experiments with various liquid propellants began to concentrate on the need for a "super thrust capacity" as a basic necessity for future space travel.

The advent of Adolf Hitler in 1933 created a period of upheaval for German scientists interested in rocket and space travel. With the increased militarization of Germany, it was decreed that their efforts should be utilized for purposes of national defense. It's ironic that the field of rocket engineering received its greatest stimulus during the World War II years. Because of the high priority given to the development of new long-range weapons, Germany poured substantial technical and financial resources into such projects.

It was in this tension-packed atmosphere that the early period of modern rocket and space technology began to grow. The German program produced an exceptional brain trust of talent. One such example was Eugene Sanger, an aeronautical engineer whose interest in rocket propulsion led him to publish *The Technique of Rocket Flight* in the early 1930s. This work came to be regarded as one of the most important contributions made to the technical literature of rocket thrust capability. Another was Hermut von

Zborowski, a friend and colleague of Sanger who, as an aircraft engineer, perfected various propellants and techniques which led to significant progress in the key area of constructing combustion chambers. A third was General Walter Dornberger, an engineer, who headed Germany's rocket development program and directed the production of the V2. With the conclusion of the war, Dornberger was employed as a consultant on rocket ballistics by the United States.

The premiere figure of the German era was Wernher von Braun. Born in Posen, in 1912, the boy quickly demonstrated a superior intellect. After a comfortable boyhood and the accumulation of a brilliant scholastic record in school, he began his technical studies at Charlottenburg Technical School and later at the University of Berlin.

It was during this period that the rocket and space mania had reached its peak in Germany. The news featured countless stories on theories and experiments. Von Braun's involvement in rocket engineering brought him into contact with other German scientists, including Dornberger. By the early 1930s, the young physicist went to work for the German Army's Ordnance Ballistics Department. By 1936, the successes of von Braun, Dornberger, and associates led to the establishment of a rocket center at Peenemunde located in the Northeast coastal area of Germany.

The next five years saw the world plunged into World War II. The research and testing at Peenemunde took on a greater urgency. Through the efforts of von Braun, and Drs. Theil, Wahrmke, and Stienhoff progress on the development of long-range rockets was considerable. Technical innovations related to the power unit and combustion chambers of the rockets were worked out. The result was the successful launching of a rocket in 1942. It was 45 feet long, weighed 12 tons, and implemented the use of 25 tons of thrust. It rose to an altitude of 54 miles and matched the speed of sound.

The German war effort was suffering by 1943, and Hitler authorized the construction of rockets for weapons. This project was placed under the direction of thirty-one-year-old Wernher von Braun. The research behind the project required experiments in multi-stage rockets and led the new director to consider the possibilities of space flight. The carnage and suffering caused by the rockets has been documented, but they were used too late in the war to alter the outcome. It was tragic irony that such was the atmosphere in which long-range rockets proved themselves and set the course for the future of space exploration.

In 1945, as the war drew to its conclusion, von Braun played a key role in the closing of the Peenemunde test site. Then the German scientists positioned themselves so they could surrender to American forces. Their surrender became part of a scientific "scramble" whereby the United States won the services of leading German scientists. "Operation Paperclip" as it was called, was the vehicle which carried von Braun and colleagues to the

United States. From 1946 until 1952, Wernher von Braun was associated with the V2 program which found a new home in the United States' rocket and space program.

The Space Race, Stage One

The defeat of Germany and Japan during the war years was in part due to the full use of the massive technological and industrial might that the United States had at its disposal. The military strategy of America and her Allies leaned more toward the effective use of airpower and the eventual development of a potent knockout weapon—the atom bomb.

During the war, a key arms race developed between the United States and Germany, revolving around the atom versus rocket power controversy. With the successful use of the atom bomb against Japan and the defeat of Germany, Americans temporarily concluded that they had the ultimate weapon—security against threats of aggression.

The defensive posture of the United States was of prime concern with the emergence of the Cold War. The psychological and physical struggle between the forces of democracy and communism put an even greater emphasis on the arms race. Despite advances in the field of airpower, the development and concentration on rocket power was second to the perfection of the atom and the development of hydrogen and nuclear weapons.

Although experiments and tests relevant to space travel were conducted, it appeared as if space was a scientific luxury to be bequeathed to future generations. At International Astronautical gatherings, bold scientific predictions were made, but it wasn't until the 1950s that both the United States and Russia were involved in programs designed to place instrument-carrying satellites into space. The man on the street was aware of the high priority given to space technology by the United States, and the race into outer space began.

Because of Wernher von Braun's work as leader of the U.S. Army's Guided Missile Division at Huntsville, Alabama, and the successful experiments of high level rocket power, the prevailing sentiment seemed to be that the United States would automatically assume the lead in the space race.

American pride was jolted severely on October 5, 1957, when the Soviet Union announced a successful launching of Sputnik I, the first man-made earth satellite. This was followed one month later by a second satellite which carried a dog into orbit. How could it be! After all, the United States had secured the services of a majority of the German rocket experts and already was simulating outer atmospheric conditions equal to 200 miles above earth. American scientists were investigating the psychological aspects of space travel and possible psychoses in manned space travel. Only a matter of months prior to Sputnik I, an American Jupiter rocket had been launched to a height of 700 miles, accelerating to 14,000 miles per hour.

The Eisenhower administration initially issued a low-key response to news of Russia's success. The President explained that the United States had a controlled space program and was not engaged in a space race and that the country's defensive structure was secure. That stated position didn't last very long as ex-President Harry Truman, members of Congress, the military, and the public began to voice loud concern. Most Americans recognized the propaganda value of the Soviet achievements. "The Americans have been beaten!" was not a digestible phrase. Communist technology triumphs over democratic technology? The international political scene would never be the same.

Dr. von Braun took advantage of the situation to emphasize publicly that a lack of finances had placed the United States in a secondary position. He called for a better public relations approach to the space program, more prestige for American scientists and their research, and a consolidation of the overall space effort. And America painfully re-evaluated her entire space program.

By early November, President Eisenhower conceded the defects of the U.S. program along with the advantages the Soviet Union had gained. Dr. James R. Killian, Jr., president of the Massachusetts Institute of Technology, was named to head up the U.S. space program. The appointment of a civilian gave credence to the rumors that competition existed between the armed forces concerning the space effort. The trauma of the 1957 space drama had a final act when the United States attempted to launch its Vanguard spacecraft. The Vanguard failed when the three-stage rocket exploded on the launching pad at Cape Canaveral.

The years 1958-1961 represented a learning experience for the United States. The consolidation of the space program was undertaken with the creation of a civilian National Aeronautics and Space Administration in April of 1958. The facilities of the armed forces eventually were absorbed into the program; thus, it eliminated a possible competitive friction.

The international aspects of space exploration continued to grow in importance as Secretary of State John Dulles called for an International Commission to control space for peaceful purposes. This agency was to function under the auspices of the United Nations, a move which gained the support of many United Nations participants, including Russia. Unfortunately, the proposal quickly bogged down in debate related to defensive considerations and would not be approved until late in December of 1958.

Earlier in the year, the United States launched its first successful satellite, Explorer I. This success was credited largely to Wernher von Braun whose research team worked on the sixty-nine foot, 68,000-pound rocket. Other satellite successes followed, but so did some failures especially with the Vanguard rockets.

The space race accelerated as the Russians launched Sputnik III and demonstrated superiority in "thrust capability." The satellite carried a payload one hundred times heavier than U.S. satellites, but it was preceded by many failures, indicating that Soviet space technology also had problems.

Space discussions concentrated more and more on manned space flights, and Dr. von Braun paved the way for the organization of volunteers for the projected launchings. NASA created Project Mercury, gave it number one priority, and aimed for a man in space within two to three years.

The moon became the source of attention; it was no longer remote and inaccessible. Observatories concentrated on the more than 30,000 craters dotting the moon's surface. Jagged mountain chains and peaks higher than Mt. Everest were brought to the public's attention. The mystery of the far side of the moon attracted considerable scientific attention. Jules Vernes' novels *From the Earth to the Moon* and *Round the Moon*, despite being published in the 1860s, were now read by thousands. Christianity even gave its blessing to space travel by indicating that it inevitably would expand man's knowledge of God.

So it was that many of the space efforts of 1959-60 were directed at the moon. The Soviet's Lunik I probed past the moon and was expected to take approximately 450 days to make a circle around the sun. Other Russian successes in this area further began to convince a wary but interested public that the United States still was behind in research and rocketry.

By March, the United States sent the second man-made planet in orbit around the sun. The success of Pioneer 4 left Americans believing that the country was only a matter of months behind in the space race. But in the fall of 1959 the Russian space scientists sent rockets Lunik II and Lunik III to the moon. Lunik II delivered an instrument package; Lunik III photographed the elusive dark side of the moon. The Soviet successes took on even more meaning in November 1959 when a United States Atlas-Able rocket aimed at the moon exploded and fell, burning in the Atlantic Ocean.

The failure of the United States to keep pace with Russia caused much concern among leaders and citizens. As the election of 1960 approached, space became a political issue in the Nixon-Kennedy campaign. Politicians and other Americans grew aware of the lack of sufficient booster power or thrust. The need for a million-pound-thrust engine became a high priority item. At the same time, the National Aeronautics and Space Administration chose McDonnell Aircraft Corporation to build the Mercury capsule for manned spaceflight. The Space Administration also selected seven volunteers as astronauts and presented them to the American public with considerable fanfare. Thus, the names of Carpenter, Cooper, Glenn, Grissom, Schirra, Shepard, and Slayton became the basis for new public interest and curiosity as they prepared to lead their nation into outer space.

Despite enormous efforts by American scientists to produce the necessary space rockets, it was conceded that the Russians held a substantial lead in this aspect of space technology. That realization was reflected at times in increased international tensions concerning the role of space. The United Nations tried to prevent any impasse by taking action through a permanent committee. The committee was organized to oversee the peaceful uses of outer space. The success of the committee was largely the result of a compromise between Russia and the United States. Both acknowledged that rivalries in space were absurd in light of the awesomeness of exploring the universe.

Many Americans fixed their attention on the Mercury program and the seven astronauts involved in their rigorous training program. The Mercury capsule was tested, and the projected manned space flight drew near. A considerable amount of attention was given to the safety of placing a man in orbit. The United States' media took great pains to point out the elaborate safety precautions that were part of the American space program.

Manned Flights, Stage Two

The human dimension of space travel became a reality on April 12, 1961, when Yuri Gagarin, a Soviet cosmonaut, orbited the earth once and became the first recorded space traveler. This orbit fulfilled predictions made earlier by Soviet officials, including Premier Nikita Khrushchev. Gagarin, a 27-year-old air force pilot, accomplished his feat using a 10,395-pound space vehicle named Vostok I. In congratulating Gagarin, Khrushchev stated, "Let the capitalist countries try to catch up with our country which has blazed a trail into space and which has launched the world's first cosmonaut."

The new American President John F. Kennedy had given the United States space program a top priority when he took office. Not surprised by the Russian's success, Kennedy declared the American intention to be first in the race to put a spaceman on the moon. He told Congress, "No single space project will be more exciting, more impressive, or more important, and none will be so difficult or expensive to accomplish."

This new commitment to the space effort was exactly what space officials and many Americans wanted to hear. But with the possibility of increased costs, certain segments of the media and the public began to ask openly if the expenditures were justified. This seemed to be a valid question in view of the need for internal improvements in the country and the ever-increasing amounts of foreign aid sent abroad.

Then the Soviets scored a second coup in August when Major Gherman Titov blasted off in Vostok II for a 25-hour mission that took him on seventeen trips around the earth. The United States edged into manned space flight in 1961 with two suborbital flights.

Commander Alan Shepard, Jr., became the first U.S. astronaut in space May 5, 1961. He was launched in Freedom 7, a 4,000-pound Mercury capsule which propelled him 116 miles into space on a fifteen-minute flight. On July 21, Air Force Captain Virgil Grissom completed a similar flight lasting eighteen minutes. Grissom experienced some anxious moments as his capsule sank after splashing down in the Atlantic. Abandoning the capsule, Grissom swam to safety and the mission was a success.

Armed with these successes, President Kennedy appealed to Congress and the American public to authorize an accelerated program which would place an American on the moon before 1970. Interestingly, the President emphasized the need to achieve this goal as a requisite for strengthening the United States military and economic image before the world. He called for a program of overall improvements to cost an estimated $7-9 billion and to be spread out over a five-year period. Later, in the fall of 1961, NASA announced plans to build a research and command center in Houston, Texas, for the Project Apollo Moon program. In November, North American Aviation Inc., was given the contract for the design and construction of an Apollo spaceship.

By the end of the year, both Russia and the United States had launched numerous rockets for purposes of gathering reconnaissance, weather and general space data all of which seemed to be aimed at contributing to the final assault on the moon. These activities as well as the extraordinary increase in space activities led the United Nations to adopt a resolution barring national appropriation of celestial bodies.

The United States space ventures had a rewarding year in 1962. Three successful orbital flights were completed suggesting that the rough spots that often had plagued the space program were eliminated.

Because of the complete coverage by U.S. media, the five-hour flight of Marine Lieutenant Colonel John Glenn in Friendship VII on February 20, 1962, was viewed by millions. For the first time, the real story of space travel was seen as Glenn circled the earth three times before splashing down in the Caribbean. Lieutenant Colonel Glenn's mission was a matter of pride to most Americans who began to share the sense of adventure which had become a vital part of this new frontier.

The media also was on hand to record the events surrounding the three orbital trips of Navy Lieutenant Commander Malcolm Scott Carpenter which were made on May 27. His ship, Aurora VII, blasted off from Cape Canaveral in the nose of an Atlas booster, and, like Glenn, he experienced hours of weightlessness as the craft attained a speed of 17,532 miles per hour.

Not to be outdone, the Russians performed a space spectacular three months later. This consisted of launching Major Andrian Nikolayev in Vostok III on August 11 and the next day launching Lieutenant Colonel Pavel Popovich in Vostok IV into practically the same orbit. Both space vehicles were brought down August 15. Nikolayev circled the earth a record 64 times, and Popovich completed 48 orbits. The launchings were so accurate that both cosmonauts were able to contact each other, and Nikolayev reported that he could see Popovich's craft through his port window. Thus, the "space twins" were able to demonstrate that Russia was still very much in this competitive race to the moon.

Commander Walter M. Schirra became the third American to be sent into orbit. Schirra's flight aboard Sigma VII October 3, 1962, was one of the most successful in the American program. He spent almost nine hours in space, orbited the earth five and three-quarters times, and splashed down in the central Pacific less than four miles from the waiting carrier Kearsarge.

The success of the Mercury program did not insulate the Kennedy administration from continued severe criticism of the costs of space travel. The space budget was at $5.4 billion a year already, and all indications were that the costs would continue to increase. Vice President Johnson answered some of the critics in the fall of 1962 when he declared, "Because the space age is here we are recruiting the best talent regardless of race or religion, and the senseless patterns of discrimination in employment are broken up."

A continuance of the space efforts was clear with the selection of nine new astronauts in September 1962. The list included both military and civilian selections, all having extensive flight experience, all being less than thirty-five years old, and all under six feet tall. The new astronauts to complete the final stages of the moon quest were Neil Armstrong, Frank Borman, Charles Conrad, Jr., James Lovell, Jr., James McDivitt, Elliott See, Jr., Thomas Stafford, Edward White, and John Young.

Target Moon, Stage III

The Gemini Space Program was officially begun in 1964. It was coordinated out of the Johnson Space Center, Houston, Texas under the direction of Dr. Robert R. Gilruth. The objectives of the program were directed toward experimenting with long duration flights, to effect rendezvous and docking procedures with two orbiting vehicles in space, to perfect reentry methods and landing techniques, and to continue the study of the effects of weightlessness and physiological reactions of crew members.

During the year, the American space enthusiasts had to be content with two unmanned Gemini flights undertaken for purposes of scientific testing. Russia, however, continued to add still another first with the successful launching of a spaceship carrying a three-man crew. The craft, named the Voskhod I, spent over twenty-four hours in orbit.

On March 23, 1965, the first of the manned Gemini flights was launched from Houston. Nine more manned space shots followed between March 1965 and November 1966. Astronauts Virgil Grissom and newcomer, John Young, piloted the three-orbital-flight. The Gemini sequence was so concentrated that it began to produce a blasé attitude among many Americans. Those familiar with the early ventures of Shepard, Glenn, et. al., now had a difficult time remembering both the flights and the names of the new astronauts. It was with the Gemini space program that the United States appeared to draw even with the Russians although the Soviet achievements still seemed more spectacular to most observers.

A case in point was the March 1965 space walk by Colonel Pavel Belyayev. The Russian cosmonaut operated out of Voskhod II as part of a two-manned effort, and he successfully performed a series of tests during a ten-minute space walk.

The duration objective of the Gemini program was accomplished through flights five and seven. Gemini V, with astronauts L. Gordon Cooper and Charles Conrad, Jr., was in orbit for eight days between August 21-29, 1965. The total flight time was near 191 hours. Gemini VII, with astronauts Frank Borman and James Lovell, Jr., recorded a fourteen day mission between December 4-18, 1965. The conclusion to the flight was a touchdown in the western Atlantic just a little over six miles from the USS Wasp recovery vessel.

The first successful docking maneuvers were carried out by Gemini VIII with astronauts Neil Armstrong and David R. Scott. After six hours in space, the Gemini made contact with an unmanned spacecraft and completed the first docking of two vehicles in space. Sometime later Charles Conrad and Richard Gordon, Jr. successfully completed re-entry experiments.

With the completion of the Gemini program, the United States was very near to having recorded 2,000 manned hours in space. The overall program was an unqualified success. Not only was the timetable for the moon looking good, but for the first time in the space race American technology was at the point of surpassing the Soviet Union. This tended to reverse the earlier Russian claims that communist technology was superior and more efficient than its democratic counterpart.

The final drive toward a moon landing incorporated the use of the Saturn launch vehicle program. Various unmanned flights were made for research and experiments with the rocket guidance system; and the concept of clustered rocket engines was tested and validated. The program also began using liquid hydrogen as the primary rocket fuel. This propellant provided twice the fuel economy of earlier fuels.

During this phase of the space program, the stark reality of the dangers involved became apparent when on January 27, 1967, tragedy struck at Cape Kennedy. Astronauts Virgil Grissom, Edward White, and Roger Chaffee were killed when a fire erupted inside the Apollo Module they were testing. The cause of the fire was traced to faulty wiring in the craft.

In 1968, the manned segment of the moon program was inaugurated. An October flight lasted eleven days and gave a clear indication that the intent of the program was geared toward missions taking days instead of hours. Apollo VII, manned by astronauts Walter Schirra, Don Eisele, and Walt Cunningham, was judged 101 percent successful and included the first live TV coverage from a manned vehicle.

The next three launchings brought the United States closer to the moon landing. President Kennedy's challenge and prediction of the early 1960s was on the verge of becoming reality. Apollo VIII completed ten revolutions of the moon to gather important lunar photography. Apollo X, under the direction of astronauts Thomas Stafford, John Young, and Eugene Cernan, completed thirty-one revolutions around the moon between May 18-26 of 1969. This mission came within nine miles of the moon's surface in a dress rehearsal for the actual lunar landing.

There was tremendous worldwide media buildup preceding the landing on the moon by Apollo XI. Public interest which had lagged now began to peak. The stage was set, the American space effort was poised on a green go signal while the moon patiently awaited the new arrivals.

It was July 20, 1969, at 10:56 p.m. Eastern Daylight Time. Millions of people anxiously watched their TV sets as astronaut Neil Armstrong, commander of Apollo XI, set foot on the moon. This drama culminated a national effort which began in 1961. The emotion of the moment was enormous, the historical significance forever, a new era in space travel had begun. Armstrong was equal to the occasion when he took his momentous step commenting, "That's one small step for a man, one giant leap for mankind."

Participating in this unparalleled achievement was Edwin Aldrin, the pilot of the lunar module. An estimated half-billion people watched on TV as Aldrin descended the ladder and began to record the total event at close range with a small television camera he carried.

After making post-landing checks of the lunar module, the two astronauts routinely began to run through a series of tests and experiments. This included the collecting of moon rock samples and setting up camera equipment to transmit several panoramic shots of the immediate area. The crew next set up a specially constructed 3' x 5' American flag. Nationalism had its moment during those historic hours on the moon, but perhaps the true meaning of all space efforts was best reflected on a plaque the astronauts unveiled and mounted. It read:

> Here Men from Planet Earth
> First Set Foot Upon the Moon
> July 1969 A.D.
> We Came in Peace for All Mankind

Aldrin and Armstrong reentered the lunar module after about two hours on the moon. A rest period followed; then the two moon walkers completed another of the tension-packed tasks of the journey. The countdown for the blast-off from the moon began at 1:54 p.m. EDT, and the world viewers held their breaths as the ascent took place without incident.

Rendezvous with the command module piloted by the third man of the team, Michael Collins, and docking took place at 5:35 p.m. EDT. The return trip was routine—without complications. The three astronauts splashed down, were issued isolation suits, and boarded the aircraft carrier *Hornet* where they were placed in a mobile isolation unit. It was there that they received the congratulations of President Nixon who was on board to welcome them back home.

Thus, the eight-day journey of the Eagle (Apollo XI) and its crew came to an end. Perhaps the highlight of the journey, besides the moon landing, was the exceptional amount of television exposure that the millions of viewers were able to receive from "old man moon." The international aspects of the mission were numerous. Perhaps President Nixon put it best when he spoke to Armstrong and Aldrin on the moon from the White House. Nixon told the astronauts, "As you talk from the Sea of Tranquility, it inspires us to double our efforts to bring peace and tranquility to the earth. For one priceless moment in the whole history of man all the people on this earth are truly one."

Between November 1969 and December 1973 there were five more missions that accomplished lunar landings. Each effort was directed at exploring various geographic areas of the moon. The amount of time spent by each crew was increased to the extent that Apollo 17, the last of the series, spent better than twenty-two hours on the lunar surface.

Not content with the conquest of the moon and number one ranking in the space league, the United States (during most of 1973 and into 1974) conducted the Skylab space program. This approach made full use of both military and civilian participants. The overall objective was to conduct extended missions to test the endurance of both the crews and the space vehicles. Three such skylab shots were conducted. The final mission, Skylab IV, had a space journey of eighty-four days, one hour, and sixteen minutes. Composed of astronauts Gerald P. Carr, William R. Pogue, and Edward Gipson, the craft made 1,214 revolutions of the earth.

At the end of the Apollo Skylab program the United States had completed thirty-one flights using forty-seven astronauts and accumulating 22,432 hours in space. Americans had good reason to be proud of those accomplishments in the field of space, technology, and communications. There was, however, the question of cost which became a burning issue during the inflationary periods of the late 1960s and 1970s. The estimated cost of the Mercury through Apollo-Skylab programs was $30 billion.

International Space, Stage Four

Understanding the competitive aspects of the space race which involved Russia and the United States, the organization of the first international manned space flight seemed appropriate. Through this effort the bond of world unity which space travel seemed to effect took on real meaning.

The Apollo-Soyuz test project was conducted between July 15-24, 1975. The objectives of the mission were considerable aside from the international-political factors. They included spacecraft rendezvous, docking, undocking, crew transfer, interaction of control centers, and interaction of spacecraft crews.

The launching phase was a two-stage operation. The Soyuz with cosmonauts Alexey Leonov and Valeriy Kubasov was launched from Baikonur, Kosakhstan in Russia on July 15. Seven hours later, the Apollo blasted off from the Kennedy Space Center with Thomas Stafford, Vance Brand, and Donald Slayton making up the crew.

The entire mission lasted better than nine days and achieved all of the objectives previously stated. The harmony and good will created by this joint mission was perhaps the most important aspect of the flight.

Currently the United States' Space Program is involved in the research and testing of various models and crafts to be used in space shuttles. Such efforts will lead to interplanetary space travel based on the research and data collected from the universe.

Towards that end the 54½-hour journey of the space shuttle Columbia, April 12-14, 1981 represented a significant breakthrough for the United States. Despite financial problems and technical delays, pilots John Young and Robert Crippen blasted off the Cape Canaveral launching pad and guided as well as maneuvered the 102-ton flying machine to a practically flawless journey.

The Columbia's feat clearly established the feasibility of shuttle flights for future space projects. Equally important is the fact that the success of Young, Crippen and the Columbia boosted both the morale and interest of the American public in space travel. Not since the heady days of the moon landings a decade before had the nation revealed such enthusiasm for America's role in space.

Suggested Bibliography

Clark, Arthur C. (ed.), *The Coming of the Space Age: Famous Accounts of Man's Probing of the Universe* (Meredith Press, New York, 1967), endeavors to bring together a wide sampling of man's early and developing interest in space and the universe. The significance of the work is it allows the reader an opportunity to see the continuity of interest in the space age and how that trend relates to modern successes and ventures into space.

Eisenhower, Dwight D., *The White House Years: Waging Peace, 1956-1961* (Doubleday & Co. Inc., New York, 1965). This autobiography is Mr. Eisenhower's recollections of his second term in the presidency and the real beginning of the American surge into space following the successful Russian launching of Sputnik I. President Eisenhower's attitude towards space development and the United States' role in the space drama was a constantly changing one. The volume enables students to understand the times and pressures operating on the Eisenhower administration related to space.

Emme, Eugene M., *Aeronautics and Astronautics: An American Chronology of Science and Technology in the Exploration of Space, 1915-1960* (NASA, Washington, D. C., 1961), probes into the complex technology of space development. Beginning in the World War I years, the author seeks to explain, in a detailed fashion, the painstaking amount of research and experimentation in the United States up to 1960.

Emme, Eugene M., *A History of Space Flight* (Holt, Rinehart, and Winston, New York, 1965), develops the saga of space flight from various theories and shows the advances made in terms of the planning and experimental stages, culminating with man's flight into space in the mid 1960s.

Gartmann, Heinz., *The Men Behind the Space Rockets* (Weidenfeld and Nicolson, London, England, 1955), provides a concentrated investigation of the men and minds that preceded the successful ventures into space. Special emphasis is paid to the early pioneers and individual efforts that each made. The volume clearly establishes that the newness of space is, in reality, the drawing together of the genius of the past as represented by the early pioneers and scientists.

Green, Constance M. and Lomask, Mitton, *Vanguard: A History* Smithsonian Institution Press, Washington, D. C., 1971), develops the complete background and history of the attempts of the U. S. to achieve successful space launchings using the Vanguard rockets. The volume is especially complete in pointing out the areas of difficulty causing many of the launchings to fail.

McDonald, Robert L., Hesse, Walter H., *Space Science* (Charles Merrill Publishing Co., Columbus, Ohio, 1970), guides the reader into a general orientation to the vastness of space science. The layman is offered a view into the philosophy which pervades any attempts in conquering space.

Hunter, M. W., *Thrust Into Space* (Holt, Rinehart, and Winston, New York, 1966), deals with thrust capability as the most important single element of space travel, and propulsion as a key to further space exploration and exploitation. The volume is geared towards the technically orientated high school or early college student.

McGraw-Hill Encyclopedia of Space (McGraw-Hill Book Co., New York, 1968), is a general source providing quick, concise, useful information for individuals seeking knowledge concerning space language or descriptions of space exploits.

NASA Facts, Educational Publication of the National Aeronautics And Space Administration (U. S. Government Printing Office, Washington, D. C., 1977), is a detailed publication allowing the reader to trace the role and programs of the National Aeronautics and Space Administration. The order of development makes the source helpful to individuals seeking an organized insight into the United States primary space agency.

Rickert, Russell K., *Astronomy and Space Exploration* (Addison-Wesley Publishing Co., Reading, Mass., 1974), notes the importance of astronomy to the successful understanding and exploration of space. The work demonstrates that space vehicles or space travelers are functioning in an atmosphere which is constantly revealing itself to mankind.

Sobel, Lester A. (ed.), *Space: From Sputnik to Gemini* (Facts on File, Inc., New York, 1965), represents the most complete work available on the American space effort from 1957 to 1965. The work blends together a narrative of the events dealing with the early U. S. space lag and the course charted that resulted in the U. S. successful participation in the space race and a new era for mankind.

Burning discarded automobile batteries near Houston, Texas, 1972. (EPA-Documerica, U.S. Environmental Protection Agency)

Battling the Environment: Conservation Turns to Ecology

Warren B. Johnson

In his 1970 State of the Union address, President Richard Nixon declared, "The great question of the seventies is, shall we surrender to our surroundings, or shall we make our peace with nature and begin to make reparations for the damage we have done to our air, our land, and our water?" He went on to devote a large part of that address to environmental issues. Less than three months later another event emphasized the heightened public concern about ecology and the environment when Earth Day was celebrated on April 22, 1970. For the first time the environment had become a "grassroots" political issue and one with which the average citizen could identify.

How to explain why this intense public interest surfaced at this particular time (opposition to the Vietnam War was entering its bitterest phase) is not easy. It is certain, however, that alarm about the environment did not originate with the American President or with Earth Day organizers. As one author has pointed out, the Romans debated the handling of waterborne sewage, and in 1273 Edward I of England ordered a ban on the burning of sea coal in London to relieve air pollution. In the fourteenth century Richard II handed down a decree forbidding river pollution. The roots of environmental concern extend deep into history.

Why did public interest in environmental matters appear in the 1970s rather than at some earlier time? The answer is probably impossible to state with certainty, but the growing interest in pollution control in the post-World War II era suggests several factors which, taken together, could explain this phenomenon.

Affluence would likely head any list of factors, both as part of the cause and part of the solution. The phenomenal postwar production created a standard of living that used up resources at an alarming rate, never before witnessed. The environment became polluted as never before, creating a mountain of waste which gave no evidence of stopping. Production growth was matched with population growth and urban expansion ("urban sprawl"). Citizens of the affluent society were becoming painfully aware of the consequences of growth and were beginning to doubt that "bigger was really better."

Affluence had produced the problem, but ironically, it was only an affluent society that could afford to attempt to solve the problem. In many ways concern with the environment is a luxury that only a wealthy nation can afford. A wealthy society with ample leisure time can afford to concern itself with recreation and aesthetic matters. It can also afford to bring the necessary resources together to attack the problem of the environment.

Finally, cleaning up the environment has become an attractive issue to politicians of all persuasions. As noted above, Richard Nixon, a public figure not known for his liberal leanings, saw the environment as a current and lively topic of national concern.

"Ecology" and "environment" were not household words in the last century, but already there were movements afoot which eventually would culminate in the Earth Day observance of 1970. Three distinct (but related) movements were under way which were clearly the ancestors of the Environmentalists of the 1970s. These three were: (1) the preservation movement, associated with persons such as John Muir: (2) the parks-boulevards-city beautiful movement, typified by Frederick Law Olmsted: and (3) the conservation movement, represented by Theodore Roosevelt and Gifford Pinchot. Yet even these were not the beginning of the environmental movement in this country.

Environmental awareness arrived with some of the first colonial immigrants. William Penn began his colony with the careful planning of Philadelphia. James Oglethorpe put considerable effort into a design for Savannah. In 1791 the Founding Fathers engaged the engineering genius of Washington's continental army staff to draw up a plan for the new national capital. These are a few of the early instances, all of them aimed at improving the aesthetic.

As towns and cities in the nineteeth century began to grow more extensively, modest efforts of preserving and creating a natural environment were begun. Tree planting programs were started in Charleston, Albany, and New York City in the 1820s, where these cities passed ordinances protecting such efforts. Still later (in the 1830s) environmental attention spread to creating promenades and public squares.

In the 1830s a movement began to design and construct sylvan cemeteries on the outskirts of large cities. The first, Mt. Auburn in Cambridge, Massachusetts outside of Boston, soon became an important recreational attraction for Bostonians, cramped for space and starved for views of natural beauty. One contemporary visitor described the scene as follows:

> The avenues are winding in their course and exceedingly beautiful in their gentle circuits, adapted picturesquely to the inequalities [sic] of the surface of the ground, and producing charming landscape effects from this natural arrangement . . . The gates of the enclosure are opened at sunrise and closed at sunset, and thither crowds go to meditate, and to wander in a field of peace.

Many other cities followed the lead of Cambridge and built rural cemeteries on their outskirts with many of them clearly planned as recreational space, in addition to their primary function. So popular did these places become that, for example, in a nine-month period in 1848 some 30,000 people visited the Laurel Hill Cemetery outside Philadelphia. Municipal guidebooks of the time called visitors' attention to Greenwood Cemetery in New Orleans and Cave Hill Cemetery in Louisville. Rural cemeteries soon were too popular as recreational sites, and it became evident that a substitute would have to be found to fill this public need.

Andrew Jackson Downing, an early landscape architect and writer, whose aim was to bring nature into design and architecture, noted this trend and urged cities to establish regular public parks designed along the lines of the rural cemeteries. As the editor of the popular journal, *The Horticulturist*, his advice was widely sought and his ideas influenced many designers and builders in the 1840s. At the time of his death in 1852 his landscape firm was working on the landscaping of the mall in the Nation's capital. His social outlook was clearly stated in one of his writings:

> The true policy of republics is to foster the taste for great public libraries, sculpture and picture galleries, parks and gardens, which all may enjoy, since our institutions wisely forbid the growth of private fortunes sufficient to achieve these desirable results in any other way.

The urban parks movement began in the 1840s when *New York Post* editor, William Cullen Bryant, opened a campaign to provide the nation's largest metropolis with a suitable recreational area. The result was Central Park, the country's first major urban park, begun in 1853 and destined to be imitated by many other cities.

The designer of Central Park was Frederick Law Olmsted, a friend of Downing who had developed an interest in landscape design, and his collaborator, Calvert Vaux, Downing's business partner. Together they created a park which emphasized natural features and disturbed original topography as little as possible. The design was in sharp contrast to the stylized form of the European park. Olmsted noted that this approach was more economical, but the main justification was philosophical and aesthetic.

Olmsted believed in the need to consider the city in relation to the total physical environment. The aim was to preserve the natural rural atmosphere in an urban setting. The benefits to city folk would be aesthetic and therapeutic ("tranquility and rest to the mind") but in no way was Olmsted anti-city. He accepted urban growth, and the idea of a great park was simply to make the city more livable.

The success of Central Park established a reputation for Olmsted which made him much in demand as a consultant and designer for parks in cities across the nation. Although he wrote nothing that presented his ideas in any systematic form, an examination of various prospectuses and plan statements emphasize his basic belief that landscape should blend delicately into cityscape. A well-designed suburb could be the vehicle to accomplish this.

By the 1870s, as urban growth accelerated, a growing number of park and boulevard planners began to urge cities to plan for and acquire park and recreational land while it was still available. Persons such as Henry W. S. Cleveland, an associate of Olmsted, and George Kessler, designer of the Kansas City, Missouri, park system, stressed the need for quick action to assure environmental quality for future generations, and particularly, the value of a harmonious environment in generating civic pride.

These early landscape architects and park designers were really city planners. Their ultimate goal was frequently revealed in their words and writings, the desire to create the ideal city—to bring the natural environment into harmony with the man-made—to lead to the ultimate of well-adjusted and content citizens.

The City Beautiful movement, which peaked in the pre-World War I era, was an outgrowth of the earlier parks and boulevards movement and the Chicago Columbian Exposition of 1893. Daniel H. Burnham, a well-known Chicago architect and civic promoter, was the prime mover behind the project which was to celebrate the 400th anniversary of Columbus' voyage and, incidentally, the resurgence of Chicago since the 1871 fire.

In planning for the exposition, which was to have as its theme the rise of the city, Burnham enlisted the aid of Olmsted, who was to design the grounds, and various other architects, landscape architects, sculptors, planners, and engineers. An observer remarked after attending one of the conferences that it had been the greatest gathering of artists since the fifteenth century. What eventually was created at Jackson Park in Chicago was a complete new city with all the required urban services, including water, sewage disposal, transportation facilities, police and fire protection. Olmsted's landscaping created an Elysian environment for Burnham's white buildings. Seven thousand workers completed the project, and when the gates closed in October 1893, 27 million admissions had been counted.

The White City, as the exposition grounds came to be called, became the inspiration for further development in Chicago and other cities, as an urban renaissance of park-building and city beautification took root across the nation.

However, some Americans saw deeper issues involved than merely cosmetic ones. One early voice of alarm raised against private exploitation of natural resources was that of Lester F. Ward, probably the first American sociologist and one who argued strongly for increased state control and regulation. His most famous work, *Dynamic Sociology*, published in 1893, argued, among other things, for public ownership of utilities, a radical idea at that time.

Conservation began to interest other members of the American intellectual community. The Society for the Study of the National Economy, a subgroup of the American Economic Association, was formed in 1884. The organization's constitutional platform called for planning to utilize effectively the nation's resources, and specifically charged the state with the duty to set aside sufficient forest reserves to meet future needs. The group further urged changing current land laws to encourage a class of farmers whose interest in agricultural management would coincide with the public interest. Ideally, these farmers would use the best machines, the best farming methods, and develop the best breeds of livestock. Furthermore, each section of the country would specialize in what it could produce best. Effective planning and a rational approach to problems obviously attracted much of their attention.

Another strong academic voice for conservation was Richard T. Ely, economist from the University of Wisconsin and one of the founders of the American Economic Association. He favored a stepped-up forest conservation program, re-forestation, a training program for professional foresters, and, by 1900, was urging the conservation of mineral resources. Many of these ideas are expressed in his work, *Foundation of National Prosperity*, published in 1917.

Gradually state governments began to show increasing interest in conservation as fish and game commissions were established in the late 1860s and 1870s. Between 1885 and 1900 thirteen states founded forestry agencies, and five states began park systems. By 1900 ten states had provided for geological surveys, and eight had passed laws to prevent waste of oil.

One of the best known nineteenth-century conservation spokesman was John Muir. Educated as a botanist and geologist at the University of Wisconsin, he became famous as a naturalist writer who wrote hundreds of newspaper articles and several books on the wilderness that he knew so intimately. Muir spent several years living in the Yosemite area in the 1860s, and it was largely through his efforts that the national park there was created. He traveled throughout the wilderness areas of the United States, Alaska, Canada, and even to the Arctic before his death in 1914. His role was mainly that of a propagandist for conservation, but particularly, for wilderness preservation.

As industrialism and urban growth proceeded, a small number of Americans began to be concerned about availability of natural resources in the future. As early as the Civil War many great forests, some in the recently settled Great Lakes region, had already disappeared. State and local efforts were not enough to prevent the depletion of the country's forest resources. In 1873, as the result of a national movement to save forests, President Benjamin Harrison set aside 13,416,710 acres of forest land. President Cleveland followed the lead of his predecessor, and during McKinley's presidency the total acreage of national forests was increased to over 46 million acres.

Besides the creation of national forests, other conservation measures were underway. In 1877 the Desert Land Act was passed which authorized the government to sell up to 640 acres of arid land for $1.25 per acre if the purchaser would begin reclamation within three years. Some irrigation took place, but there was also much fraud as unscrupulous land-greedy persons simply dumped a bucket of water on the ground to "fulfill" their part of the agreement. Under the Carey Act (1894) arid federal land in the West could be ceded to states if the state caused the land to be irrigated and settled upon. Over a million acres were irrigated under this program.

Mention the word "conservation" to most Americans and the name of Theodore Roosevelt immediately comes to mind. What had in the past attracted the interest of a minority of naturalists, intellectuals, planners, social critics, artists, and other visionaries now became a cornerstone of the reform movement of the early twentieth century. Under Roosevelt, conservation became a major national political issue and eventually a moral crusade.

When Roosevelt entered the White House in 1901 he projected the image of the vigorous, robust life of the "roughrider," the Easterner who had adopted the West, the love of nature, and one who personally hiked through the forests and over the mountains of the western wilderness. His intellectual associates included western writers such as John Muir, Owen Wister, John Burroughs, and Stewart Edward White, geologist Clarence King, and Forester Bernard Fernow.

Although conservation did not begin with Roosevelt, it was in his administration that the movement grew and developed strong and broadly–based national support. Forest reserves were increased from 45 million to nearly 200 million acres by 1908. Before Roosevelt there was no comprehensive federal forest program, and he was responsible for beginning the Reclamation Service and placing the forest program under the Department of Agriculture.

Roosevelt's conservation policies had wide public support, but they also developed bitter opposition. Many in the West, including ranchers, mine operators, lumbermen and power companies fought his program. In 1905 Senator Charles W. Fulton of Oregon demanded that Roosevelt cease this rigorous enforcement of conservation, especially since a federal investigation in that state had led to prosecutions and convictions that put several loyal Oregon Republicans in prison.

Congressional opposition mounted in 1907 when a bill was passed limiting the authority of the president to create forest reserves in the six western states. However, before signing the bill Roosevelt added or increased the size of thirty-two national forest reserves, and Chief Forester Gifford Pinchot designated 2,500 potential power sites as "ranger stations." Needless to say, western congressmen were irate.

In 1908 following the urging of the President, three important national conservation meetings were held. The first was the National Conservation Congress which was attended by forty-four governors and was the forerunner of today's National Governors' Conference. By 1910, under the influence of this meeting, forty-one states had created conservation commissions of their own. The other two national conservation meetings held in 1908 were the Inland Waterways Commission and the National Country Life Commission, both designed to promote state support for a stronger national conservation program.

The incident which became a national symbol of the conservation movement was the Ballinger-Pinchot controversy, which broke out during the Taft administration in 1909. Pinchot, the chief forester in the Agriculture Department and the most outspoken supporter of conservation next to Roosevelt himself, accused Secretary of Interior Richard A. Ballinger of not being forceful enough in protecting the nation's resources. Amid the charges and counter-charges that resulted, Pinchot was dismissed from his post by Taft. This cause celebre provided a rallying point for the nation's conservationists. Even Roosevelt turned against Taft in his support for Pinchot. The cause of conservation was strengthened, Pinchot was vindicated, and Taft had to back down, but not before suffering some permanent political setbacks. The progressive rebellion of 1910 grew out of the Ballinger-Pinchot affair, and in the end it was to be Taft's undoing.

On the surface the issue of conservation versus uncontrolled exploitation of natural resources seems a rather simple issue. Recent scholarship, however, has revealed a rather complex picture. Conservationists themselves were split over the issue of preservation. (John Muir and his followers urged the creation of wilderness areas, while Pinchot and his supporters were in favor of scientific resource management and sustained yield policies.) Pinchot wrote:

> The object of our forest policy is not to preserve the forests because they are refuges for the wild creatures of the wilderness, but the making of prosperous homes. Every other consideration comes as secondary . . . . The test of utility . . . implies that no lands will be permanently reserves which can serve the people better in any other way.

Although Roosevelt made conservation a moral crusade, modern scholars are inclined to see a more rational and practical side, emphasizing the ideas of efficiency. The language was moralistic, but the goals were efficiency. Walter Lippman, in his book *Drift and Mastery* (1914) expressed this as clearly as anyone possibly could.

> You have to make a survey of the natural resources of the country. On the

basis of that survey you must draw up a national plan for their development. You must eliminate waste in mining, you must conserve the forests so that their fertility is not impaired, so that stream flow is regulated, and the water-power of the country made available. You must bring to the farmer a knowledge of scientific agriculture, help him to organize cooperatively, use the taxing power to prevent land speculation and force land to the best use, co-ordinate markets, build up rural credits, and create in the country a life that shall really be interesting.

Roosevelt had been profoundly disturbed by the social unrest of the 1880s and 1890s and feared this might lead ultimately to a prolonged class struggle. The struggle between big business and farmers and labor only made the situation worse. He strongly believed that the nation's social and economic problems could and should be solved by experts. Conservation afforded wide opportunity for government by these experts to apply principles of efficiency through planning, organization, and investigation. Roosevelt's conservation crusade, which emphasized agrarianism, the outdoor life, and middle-class values of individual initiative, thrift, equal opportunity, and political democracy, was strong in moral qualities and set the political tone which brought wide support from groups who feared the uncertainties of the advancing technological age. The middle class, in particular, saw a vigorous and purposeful government as the only protection, and the conservation movement provided the opportunity to oppose the trusts.

The Progressive Party platform of 1912 strongly endorsed the principle of conservation of natural resources. It clearly supported programs to protect forests, mineral resources, grazing lands, and water resources. Specifically, the platform identified the need for:

> . . . national obligation to develop our rivers, and especially the Mississippi and its tributaries, without delay, under a comprehensive general plan covering each river system from its source to its mouth, designed to secure its highest usefulness for navigation, irrigation, domestic supply, water power, and prevention of floods.

The above statement would appear to anticipate later projects like the Tennessee Valley Authority of New Deal times. Furthermore, prominent Bull Moose conservationists, such as Harold Ickes, Edward P. Costigan, and Bronson Cutting were to become New Deal conservation supporters twenty years later.

By the end of the Progressive era, the idea of conservation had been indelibly etched on the public consciousness. Conservative opponents who had hoped that the issue would "blow over" would be sadly disappointed. There would be occasional setbacks (e.g. the Teapot Dome scandal of the Harding Administration) but never another confrontation on the scale of the Ballinger-Pinchot affair. Conservation had become a matter of national policy.

During the 1920s the Forest Service quietly added to the country's forest reserves. Both Harding and Coolidge tried to end federal development of dams and nitrate plants at Muscle Shoals on the Tennessee River and allow private power companies to take over. It was only through the efforts of Senator George Norris of Nebraska that this was averted. The area became famous during the 1930s under President Franklin Roosevelt as the Tennessee Valley Authority (TVA).

The Depression and the New Deal period saw no specifically designated conservation or environmental program being pushed. Conservation did advance but only as an adjunct to the attempt to solve some of the economic and human problems of the time. Thousands of unemployed city boys found themselves in the Civilian Conservation Corps building nature trails, planting seedlings in national forests, and otherwise improving the rustic environment. The Soil Conservation Service was created in 1935 and made a part of the Department of Agriculture. Many more acres were added to national forests, and the federal government was given stronger control over western grazing land. This law, the Taylor Grazing Act of 1934, attempted to deal with the ecological problem of the "dust bowl" by setting aside eighty million acres of public domain for grazing purposes. One conservation measure, the Guffey–Snyder Coal Conservation Act, was declared unconstitutional in 1936.

Another aspect of the New Deal period which had some bearing on the matter of conservation and environmental concerns was the fact that planning became widely accepted. The President set up the National Resources Planning Agency. The Public Works Administration established a national planning board to select and guide its projects. The National Resources Committee was headed by FDR's uncle, Frederick A. Delano, a veteran city planner.

The urban environment was affected by many WPA (Works Progress Administration) projects, and an imaginative new experiment to create new planned communities in the Greenbelt Program was launched. The essential goal of the New Deal was to attack the nation's economic problems and in particular, unemployment, but in the process many broader issues, such as the environment, were touched. The precedent for experimentation had been set and new areas would be easier to enter in the future.

The 1950s witnessed some backsliding as far as conservation was concerned. The Eisenhower Administration, business dominated and states' rights oriented, supported some anti-conservation legislation. The Submerged Lands Act of 1953 gave in to pressures from oil interests and states by transferring federally-owned crude oil deposits off the coasts of California, Louisiana, and Texas to the states. Western conservationists, environmentalists, and public power interests were angered in 1953 when the administration allowed a private concern, the Idaho Power Company, to build a series of low dams on the Snake River in Hell's Canyon, one of the few remaining wilderness areas in the nation. The same year the administration completed the Dixon-Yates contract to supply power to the Atomic Energy Commission, despite available TVA power. This was seen by many as an attempt to weaken and eventually destroy the TVA.

By the mid 1960s the Johnson Administration was asking for legislation to protect the consumer, rebuild the cities as well as asking Congress for laws dealing with air, water, and land pollution. "Great Society" programs contained more progressive measures proposed than at any time since the 1930s. The proposals were not so unusual, considering some of the major political and social changes that had occurred. A basic political shift had taken place in the late 1960s and into the seventies as young, middle-class, educated liberals replaced early liberals whose programs had been based mainly on economic or ethnic issues. The new group was much more broadly based and more interested in social issues and problems of the environment.

America's social activists were beginning to realize that the country's problems, besides being human, were also environmental. Natural beauty was being threatened by urban sprawl and endless concrete ribbons of superhighways. In California alone land developers consumed between 50,000 and 100,000 acres annually. Everywhere the nation faced a trash explosion which threatened to bury them. Technology was turning out goods which Americans threw away at the rate of over 400 billion pounds a year. This included 55 billion cans, 26 billion bottles, 30 million tons of paper, and over 7 million automobiles. By the early 1970s San Francisco Bay had already lost 250 of its 700 square miles to trash landfill. Even air and water pollution was becoming treacherous as the country collectively created 142 million tons of smoke and fumes, and each city of over 500,000 population dumped 50 million gallons of sewage into rivers, streams, and lakes each year. Detergents and insecticides killed fish and wildlife, and bodies of water such as Lake Erie were so damaged by collective pollution that they had long since been pronounced "dead."

The productive capacity of the United States economy in the postwar era began to display a negative side of the affluent society. Large numbers of the public began to raise questions about the basic value of "more" and "bigger" and suggested very strongly that quality should take precedence over quantity. The mid-1960s saw two important pieces of national legislation which dealt with environmental aesthetics eventually passed by the Congress and signed into law—the Wilderness Act of 1964 and the Highway Beautification Act of 1965. Both measures were passed after lengthy debate and strong opposition, but with equally strong and broad public support.

The Highway Beautification Act provided for banning billboards, shielding junkyards, and roadside landscaping. Support came from groups such as Garden Clubs of America and the Izaak Walton League. In opposition were scrap dealer associations, road contractors, and advertising companies, among others. In the end few could argue with the general idea of "beauty," particularly when the bill was so strongly backed by the President and his wife.

The Wilderness Bill had a much rougher legislative road to travel. The original bill had been introduced in 1956 by Senator Hubert Humphrey of Minnesota and immediately drew fire from industrial interests and their ally, Congressman Wayne Aspinal of Colorado, chairman of the House Interior and Insular Affairs Committee. Although the bill passed the Senate, it died in the House committee. In the meantime, a law favored by industry was passed—the Multiple Use Act of 1960. This brought renewed efforts to get a wilderness bill passed.

What alarmed many environmental groups was the application of the Multiple Use Act of 1960, which gave control of wilderness areas to the Forest Service and included the power to classify and declassify public lands by administrative directive.

Past experience had shown the service particularly vulnerable to industry pressure, with the tendency for consumption-oriented forces to dominate. The environmentalists particularly wanted a law that required extensive public hearings before a wilderness area could be reclassified.

The first attempt to protect the wilderness was the establishment of the National Park System in 1916, but the Park Service made no effort to designate wilderness areas. In the 1920s and thirties the first real steps were taken by the Forest Service. By the 1940s several million acres of wilderness and primitive areas had been so identified by administrative directive within national forests.

Following World War II with heavy housing demand, economic expansion, and a consumption-oriented society, the environmentalists were clearly worried about the future of wilderness. Even if the areas were set aside, they could be obliterated by overuse, as an increasing and wealthier population could afford more recreation. The problem was growing more serious, but so was its recognition. The 1964 bill was passed because of increased public support, effective political strategy by the environmental forces, and a willingness to accept some compromises. But more importantly, the passage of the Wilderness Act represented the first successful attempt to justify a major national policy on non-economic grounds.

Air and water pollution offered more immediate and practical evidence. People have long been concerned about air pollution, but mostly from an aesthetic standpoint. The real alarm from the health standpoint came in the 1930s in the Meuse Valley in Belgium when a thick fog settled over that area and six thousand cases of illness were reported in a single week in which sixty-three persons eventually died. In the United States, public alarm arose over an incident in the small industrial town of Donora, Pennsylvania, when in October 1948, a heavy smog settled over the area causing thousands of cases of illness and an estimated twenty deaths.

The worst example in recent times happened in London in 1952 when a "killer fog" resulted in 4,000 more deaths than usual during that year. There were similar episodes in London in 1957, 1958, and 1962.

Water pollution concerns have existed for a long time, but most have centered on the health effects of polluted water. In the New Deal years public works programs spent millions on the construction of sewage treatment plants. Although most American communities are now served by effective sewage treatment facilities, in some of the older communities, improper treatment or the dumping of raw sewage is the major cause of water pollution. However, other forms of water pollution, particularly wastes and oil spills, have worried the public. Since the late 1960s there have been a series of federal laws passed covering both air and water pollution.

For most Americans in the past the environment has been an obstacle and a challenge. It was something to be overcome, tamed, and exploited. At best it was taken for granted by nearly everyone, save a tiny minority. What western civilization seemed to be doing was rushing toward an environmental crisis, but few realized how fast it was approaching. It took thousands of years for human ideas to reach the point where they could overpower and destroy nature. The technology actually to accomplish this took another century. The last one hundred years have seen Western society develop a system that forces humankind to apply that power destructively as a matter of everyday life. Clearly Pogo is right when he declares, "We have met the enemy and they is us."

Suggested Readings

Early planners concerned with the urban environment are covered in John W. Reps, *The Making of Urban America: A History of City Planning in the United States* (Princeton, 1965). Olmsted and his contribution is comprehensively presented in Albert Fein, *Frederick Law Olmsted and the American Environmental Tradition* (New York: Braziller, 1972).

Conservation and the Progressive Movement is described in numerous books on Theodore Roosevelt, Gifford Pinchot, William Howard Taft, and the various other famous figures out of that era. Samuel P. Hays, *Conservation and the Gospel of Efficiency* (Cambridge: Harvard University Press, 1959), describes the progressive fascination with experts and professionals. Two books by George E. Mowry detail the Ballinger-Pinchot controversy and the other political aspects of conservation—*Theodore Roosevelt and the Progressive Movement* (New York: Hill and Wang, 1960) and *The Era of Theodore Roosevelt* (New York: Harper, 1958). Elmo R. Richardson, *The Politics of Conservation* (Berkeley: University of California Press, 1962), is an excellent and detailed study of western politics as it influenced conservation.

The literature on the current environmental crisis is almost endless with the range all the way from popular-simplistic to minutely technical. The following books occupy a middle ground between those two extremes: Lester R. Brown, *The 29th Day: Accommodating Human Needs and Human Numbers to the Earth's Resources* (New York: Norton, 1978), spells out the crisis in a straightforward manner and offers intelligent analysis and suggestions. Richard A. Cooley and Geoffrey Wandesforde-Smith are the editors of a book on the political side of the issue, *Congress and the Environment* (Seattle: University of Washington Press, 1970). J. Clarence and Barbara S. Davies, *The Politics of Pollution* (Indianapolis: Bobbs-Merrill, 2nd Ed., 1975), does an excellent job of tracing the past and present history of pollution legislation up through 1974. A first-rate collection of the writings of many outstanding environmentalists and supporters is found in Harold Helfrich, Jr., *The Environmental Crisis: Man's Struggle to Live with Himself* (New Haven: Yale University Press, 1970). One of the investigations of a Ralph Nader task force is reported in *Vanishing Air* (New York: Grossman, 1970). Roderick Nash, *Wilderness and the American Mind* (New Haven: Yale University Press, 1967), argues that America's limited amount of wilderness is irreplaceable and should not be exploited.

Current History, July 1970, devoted the entire issue to "America's Polluted Environment" and has several excellent articles on various aspects of this subject. Included are book reviews and a comprehensive list of suggested readings on the environment.